Misbeliefs about Autonomy

Attila Dabis

# Misbeliefs about Autonomy

## The Constitutionality of the Autonomy of Szeklerland

PETER LANG

**Bibliographic Information published by the Deutsche Nationalbibliothek**
The Deutsche Nationalbibliothek lists this publication in the Deutsche Nationalbibliografie; detailed bibliographic data is available online at http://dnb.d-nb.de.

**Library of Congress Cataloging-in-Publication Data**
A CIP catalog record for this book has been applied for at the Library of Congress.

Cover illustration:
Photos and collage: Attila Toró

The publication was subsidised by the Institute for the Protection of Minority Rights, Budapest/Hungary.

Institute for the Protection of Minority Rights

ISBN 978-3-631-85580-5 (Print)
E-ISBN 978-3-631-86822-5 (E-PDF)
E-ISBN 978-3-631-86823-2 (E-PUB)
DOI 10.3726/b19090



Peter Lang – Berlin · Bern · Bruxelles · New York · Oxford · Warszawa · Wien



This publication has been peer reviewed.

www.peterlang.com

# Acknowledgements

This book could not have been written without the support and encouragement of countless people. I can consider myself honoured to have been supervised throughout my PhD studies by Elisabeth Kardos Kaponyi, whose delicate balance of encouragement and criticism helped me to keep my scientific focus on track. I am also pleased to acknowledge the support of a number of researchers, academics, and university professors, as well as diplomats and politicians across Europe. In alphabetical order these are: Bakk Miklós, Bárdi Nándor, Bárður Larsen, Blahó András, Filep Béla, Graham Donnelly, Gordos Árpád, Günther Rautz, Heidi Öst, Izsák Balázs, Kalmár Ferenc, Kántor Zoltán, Kardos Gábor, Kiss Eszter, Lauri Hannikeinen, Markku Suksi, Richard Berry, Sarah Stephan, Sergiu Constantin, Tom Mullen, Tóth Norbert, Varga Attila, and Verhás Evelin.

I had the privilege to base this book on research conducted in some of the most renowned scientific centres, such as the European Academy of Bolzano/Bozen (EURAC), the University of Glasgow, and the Åbo Akademi in Finland. Furthermore, the methodological guidelines of the Corvinus University of Budapest proved to be particularly useful throughout the whole research process.

Equally essential was the financial support provided by the Balassi Institute and the Erasmus Traineeship scheme of the EU, through which I was able to conduct my research abroad. The financial contribution of the Institute for the Protection of Minority Rights was also a crucial factor in the publishing process, not to mention the fact that as an employee of this Institute, I managed to gain first-hand experience of all those rights violations which generate the self-determination demand discussed in this book.

Writing this book entailed considerable periods of absence from home, placing additional burden on my relatives. Consequently, I express my most sincere gratitude to my family, and most of all to my wife, Melinda, for her unconditional support and patience throughout this long process. Not forgetting, of course, the cheerful moments my son, Attila Jr., and my daughter, Dóra, had to offer throughout this period.

Last, but not least, following a lengthy research process, it is important to thank the publisher Peter Lang for seeing potential in this book and sharing the same vision regarding the relevance of this material.

# Contents

**List of Abbreviations** ........ 11

**List of Tables and Figures** ........ 13

**1 Introduction** ........ 15

1.1 Novelty and Relevance of the Analysis ........ 15

1.2 Structure of the Book ........ 18

1.3 Theoretical and Methodological Framework ........ 19

1.4 Primary Concepts ........ 22

1.5 Relating Concepts ........ 28

1.6 Historical Background ........ 32

1.7 What and Why ........ 38

1.7.1 Basic Features of the Draft Law on the Autonomy of Szeklerland ........ 38

1.7.2 Driving Forces Behind Szekler Autonomy Aspirations ........ 41

1.7.2.1 Linguistic Rights, Cultural and Educational Issues ........ 44

1.7.2.2 Religious Discrimination ........ 50

1.7.2.3 Economic Discrimination ........ 52

1.7.2.4 Constraints on the Use of Symbols ........ 54

1.7.2.5 Lack of Dialogue and Insufficient Administrative Practices ........ 58

1.7.2.6 Securitization of Autonomy Aspirations ........ 62

**2 Autonomy and the Constitution of a Nation State** ........ 77

2.1 Romanian Constitutional Traditions ........ 77

2.1.1 Liberal Constitutionalism ........ 77

2.1.2 Communist Period ........ 81

2.1.3 Post-communist Period ..... 82
2.1.4 Constitution in Force ..... 84

2.2 Opinion No. 405/2004 – the Essential Summary of All Arguments ..... 86
2.2.1 Substantive Objections ..... 87
2.2.2 Procedural Objections ..... 89

2.3 Decision No. 80/2014 of the Constitutional Court of Romania Rejecting the Constitutional Amendments Proposed by the Special Committee of the Parliament – the Constitutional Court and the Recognition of the National Ideal ..... 90

2.4 Political Assertions ..... 91

2.5 Similar Approaches ..... 99

**3 Deconstructing the Constitutional Barrier** ..... 105

3.1 Counterarguments to Opinion No. 405/2004 ..... 105
3.1.1 Counterarguments to Substantive Objections ..... 105
3.1.2 Counterarguments to Procedural Objections ..... 116

3.2 Counterarguments to Decision No. 80/2014 ..... 119

3.3 Legal Entrenchment – Flexible Solutions to Accommodate Autonomy Arrangements ..... 121

**4 Policy Implications** ..... 139

4.1 Romanian State ..... 142
4.1.1 Options Requiring the Amendment of the Constitution or the Adoption of a New One ..... 143
4.1.2 Options Not Requiring Constitutional Amendments ..... 144

4.2 Minority Community ..... 146

4.3 Kin-State ..... 149

4.4 International Community ..... 151

**5 Conclusions** ........ 155

**Appendix** ........ 161

**Bibliography** ........ 169

# List of Abbreviations

| | |
|---|---|
| AC | Advisory Committee of the Framework Convention for the Protection of National Minorities |
| CCR | Constitutional Court of Romania |
| CCS | Constitutional Court of Spain |
| CI | Constitution of Italy |
| CLRAE | Congress of Local and Regional Authorities of the Council of Europe |
| CoE | Council of Europe |
| COMEX | Committee of Experts of the European Charter for Regional or Minority Languages |
| CR | Constitution of Romania |
| CS | Constitution of Spain |
| CSCE | Conference on Security and Co-operation in Europe |
| DAHR | Democratic Alliance of Hungarians in Romania |
| DIICOT | Directorate for Investigating Organized Crime and Terrorism (*Direcţia de Investigare a Infracţiunilor de Criminalitate Organizată şi Terorism*) |
| DL | Draft Law on the Autonomous Status of Szeklerland |
| DNA | National Anticorruption Directorate (*Direcţia Naţională Anticorupţie*) |
| DOM-TOM | Overseas Departments and Territories (*départements et territoires d'outre-mer*) |
| DSF | Day of Szekler Freedom |
| ECHR | European Convention on Human Rights |
| ECRI | European Commission against Racism and Intolerance |
| ECRML | European Charter for Regional or Minority Languages |
| ECtHR | European Court of Human Rights |
| EU | European Union |

| | |
|---|---|
| FCNM | Framework Convention for the Protection of National Minorities |
| ICCPR | International Covenant on Civil and Political Rights |
| ICESCR | International Covenant on Economic, Social and Cultural Rights |
| LCM | Legislative Consent Motion |
| NCCD | National Council for Combating Discrimination |
| NGO | Non-Governmental Organization |
| NSAC | New Statute of Autonomy of Catalonia |
| OSCE | Organization for Security and Co-operation in Europe |
| PACE | Parliamentary Assembly of the Council of Europe |
| PD | Democratic Party (*Partidul Democrat*) |
| PDL | National Liberal Party (*Partidul Național Liberal*) |
| PSD | Social Democratic Party (*Partidul Social Democrat*) |
| SRI | Romanian Intelligence Service (*Serviciul Român de Informații*) |
| SzNC | Szekler National Council |
| TA | Territorial Autonomy |
| UN | United Nations |
| UPR | Universal Periodic Review |
| Venice Commission | European Commission for Democracy Through Law |

# List of Tables and Figures

Tables

Tab. 1: Demographic trends of Hungarian minority communities living in countries adjacent to Hungary (1989–2011) .................... 161

Tab. 2: Proportion of GDP/capita in the CDR counties, relative to the CDR's GDP/capita average (in %) ............................ 161

Tab. 3: Annual increment of GDP/capita in the counties of the Central Development Region ............................................... 162

Figures

Fig. 1: Administrative borders of the Austro-Hungarian Empire ............... 162

Fig. 2: Territorial changes due to the 1st and 2nd Vienna Arbitrations in 1938 and 1940 ............................................................ 163

Fig. 3: Changing borders of the Hungarian Autonomous Province in communist Romania ........................................................................................ 164

Fig. 4: Changes in the ethno-linguistic composition of Transylvania comparing results of the 1910 and 2002 censuses ..... 165

Fig. 5: Ethnic map of Transylvania (based on the census of 2011) ............ 166

Fig. 6: Ethnic map of Transylvania, juxtaposed with borders of the administrative and the Central-Romanian NUTS II Development Region (with bold outlines), as well as the increment of their GDP per capita income 2007–2013 ............ 167

Fig. 7: GDP per capita development in the counties of the Central-Romanian NUTS II Region, calculated in current price USD based on purchasing power parity (2000–2016) ........... 167

Fig. 8: Low income (red), low growth (blue), and other NUTS II regions (white) ..................................................................... 168

# 1 Introduction

## 1.1 Novelty and Relevance of the Analysis

With approximately 650,000 members, the Hungarian-speaking Szekler community is one of the largest nationalities of Europe that, despite corresponding efforts, has not yet obtained regional autonomy. The many public protests, demonstrations, the numerous drafts, programs, and manifestos of Hungarian political organizations, scientific institutions, and NGOs show a permanent discontent of the Hungarian minority regarding their legal status in Romania. Given that such discontent was present in different forms ever since the territorial changes after the First World War occurred, the question of the Hungarian minorities in the successor states of the Austro-Hungarian Empire (see Fig. 1) is characterized by some as one of the major unresolved questions of Central and Eastern Europe.[1] It is no great surprise, however, that this opinion is not widely shared by state officials of countries having extensive Hungarian minority communities. As a matter of fact, the most common viewpoint one would hear is that the minority question in Romania is solved in an exemplary manner. Any subject which continues to polarize the public opinion so vividly is worthy of scientific analysis.

On the theoretical, conceptual level, *Misbeliefs About Autonomy* offers a multidisciplinary approach, blending legal studies, social sciences, and history in analysing the arguments of a nationalizing state against regional autonomy.[2] The book presents a multi-tier approach to scrutinize the validity of these "nation-state arguments" based on a doctrinal legal analysis, combined with a comparative legal analysis. In this sense, the analysis presented in this book has an educational and awareness-raising core, as it aims to falsify widespread misinterpretations regarding the connection between regional autonomy and its effects on state unity and territorial integrity in general and those of Romania in particular. The book wishes to clarify various minority-related issues and present how these affect Romanian public policy decision, while also introducing, for the wider public, the Szekler community of Transylvania, and the self-determination aspirations thereof.

---

1 See, for example, Arday (2010), p. 1.

2 The term "nationalizing state" is referred to in the context of Brubaker (1996).

As regards the policy level, the book outlines a framework of policy recommendations for different spheres of politics and for different levels of implementation (including regional, national, inter-governmental, and international). The Szekler case reflects how parallel nation-building projects and historical resentments can be stronger factors in shaping public policy decisions than the rule of law, that is, respect for and implementation of international treaties and constitutional provisions. The book draws up a general framework to gauge these policy implications and summarizes the most relevant minority-related findings of international monitoring procedures, shadow reports, and case law, in order to provide a realistic picture about Romania and its treatment of minorities in general and the Hungarian/Szekler community in particular. Accordingly, the book aims to function as a guidebook that both academics and policy-makers as well as a more general audience could use to examine and understand how and why Romania is keen on building an "ethnic democracy" even to the detriment of the rule of law.[3]

Additionally, concerning the contribution to studies on Central-Eastern Europe, the book highlights the fact that the question of Szekler self-determination was a critical issue throughout the process of the 20th century power struggle in Europe.[4] In the author's opinion, Szeklerland deserves more academic attention at the international level as a region that still bears significant potential in shaping the domestic political affairs of the Romanian host country, the relations between the Hungarian kin-state and Romania in inter-state relations, and by extension also the international affairs in Central-Eastern Europe.

Despite this potential, the issue of Szeklerland remains, to date, a lesser-known case among scholars. The constitutional aspects of a Szekler autonomy arrangement were largely neglected within academia, leaving behind a gap that is very much ripe for scientific review. Furthermore, even if the topic was

---

3 The term is used in the context of: Smooha (2001).

4 For example, the question of Szekler autonomy is explicitly referred to in Art. 11 of the Treaty between the Allied and Associated Powers and Romania, signed in Paris on 9 December 1919. It was also a contentious topic during the peace building process that commenced after the Second World War, prompting the Soviet Union to pressure Romania into granting a certain degree of regional autonomy to administrative units inhabited by Szeklers, in the framework of the Romanian constitution adopted in 1952. The structure of coexistence between Szekler-Hungarians and Romanians also came to the fore during the political transition of Romania in the early 1990s, among others, in the form of ethnic clashes in the historical Szekler capital of Marosvásárhely/Târgu Mureş.

discussed, it was mostly done within the framework of the "nation-state discourse",[5] and all the conceptual restraints thereof. Against this backdrop, one of the main motivations for writing this book, and one of the core novelties of the outcome, was to surpass these constraints and challenge the most widespread, albeit false presuppositions and misconceptions surrounding the issue at hand. Hopefully, by the time one reads through this book, they will have been convinced that there are indeed no constitutional obstacles to establishing a territorial autonomy within Romania. Ultimately, we invite the reader to engage in a "mind-game" in order to deconstruct the "constitutional myth" regarding autonomy.

A further novelty of the book lies in the fact that it takes legal solutions adopted in functioning autonomy arrangements and gauges if and to what extent these can be applied to a region (Szeklerland) that lost its autonomy but wishes to regain it. The book thus demonstrates on the example of functioning autonomies (including, among others, the examples of the Åland Islands, the Basque country, South Tyrol, the Faeroe-islands, or Gagauzia) that there are manifold ways one can manage or even solve inter-ethnic disputes through flexible autonomy arrangements. I make the clear case that in the presence of political will, minority claims on decentralization can be accommodated even if the resolution requires the central state to resort to special means. From this perspective, the conclusions of the book are more solution-oriented than problem-oriented.

Taking into account the lessons of the functioning of these existing autonomies, as well as the numerous different forms of legal entrenchment used in their creation, the book draws up practical guidelines that can be applied to the establishment of a Szekler autonomy. For these parts, I used the entrenchment-typology established by Markku Suksi.[6] This typology allows to identify and distinguish various forms of legal entrenchments, as well to identify certain factors that can increase the longevity of an autonomy arrangement.

The above characteristics will hopefully make the book useful not just for researchers and academics but also for national and international decision-makers

5 Under this term I refer to the acceptance of the presupposition that territorial autonomy contradicts the indivisibility clause of the Romanian constitution.

6 The book benefited greatly from the research visit I carried out under the supervision of Markku Suksi at the Åbo Akademi in Turku, Finland in 2015. This part of the book thus relies to a large extent on: Suksi, Markku (ed.) (1998): On the Entrenchment of Autonomy, In: Suksi, Markku (ed.): *Autonomy: applications and implications*. The Hague; Boston: Kluwer Law International, pp. 151–171.

and policy-practitioners working in multinational countries with minority issues in general and Central-Eastern Europe and Romania in particular.

## 1.2 Structure of the Book

The book is organized into five main chapters. The present chapter introduces the relevance, novelty, and structure of the analysis; the main questions and objectives of the research; and the methodological and theoretical framework thereof, including, most importantly, the rationale behind the case selection. This chapter also offers the explanation of the primary concepts used throughout the book and the concepts that are in close relation to these. Furthermore, a brief historical overview of the subject matter is provided to increase the contextual understanding of the Szekler case.

The second chapter presents the arguments of various Romanian authorities against autonomy. A certain pattern emerges from the presented official documents, emphasizing similar observations as to why autonomy is in contradiction with the constitution. The main legal argument – that autonomy would eliminate the unity and indivisibility of the state – is often complemented with theoretical arguments on sovereignty and procedural observations on the feasibility of autonomy within the Romanian legal system.

All of these considerations come under scrutiny, as the third chapter explores the possible answers and counter-responses to nation-state arguments, based mainly on doctrinal analysis of legal material and comparison of the experience of other European states and their autonomous regions, as well as relevant scientific literature and the commitments that accrue from international documents ratified by Romania. While the former three groups of sources present a large variety of arguments about autonomy being an effective and flexible solution for multi-ethnic states to accommodate minority aspirations in a democratic manner, while also preserving the territorial integrity of the state, the latter sources are of relevance as they outline the extent to which Romania is encouraged or even obliged to seek more effective ways of minority protection and power-sharing. These two chapters outline the misconceptions as well as the discrepant perceptions of the majority and the minority about state, nation, sovereignty, autonomy, and their relation to one another.

The conclusions of the study are split into two chapters. The fourth chapter considers the policy implications that accrue from the analysis for the territorial state, the kin-state, the Szekler community, and the international community. Finally, the fifth chapter summarizes the findings of the research and underpins the hypothesis of this book, that there are no constitutional legal barriers to establishing an autonomous Szekler region within Romania. There are only political obstacles that are conceptualized as constitutional legal barriers as a means to avoid any kind of dialogue with members of the Szekler community on regional power-sharing.

## 1.3 Theoretical and Methodological Framework

The Romanian legislature rejected the Draft Law on the Autonomous Status of Szeklerland (DL) four times in a row: on 30 March 2004, 12 October 2005, 29 May 2018, and 29 April 2020.[7] Opinion no. 405/2004 of the Legislative Council of the Parliament,[8] elaborated after the first submission of the statute draft, argues in favour of the rejection, as this DL is contrary to the constitution for various reasons – an opinion that was reinforced in the three other subsequent occasions.

This theoretical conception arises from the misinterpretation of the connection between state and autonomy and as such can be falsified by the experience of functioning autonomies as well as by international law and the corresponding scientific literature. Consequently, my main hypothesis is that the territorial autonomy of Szeklerland does not contradict the Constitution of Romania (CR). There are in fact no provisions in the Romanian constitution that represent a material legal obstacle for the establishment of an autonomous territorial entity. The only obstacle that exists is a political one, which derives from the dissenting interpretation of the same legal materials. A phenomenon that is mostly fuelled from the side of Romania by an ethno-centric political culture.

The applied methodology to prove this main hypothesis is twofold. The analysis presented in the book is largely a doctrinal legal analysis that first

7 These dates refer to the days when the Senate rejected the DL. Under the special asymmetrical bicameral legislative system that exists in Romania, Art. 75 (1) of the Constitution enumerates the questions that need to be debated and adopted by the Chamber of Deputies, as a first notified Chamber, while all other bills or legislative proposals shall be submitted to the Senate, as a first notified Chamber, for debate and adoption. Accordingly, bills pertaining to "the organization of local public administration, territory, as well as the general rules on local autonomy" (Art. 73 (o)) need to pass the Chamber of Deputies first, before transferring it to the Senate for the final decision.

8 According to Art. 79 (1) of the Constitution, the Legislative Council shall be an advisory expert body of the parliament, which advises draft normative acts for the purpose of a systematic unification and coordination of the whole body of laws. It shall keep the official record of the legislation of Romania.

explores the misinterpretations of autonomy by Romanian authorities, then it presents a dissenting interpretation and provides evidence supporting it. Parallel with this, a comparative legal analysis is conducted, based on the relevant legal material, that is, the Constitution of Romania; Laws of Romania; Opinion 405/2004 of the Legislative Council of the Parliament of Romania on the rejection of the DL; Decision No. 80/2014 of the Constitutional Court rejecting the constitutional amendments proposed by the Special Committee of the Parliament; relevant decrees of the Prefect's of Romania; the statutes of European autonomies, as well as the constitutions and laws of their host countries; and international legal documents ratified by Romania.

In order to understand the misbeliefs surrounding the issue of autonomy, one first needs to reconstruct the way in which the Romanian political system conceptualizes autonomy arrangements, understand the historical root causes of this interpretation, and provide a dissenting viewpoint that reviews and overcomes the presuppositions and misbeliefs embedded in this conceptualization. Consequently, the scope of the subject of the book required a multidisciplinary approach to it, which integrates three different scientific fields: legal studies, political science, and history, among which the former is the dominant field.

The case selection for the study was done bearing in mind the main features of the specific region (Szeklerland) and its host country (Romania) that serve as the basis for comparison. In this respect, I write about territorial autonomies (given the fact that Szekler autonomy aspirations pertain to territorial self-government, as opposed to other forms of autonomy) in regions where a specific minority represents the majority and which exist in unitary states (as opposed to federal ones). Applying this analytical framework, the core group of selected cases can be identified as follows: South-Tyrol in Italy, the Basque Country and Catalonia in Spain, Scotland in the UK, and the Åland Islands in Finland. These main cases, which are relevant to all the questions raised by the documents outlined in Chapter 3, are supplemented by examples that are important only in some particular aspects. More specifically, state approaches to autonomy that are similar to Romania's are mentioned, like the case of Corsica in France and the Russian community in Estonia. In particular, French reactions to, and arguments against, Corsican autonomy have remarkable similarities with Romanian arguments.[9]

9 Due to the fact that Corsica hasn't received law-making powers, hence the Corsican Assembly has only limited authority to adapt regulations in its areas of administrative competences and to propose modifications to specific legislation and regulations, scholars usually do not consider Corsica to be an entity vested with territorial

The legal entrenchment of the autonomy of the Faroe Islands and Greenland in Denmark is discussed, as well as the experience of the only minority territorial autonomy of Central - Eastern Europe, Gagauzia. While federal states in general fall outside the scope of the analysis, some brief references to the special legal entrenchment of autonomies in federal states are mentioned only for the purpose of illustrating the manifold ways an autonomy arrangement can be embedded in a given constitutional system.

In practice, content analysis of legal texts and relevant scientific literature was performed in order to deepen the understanding of the functioning of regional autonomy and the way the various autonomy arrangements fit into the legal systems of their host countries. Between 2011 and 2021, three-to-five-month-long research visits were conducted in South-Tyrol, Scotland, and Finland under the auspices of the European Academy of Bolzano/Bozen (EURAC), the University of Glasgow, and Åbo Akademi, respectively, enabling focused scientific exchange and the implementation of interviews with academics and lawyers, as well as with diplomats and local politicians. Shorter visits to Wales, the Basque Country, Catalonia, and Flanders were also carried out in the mentioned time period.

Regarding the conclusions of this study, my main scientific expectation is to prove that territorial autonomy, as an institutional arrangement, in general does not contradict the constitutional order of Romania. The misbeliefs surrounding autonomy can be traced back to a tacit agreement regarding the aspirations of the Hungarian minority and the national character of the Romanian state. If one puts aside these historically rooted resentments and takes into account the international legal documents ratified by Romania regarding minorities and interprets the country's domestic legislation accordingly, then "the road is paved" for recognizing the legitimate nature of Szekler autonomy aspirations. The book thus challenges readers to "think outside the box", look at things from a different perspective, and question certain ideas, even if these appear to be adamantly resilient in certain political discourses. Put differently, the book uses scientific analysis as a means to replace unsubstantiated beliefs on a politically contentious issue, with factual observations underpinned by law and social sciences.

Besides this main scope, there is the additional dimension of the following question that needs to be addressed. Even if we verify the general assumption that territorial autonomy as an institutional solution is in conformity

---

autonomy. See, for example, Suksi (2011), pp. 16–17. Nonetheless, this case is relevant from the point of view of the state reaction and will be discussed exclusively from that perspective.

with the Romanian constitution, does that automatically mean that the DL is implementable without having to amend the constitution first? As I will argue, when it comes to the specific statute draft, some legal obstacles arise, whose solution would require a dialogue between the given minority community and the central state. Additionally, even if there was a possibility to implement a statute without the amendment of the constitution, it might result in an autonomy without adequate legal entrenchment, which could undermine the stability of the whole autonomy arrangement.

## 1.4 Primary Concepts

Reading the scientific literature on autonomy and self-governance, one cannot help but notice the diversity of concepts, often describing seemingly identical phenomena. Given the fact that the book revolves mainly around legal issues, if available, I use the definition of concepts existing in relevant international hard or soft law, not neglecting the manifold definitions provided by scientific literature.

*Autonomy:* Defining the most relevant concept for this book poses challenges in the sense that the term "autonomy" has not yet been explicitly defined in any international legal material. The concept of autonomy has appeared in many different disciplines (sociology, psychology, political science, law), described by a diverse range of typology. Generally, autonomy in minority rights-related literature refers to self-government of a group or territory within a state and can be divided, most simplistically, into territorial and personal autonomy.

The main difference between these two, according to Brunner and Küpper, lies in the legal subject. While the former is based on the whole population of a territorial unit, the latter is based on the members of a specific minority.[10] Lapidoth adopts a similar approach and completes these basic two categories with that of sovereignty, suggesting an eclectic description of autonomy. Cultural (or personal) autonomy might be given to groups whose members are dispersed geographically throughout the population. Sovereignty refers to state sovereignty as possessing absolute authority within the state's boundaries, while territorial political autonomy in this sense is "an arrangement aimed at granting to a group that differs from the majority of the population in the state, but that constitutes the majority in a specific region, a means by which it can express its distinct identity".[11] In an attempt to provide a terminology more suitable to describe the

10 Brunner et al. (2004), p. 474.
11 Lapidoth (1997), p. 33.

numerous forms of autonomy, Tkacik differentiates between five levels. Rejecting the approach of Lapidoth, which "collapses personal and cultural autonomy", he distinguishes these two adding that unlike cultural autonomy, personal autonomy can mean the guarantee of certain basic rights to the individual *per se*, and not as a member of a specific group. Furthermore, Tkacik also tries to avoid the use of territorial autonomy, as a "vague and inconsistent" term that "suffers from varied usages", and identifies instead functional, administrative, and legislative autonomy, concentrating on the scope of autonomous competencies.[12] Heintze differentiates between four types of autonomy.[13] *Territorial autonomy*, understood as an arrangement that comprises of self-government organs vested with competences that are of particular importance to the minority or group, and three subcategories of non-territorial autonomy. These latter three are: *cultural autonomy* (the self-government of cultural affairs by a distinct group or minority); *personal autonomy* (where the subjects of the autonomous competencies are persons, and not a group); and *functional autonomy* (the transfer of specific state functions to private organizations administered by a minority group).[14] A similar approach is adopted by Légaré and Suksi when assessing the spatial and the normative scope of autonomy arrangements. Accordingly, they differentiate between territorial autonomies with legislative competencies (like the Åland Islands, Catalonia, and South Tyrol); territorial autonomies with regulatory powers only (like Corsica and Wales, adding that these self-governing territories may not be characterized as autonomies insofar as we treat legislative powers as a prerequisite of the concept of autonomy); non-territorial autonomies with legislative powers (difficult to find concrete examples; one would be the Millet system of Turkey); and finally non-territorial autonomies with regulatory powers (mainly all cultural autonomies fit in this category, like the ones existing in Estonia, Hungary, or Slovenia).[15]

Provided that autonomous arrangements most often accrue in response to minority claims, the term "minority territorial autonomy" is also used.[16] Tóth describes this as "an area of a given state that has relatively exact political and administrative borders and its population is being conferred with the power of legislation and law-enforcement at least in some fields having relevance to the

12 Tkacik (2008), p. 370.
13 A typology also used by Weller et al. (2010), pp. 2–6.
14 Heintze (1998), pp. 18–24.
15 Légaré et al. (2008), pp. 146–147.
16 See, for example, Henders (2010), p. 12.

goal of the autonomy, aiming first of all the preservation of the special identity of the minority community in a majority situation of the autonomous territory".[17]

Even when narrowing down the scope of analysis to autonomies and their relation to constitutional law – the main concern of this analysis – one finds a large variety of typologies. Among these, throughout the book I have used the typology of Suksi, who distinguishes between six possible ways of legally entrenching an autonomy arrangement: *regional entrenchment* (possibility of regional reaction to amending the statute of autonomy); *special entrenchment* (special amendment rule of the statute); *general entrenchment* (regulating autonomy in the national constitution); *semi-general entrenchment* (regulating autonomy at the level of organic laws); *international entrenchment* (having two types: a) *open*: without a formal treaty, such as the Åland-islands, and b) *treaty based*: where the autonomous competencies are being enshrined in a treaty, such as the case of South Tyrol); and *entrenchment under the right to self-determination* (insofar as the population of the area can be viewed as a peoples).[18] Hannikainen lists the constitutional criteria of every autonomy arrangement. These are: a) the autonomous status should be inscribed in the constitution of the state or at least in legislation, above normal laws in the hierarchy of norms; b) presence of a democratically elected legislative body and a local government that is subject to scrutiny of this legislature; c) jurisdiction should be either exclusive or shared, with the possibility from the side of the autonomous region to insert its preferences; d) a different language, if there is one, should have official status in the region; e) the creation of a special bilateral organ composed of delegates of the state and autonomous region dedicated to address contentious issues; f) opportunity for the autonomous region to effectively take part in the decision-making process on the national level; g) the involvement of local court in the autonomous machinery; h) sufficient taxation powers; i) the right to external cooperation; and j) limited powers to the official, representing the State within the autonomous region. This typology discusses the democratic prerequisites of autonomy, showing that it is an institutional construction that is not easily separated from democratic decision-making.[19] Benedikter describes the various forms of government based on the constitutional legal relation between the constituent parts of a state. He separates regional territorial autonomy from other forms of power-sharing through the following criteria: *Reservations* do not have representation

17 Tóth (2014), p. 20.
18 Suksi (1998), p. 170.
19 Hannikainen (1998), pp. 91–93.

within the national parliament of their host country; *dependent territories* are not part of the motherland or mainland, and they mostly represent a different order of separation; *associated statehood* includes the possibility to revoke the association at any times (as was the case with the Marshall Islands, Palau, or Micronesia, e.g.), while autonomous status does not encompass unilateral secession, and it cannot be revoked unilaterally by the autonomous region; *federal arrangements* pertain to the whole territory of a given state, while autonomies are created in one or few units only;[20] other forms of self-government might contain *administrative autonomy* (regions without legislative competencies such as Corsica) or *cultural autonomy* (or non-territorial ethnic autonomy).[21] Hannum et al. assess the common features of autonomies with regard to their internal institutions and the potential international legal personality of that entity by measuring the degree of independent control over their own affairs. With regard to the first aspect, he finds that the vast majority of autonomous entities have executive as well as legislative powers, some degree of local judicial authority, and possible joint responsibility in areas of common concern. Regarding the second aspect, there are three primary issues that point out the international legal personality of autonomies: police and security arrangements, land ownership and natural resources, social services, financial and economic issues, and cultural, religious, and internal minority group concerns. With this analysis, Hannum et al. define the place of autonomies relative to internal and international legal circumstances.[22]

Lastly, turning to territorial autonomy described in legal materials, as mentioned earlier, the concept has not yet been explicitly defined in international "hard law". There are some hints, however, in "soft law" instruments, like the Explanatory Memorandum of Resolution 361 (2013) of the Congress of Local and Regional Authorities of Europe (CLRAE) of the CoE, on Regions and territories with special status in Europe: "Special status entails the legal guarantee of more powers (legislative and/or administrative and/or financial), at least quantitatively in terms of legislation, and normally privileged forms of representation and negotiation – often by means of bilateral channels with the state – for specific territorial authorities. Such authorities always enjoy political and administrative autonomy, while formal legislative autonomy depends on the constitutional setting of each country.... As a rule, special status only affects specific territories

20 See the differences between federalism and autonomy in more detail under section 1.4.

21 Benedikter (2007), p. 22.

22 Hannum et al. (1981), p. 861.

(regions) of a state where there is no wish or need to introduce a fully-fledged federal system".[23]

Bearing all the above in mind, for the purposes of this book, territorial autonomy connotes a special legal arrangement that grants legislative and executive powers to an administrative unit, whose majority possesses an identity other than that of the majority of the state, to govern their domestic affairs through their own decision-making institutions.

*National minority:* While there are many difficulties in elaborating an internationally accepted definition on minorities,[24] I will use the generally accepted concept, established by Recommendation 1201/1993 of the Council of Europe (CoE). Accordingly, the expression "national minority" refers to a group of persons in a state who: a) reside on the territory of that state and are citizens thereof; b) maintain long-standing, firm, and lasting ties with that state; c) display distinctive ethnic, cultural, religious, or linguistic characteristics; d) are sufficiently representative, although smaller in number than the rest of the population of that state or of a region of that state; and e) are motivated by a concern to preserve together that which constitutes their common identity, including their culture, their traditions, their religion, and their language.

At this point, it is vital to allude to the connections between the concept of the protection of national minorities and autonomy. Minority rights are a specified field within the international system of human rights that exists to protect persons belonging to national minorities. The United Nations (UN) categorizes minority rights into four main pillars: I) protection of existence, II) protection of culture and identity, III) non-discrimination, and IV) effective participation in decision-making.[25] Autonomy arrangements granted to minority communities fit in this latter pillar, as an instrument that was acknowledged by many international organizations as one of the most effective means of ensuring the proper participation of minorities in decision-making (see section 3.1.1 for more detail).[26] This means that as special and unique as each and every autonomy arrangement is, in the above context they also fall within this very important general aspect of the international protection of minority rights.

---

23 Section II/a paragraphs 9 and 10, available at: https://wcd.coe.int/ViewDoc.jsp?id=2107887&Site=COE#P128_6478, accessed: 2015.04.10.

24 For a useful summary of these challenges, see: Packer (1999), pp. 223–273.

25 See, for example, paragraph 41 of the Secretary-General of the United Nations (2014): Guidance Note on Racial Discrimination and Protection of Minorities. Geneva: UN.

26 See, for example, relevant documents of the OSCE and its predecessor the CSCE.

*Nation*: While this concept is construed most widely as a set of common values and/or features producing a "specific sense of solidarity between the members of one group",[27] no commonly accepted legal definition exists. This was also the conclusion of the Committee on Legal Affairs and Human Rights when the Parliamentary Assembly of the Council of Europe (PACE) called upon them to adopt such a definition. What matters for the purposes of this book, however, was this Committee's report that concluded that while no common conception exists, it is possible to list all the various forms this term is being used in law in present-day Europe. Based on this report, "the constitution of Romania enshrines clearly the concept of the civic nation, composed of all Romanian citizens".[28]

*National state*: Nation state or national state in political science usually refers to a state whose borders coincide with the geographical distribution of a given nation. In other words, this concept was classically defined "in terms of congruence between a territorial state on the one hand and, on the other, a sovereign national community conceived as having a single homogeneous culture".[29] According to Art. 1 (1) of the Romanian Constitution, "Romania is a sovereign, independent, unitary and indivisible National State" (*România este stat național, suveran și independent, unitar și indivizibil*). The official English translation makes it clear that the term "national" in the above quoted form was not meant to be a mere adjective to the word "state", but a substantive part of the noun itself. Thus, the concept of "national state" is the same as "nation state".

This political concept is rarely, if ever, mentioned in constitutions (the Romanian constitution being the only one in Europe), most likely in order to avoid confusion, and potential conflict with some peremptory norms of international law, as well as other provisions usually enshrined in constitutions pertaining to the equality of all citizens. As the analysis will show, generally accepted principles of international law, international documents ratified by Romania, and certain general provision of the Constitution of the country are all clearly at odds with conceptualizing Romania as a national state exclusively designed for ethnic Romanians.

---

27 See, for example, Weber (1922), p. 673.

28 Paragraph 34 of the Explanatory Memorandum of Doc. 10762 of 13 December 2005 of the CoE on the concept of "nation".

29 Smith (2012), p. xii.

## 1.5 Relating Concepts

There are some concepts which are used as substitutes for the term autonomy. Most notably, autonomy and *self-government* have generally been treated as synonyms,[30] as were the terms *home rule* and *self-rule*. *Devolution* describes the process through which a constituent part of a state receives direct competencies of public authority, as opposed to merely exercising public power on behalf of another superior state agency.[31]

*Federalism* and autonomy share many similarities, but they also differ in even more aspects.[32] Except for some cases (like Switzerland or Bosnia-Herzegovina), federalism is seldom based on ethnicity and revolves much more around shared competencies rather than the exclusive ones exercised by an autonomous region. In this sense, federalized administrative units exhibit more symmetry in their powers, while a marked asymmetry is more typical of autonomy arrangements. Consequently, autonomy is more flexible than federalism.[33] Another relevant difference is that while the federated states or regions are generally involved in policymaking of the central state, autonomous entities rule themselves and do not necessarily have any special rights regarding the central power.[34] There are also notable differences from a constitutional legal point of view. The constitution of a classical federation would have a bicameral legislature on the federal level with enumerated powers and residual powers at the sub-state level, while territorial autonomies would have enumerated powers inside a state with a normally unicameral legislature having residual powers.[35] In federal countries, the representation of the constituent states in the national legislature is ensured in some generalized way, while such arrangement would normally not be present in an autonomous territory whose citizens can win representation in the national parliament through the same general electoral mechanism as other citizens of the state.[36] While the amendment of the constitution of federal states requires the consent of several constituent parts, the consent of the institutions of an

---

30 Heintze (1998), pp. 7–8; Hannikainen (1998), p. 79.

31 Weller et al. (2010), p. 4. For an overview about the difficulties of the concept of devolution, see: Suksi (2011), pp. 114–123.

32 Some scholars do not even closely connect the two concepts. See: Bernhardt (1981), p. 23.

33 Ghai (2013), pp. 16–17.

34 Benedikter (2007), p. 15.

35 Suksi (2011), pp. 130–131.

36 *Id. at* pp. 403–405.

autonomous region to amend the constitution is not required (at least insofar as the amendment does not affect autonomous competencies).[37]

Lastly, the concept of *federacy* refers to a specific category of autonomies that were established within unitary states.[38] According to Stepan et al., a federacy is "a political-administrative unit in an independent unitary state with exclusive power in certain areas, including some legislative power, constitutionally or quasi-constitutionally embedded, that cannot be changed unilaterally and whose inhabitants have full citizenship rights in the otherwise unitary state".[39] Bolleyer et al. substitute the concept of federacy with that of *regionalized arrangements* (as opposed to confederal or federal structures), where "the centre has the final say, notwithstanding the presence of lower tiers of government with legislative powers (that may or may not be constitutionally entrenched)".[40] *Subsidiarity* is another important concept mentioned frequently as a principle whose aim is to "guarantee a degree of independence for a lower authority in relation to a higher body or for a local authority in relation to central government".[41]

*Self-determination*: The right of the peoples to self-determination, as set out by Art. 1 of Charter of the United Nations, the International Covenant on Civil and Political Rights (ICCPR), and the International Covenant on Economic, Social and Cultural Rights (ICESCR), is probably the most contentious concept that can be linked to autonomy. Although this book does not engage in a debate about the many question marks surrounding this concept,[42] it cannot fully neglect it either, for at least two reasons. On the one hand, this right has been referred to in conflicts between nationalities and their host countries, including the Szekler context,[43] and on the other, the legal doctrine is constantly evolving and expanding.

---

37 Watts (2008), pp. 157–170.

38 From a legal point of view, the term might be misleading in the sense that it insinuates the presence of a voluntary association between an autonomous entity and the unitary state, which is not the case in practice.

39 Stepan et al. (2011), p. 204.

40 Bolleyer et al. (2014), p. 370. States having such asymmetric regionalized arrangements, are often called *regionalist- or regionalized states*. See, for example, Benedikter (2007), p. 16.

41 European Parliament (2015), p. 2.

42 For a useful summary of these question marks, see, for example, Summers (2010).

43 A good example would be that of the Ibarretxe plan, named after *Lehendakari* (president of the Basque Country) Juan José Ibarretxe, adopted by the Basque Parliament on 30 December 2004, envisaging a free association with the Spanish state based on a

While the "conventional" viewpoint is that the right to self-determination had its own historical course in the context of de-colonization, there is an increasing recognition that self-determination has internal aspects that require full and effective participation by all groups in society, including national minorities. As far as academics are concerned, some are sceptic as to how generally the concept of internal self-determination has been accepted, let alone realized within existing states.[44] Others recognize the existence of such a division between internal and external forms of self-determination, as a dimension of this right that provides manoeuvring space for national minorities and sub-state entities to redefine their relationship with their own state or government (a redefinition that could range from federalization to autonomy).[45] While there are also scholars who recognize the internal aspect of self-determination, but remind that the term is understood as a right of the whole population of a given state to be free from any external coercion in determining their political status, and not the right of a minority peoples within that state for greater self-rule.[46]

The biggest question mark in the relation between "self-determination" and "autonomy" is whether there is an obligation in international law on states to facilitate autonomy for minority groups as part of the right to self-determination. Turp and Sanjaume-Calvet, for example, talk about the emergence of a democratic right to self-determination. This entails the right of peoples to freely determine their political status, as part of implementing their right of self-determination, which comes with an essential corollary, the obligation for States to negotiate.[47] This theory draws inspiration from the views expressed by the Supreme Court of Canada in its 1998 Opinion on the secession of Quebec, which argues that the democratic principle "dictates that the clear repudiation of the existing constitutional order and the clear expression of the desire to pursue secession by the population of a province would give rise to a reciprocal obligation on all parties to Confederation to negotiate constitutional changes to respond to that desire".[48]

---

plebiscite, and a separate Basque citizenship, all under the right of the Basque peoples to self-determination.

44 Hannikainen (1988), p. 357, Tomuschat (1992), p. 39.

45 Rosas (1993), p. 228; Thornberry (1993), 101; Alfredson (1996), p. 59.

46 Cassese (1995), p. 346, Hannum (1996), p. 49.

47 Turp & Sanjaume-Calvet (2016), p. 252. See also: Turp (2020).

48 Para. 88 of Reference re Secession of Québec [1998] 2 Supreme Court Reports [S.C.R.] 217. Available at: http://scc-csc.lexum.com/scc-csc/scc-csc/en/1643/1/document.do, accessed, 2021.03.11.

Gilbert concurs by arguing that while there is no general international minority rights treaty granting autonomy, there is an emerging right to autonomy "that has developed from the right to self-determination, but which is in fact broader than self-determination, and is not confined to peoples", but includes national minority groups as well.[49] As he points out, existing international instruments support the idea of a right to autonomy for minority groups in society as a "necessary consequence of the combined effect of the right to self-determination and the rights of persons belonging to minorities to enjoy their own culture".[50]

Szalayné even argues that within the evolution of the right to self-determination, the emphasis is shifting, on the one hand, to peoples representing a minority in a state rather than peoples under colonial oppression and, on the other hand, to effective participation in public life, rather than secession. She also argued that such an evolution of this right is plausible as this is the way through which it can remain an effective part of international law and avoid being utterly "drained" as a legal instrument.[51] These ideas were already foreshadowed by Eide when he noted that "if effective political participation is denied to a minority and its members, this might in some cases give rise to a legitimate claim to self-determination".[52]

One can also find international documents underpinning the existence of internal self-determination. The Venice Commission confirmed that internal self-determination may be exercised by the "assertion of specific fundamental rights, with a collective character, in particular in the cultural sphere, or even by federalism, regionalism or other forms of local self-government within the state with all due regard to territorial integrity. Apart from the aforementioned cultural autonomy, federalism, regionalism, and possibly local self-government, may be mentioned".[53] Furthermore, in the CLRAE`s viewpoint: "In some case, especially when special status is established in order to accommodate ethno-cultural minority groups, it is considered to be the most genuine expression of internal self-determination of peoples".[54]

Lastly, case law is also available in the matter. Para 126 of the already mentioned Opinion [1998] 2 S.C.R. 217 of the Supreme Court of Canada on the legality of Quebec`s secession from Canada concludes that "the recognized

49 Gilbert (2002), p. 310.
50 *Id*, p. 353.
51 Szalayné (2003), p. 34.
52 Eide (2001), at para. 19.
53 Venice Commission (1999), p. 13.
54 See Section I/6. of the Explanatory Memorandum on CLRAE Resolution 361 (2013).

sources of international law establish that the right to self-determination of a people is normally fulfilled through internal self-determination – a people's pursuit of its political, economic, social, and cultural development within the framework of an existing state. A right to external self-determination (which in this case potentially takes the form of the assertion of a right to unilateral secession) arises in only the most extreme of cases and, even then, under carefully defined circumstances".[55] The autonomy statute of Gagauzia supports this approach as well. Article 1 (4) stipulates that in case of a change of the status of the Republic of Moldova as an independent state, the people of Gagauzia shall have the right of external self-determination.[56] This also presupposes that *Gagauz Yeri* otherwise exercises the internal right to self-determination through the institutions of the autonomy arrangement in force.

## 1.6 Historical Background

In this brief overview, I summarize the history of Hungarian minority affairs within Romania, with an emphasis on autonomy aspirations and their international context. In doing so, I have kept in mind the four relevant actors of such a discourse: the given minority communities, the host country, the kin-state, and the international community.

Central and Easter Europe has always been a buffer zone between the western parts of Europe and the larger foreign civilizations surrounding the continent.[57] Accordingly, this territory has always been a terrain where major powers have clashed, constantly intersecting the lives of the local population, as well as the borders they share with each other. Due to the Treaty of Trianon, the Hungarian Kingdom has lost two-thirds of its territory and population (including, at that time, more than 3.5 million ethnic Hungarians mostly living directly next to the newly established borders) as well as 80–100 % of its oil, gas, gold, silver,

---

55 Declaration 2625 (XXV.) of the General Assembly of the UN on Principles of International Law describes these circumstances and their consequences as follows: "subjection of peoples to alien subjugation, domination and exploitation constitutes a violation of the principle and is therefore prohibited. Such forcible action entitles the given peoples to seek and to receive support in accordance with the purposes and principles of the Charter, and at the same time disables the host country to invoke the principle of territorial integrity, as they lack a government that would represent the whole people belonging to the territory without distinction as to race, creed or colour".

56 The "change" in the status of Moldova refers, above all, to the country's possible union with Romania.

57 Mackinder (1904), p. 435.

iron ore, salt, and wood supplies.[58] A Treaty that caused a collective trauma for the Hungarian national community that is still tangible even after over a hundred years.

On the other hand, if we look at some of the most relevant Treaties concluded by Romania in the 19th and 20th centuries, we recurrently find provisions on religious and ethnic equality, as well as minority protection. This was true of the Treaty of Paris (1856), which granted autonomous status to Wallachia and Moldova within the Ottoman Empire, as well as the Treaty of Berlin (1878), which provided international recognition for Romania, the Treaty of Versailles (1919), which significantly expanded the borders of the country, and finally, the Treaty of Paris, which reaffirmed these expanded borders (1947).[59] These treaties were all contingent on accepting constraints on the country's authority regarding the treatment of minorities.[60] Moreover, after the First World War, monitoring and enforcement mechanisms were established within the League of Nations to safeguard the implementation of minority rights.

From a historical perspective, it's important to allude to the Treaty between the Principal Allied and Associated Powers and Romania, signed in Paris on 9 December 1919. By signing this treaty, Romania gave its consent to recognize the constitutional nature of some provisions that pertained to the acquisition of citizenship, as well as the enjoyment of civil and political rights without distinction as to race, language, or religion.[61] More importantly, Art. 11 of this treaty stipulated that "Romania agrees to accord to the communities of the Saxons and Szeklers in Transylvania autonomy in regard to educational and religious matters". The guarantor of this treaty was the League of Nations, as well as the Permanent Court of International Justice. In practice, this meant that Romania

58 For a vivid illustration of the economic and social consequences of the Trianon Peace Treaty, see the 73 maps in Emich et al. (1920).

59 This list can be further expanded as Romania made unilateral commitments to implement the documents of the CoE when acceding to the organization in 1993 and has similar commitments as a member state of the EU whose founding Treaties and secondary law also contain provisions on minority protection and the preservation of cultural and linguistic diversity (see, e.g. Art. 2 and 3 of the Treaty on the European Union or Art. 167 of the Treaty on the Functioning of the European Union).

60 Krasner (1999), pp. 73–105.

61 Article 1 of the treaty states that provisions contained in Art. 2 to 8 of the Treaty "shall be recognised as fundamental laws, and that no law, regulation or official action shall conflict or interfere with these stipulations, nor shall any law, regulation or official action prevail over them".

agreed that any member of the Council of the League of Nations shall have the right to bring to the attention of the Council any infraction, or any danger of infraction of these obligations, and that any difference of opinion regarding these obligations shall be referred to the Permanent Court of International Justice, the decisions of which shall be final and indisputable. Additionally, there was also the Declaration of *Alba Iulia/Gyulafehérvár*, adopted by the Romanian National Council in 1918, that - despite its essentially symbolic nature - promised "full national freedom for the co-existing peoples", adding that "each people will study, manage and judge in its own language" and that "equal rights and full autonomous religious freedom for all the religions in the State shall be granted".[62]

Contradicting these commitments on minority protection, in practice, Hungarians were deprived of their citizenship even years after the annexation of Transylvania (through Citizenship Law of 1924); their lands and property were subject to confiscation (as of the occupation of Transylvania); the use of the Hungarian language was systematically persecuted (as the Constitution of 1923 did not have any provisions on minority language protection); and later on, persons belonging to the Hungarian minority were even subject to pogroms and executions (as of 1944 onwards) carried out by paramilitary groups, most notably the so-called Maniu Guards.

The malleable political environment of the late 1910s and early 1920s gave birth to numerous plans on the future of Transylvania, coming from Hungarians, Romanians, and Germans (Saxons) alike. These plans included the establishment of a confederation of nationalities, based mainly on the Swiss model: territorial revision, population exchange in order to increase the homogeneity of a given region, the foundation of an independent Transylvanian state, and the establishment of various autonomous arrangements.[63]

During the interwar-period and throughout the course of the Second World War, Hungary's *raison d'état* was to regain the territories lost after the First World War. Due to the First and Second Vienna Awards concluded in 1938 and 1940 (see Fig. 2), territories in south-eastern Czechoslovakia, north-western Romania, and northern Yugoslavia, inhabited mostly by Hungarians, came

62 It was this gathering of the Romanian National Council which declared the union of Transylvania with Romania on 1 December 1918, a national holiday in Romania today. For the historical context, it is important to note that this declaration was not made by the Romanian state but by a group of Romanian-speaking individuals, most of whom were citizens of the Austro-Hungarian Monarchy at that time.

63 Bárdi (2004), pp. 330–331.

under Hungarian rule again. These Awards were annulled by the Paris Peace Treaties in 1947, re-establishing the pre-1938 borders.

After the Second World War, both Romania and Hungary were integrated into the "Eastern bloc". The Romanian communist party was pressured by its Soviet counterpart to grant autonomy to the territory populated overwhelmingly by the Hungarian-speaking Szekler community.[64] Articles 19–21 of the 1952 Constitution were adopted accordingly to establish the Hungarian Autonomous Province.[65] Support for Hungarian autonomy was seen as a bargaining chip by the Soviet Union, providing leverage over Romania. Having been incorporated into a totalitarian political system, void of democracy and the rule of law, the Hungarian Autonomous Province cannot be characterized as a political territorial autonomy, in modern terms, as the central state did not actually confer any legislative or executive powers to the Province under the auspices of decentralization (it did, however, bring forth a more widespread use of the Hungarian language).

The borders of the Province were changed already eight years later, on 24 December 1960, by expanding the western borders with Romanian-majority territories (*Ludas, Sármás* and *Dicső rajons*), and at the same time detaching the overwhelmingly Hungarian rajons of Sepsi (85.3 % Hungarian) and Kézdi (91.2 % Hungarian),[66] decreasing the overall proportion of Hungarians from 77.3 to 66.2 % .[67] This so-called Maros-Hungarian Autonomous Province was then entirely abolished by the administrative reform of 1968,[68] establishing the currently existing administrative division of Romania (for these border changes, see Fig. 3).[69]

64 For more background information on the subject, see: Bottoni (2008).

65 77.32 % (565,510 persons) of the total population (731,387) of the Province was of Hungarian origin according to the data of the Statistical Office; the number rises to 78.71 % if we count the Hungarian-speaking population (containing in that case also other minorities, mostly Jews, whose second identity was closer to Hungarian); see: *Directia Centrala de Statistica – Directia Regionala de Statistica* (1960), pp. 4043.

66 Rajons were administrative sub-division of Counties.

67 See: Miklósné Zakar (2010).

68 In this sense, this short-lived Szekler autonomy joined the ranks of other autonomy arrangements that were abolished due to continuous resistance of the central government (e.g. Chittagong autonomy in Bangladesh under the Chittagong Hill Tracts Accord 1997, South Sudan under the 1971 Addis Abeba Agreement, or the repeal of Eritrea's autonomy under the UN in 1962. Examples mentioned in Ghai (2011), p. 96.).

69 In fact, Law No. 2 of 1968 on the administrative organization of the territory of the Socialist Republic of Romania is still in force (a subsequent amendment from 1981 deleted the word "Socalist Republic" from the title).

The fall of the "Iron Curtain" and the dissolution of the Soviet Union and Yugoslavia put the question of self-determination and minority rights in the spotlight again, at a time when Romania was facing internal unrest on the one hand, and seeking to reorganize its international relations on the other, firstly, by acceding to the CoE.[70] The Hungarian minority played an important role in this period as the political transition in Romania was ignited by the harassment of Hungarian clergymen Tőkés László, and also because of the so-called Black March. The latter refers to events that occurred in the historical capitol of Szeklerland, *Marosvásárhely/Târgu-Mureș* between 16 and 21 March. Following a series of protests aimed at achieving education in Hungarian language, the far right, nationalist organization *Vatra Romanesca* gathered Romanians from surrounding communes and engaged in violent clashes with protesting Hungarians, resulting in five dead (three Hungarians and two Romanians) and almost three hundred wounded. While some of the details of this incident are still vague, one of the possible explanations is that members of the *Securitate*, the communist secret service, wanted to secure their positions for after the political transition and fabricated an ethnic conflict to underpin the relevance of their presence in a newly formed security agency.[71]

Romania's accession to the CoE and the adoption of Recommendation 1201 in 1993 by the PACE were all favourable developments,[72] placing the question of autonomy in the focal point of the identity-building activity of the sole representative organization of the Hungarian community, the Democratic Alliance of Hungarians in Romania (DAHR, or in Hungarian: Romániai Magyar Demokrata Szövetség - RMDSZ). The draft Law on Minorities and Autonomous Communities, adopted in 1993 on the 3rd annual Congress of the DAHR, foresaw the establishment of a three-pillar system: 1) cultural (or personal) autonomy for members of a minority, 2) the establishment of special statuses for municipalities where a given minority forms the majority, 3) and regional territorial autonomy accruing from the assembly of municipalities with special status.[73] Senator of DAHR, Csapó József further elaborated the 3rd pillar of the above system by

70 Romania joined the CoE on 7 October 1993, NATO on 29 March 2004, and the EU on 1 January 2007.

71 See such argument, among others, in Kincses (1990).

72 As part of their application for membership in the CoE, a written declaration was adopted, which states that Romanian authorities commit themselves to basing their policy regarding the protection of minorities on the principles laid down in Recommendation 1201 (1993). See para 5 of Opinion 176 (1993) of the PACE.

73 See: RMDSZ (1993).

drafting an autonomy statute for Szeklerland (referred to earlier as DL). This draft became the fundamental document of the Szekler National Council (SzNC), founded by Csapó as a representative body – a proto-parliament – for the Szekler Communes in 2003, with the sole purpose to achieve territorial autonomy for Szeklerland.[74] This document is of particular relevance as the only draft which the Parliament of Romania has voted on and reacted to in official documents (I will discuss these reactions in detail in the following chapters).

Meanwhile, the kin-state, Hungary, made attempts to develop an internal minority policy that could serve as a positive example for the countries of Central and Eastern Europe.[75] For this purpose, the country has granted cultural autonomy for all thirteen recognized minorities of the country[76] and voiced the relevance of such an approach *expressis verbis* during the elaboration of a new constitution in 2010, which led to the current Fundamental Law stipulating that "the nationalities of the country form part of the Hungarian political community and are constituent parts of the State".[77] Additionally, consecutive Hungarian governments implemented various kin-state activities: they established the structure of financial and cultural support through various funds; created the public television Danube TV (Duna TV), originally intended to broadcast programs to/and about Hungarians living abroad

74 It was in the same year (2003) that the ethno-regional party palette started to pluralize, as members of DAHR who were unsatisfied with the party's achievement regarding autonomy and minority rights started to establish their separate organizations. Consequently, there are five relevant political organizations advocating the interest of Hungarians in Romania today: DAHR, the Civic Party, the Transylvanian Hungarian People's Party, the Transylvanian Hungarian National Council, and the Szekler National Council.

75 This approach was not a novelty from the Hungarian political elite. As Krasner reminds, domestic support for minority protection in Hungary was present from the end of the First World War, as the country perceived these provisions as a means of protecting their co-ethnics in other countries. See: Krasner (1999) *Supra note*, p. 95.

76 According to Act LXXVII of 1993 on the Rights of National and Ethnic Minorities, the recognized minorities are: Bulgarians, Greeks, Croatians, Poles, Germans, Armenians, Roma, Romanians, Ruthenians, Serbians, Slovaks, Slovenes, and Ukrainians. This Law was replaced in 2011 by Law CLXXIX on the Rights of Nationalities. In this Law, as well as in the Constitution of Hungary, the term "nationality" is being used consistently in order to signal that Hungary recognizes the existence of collective minority rights.

77 Source: Preamble of the Fundamental Law of Hungary. The same pledge, phrased differently, was already present in the legal system of Hungary following the political transition due to the constitutional amendments adopted as of 1989.

(Antall government: 1990–1994); concluded a series of bilateral Treaties with surrounding countries on good neighbourly relations and cooperation addressing the importance to have a historical reconciliation between Hungary and its neighbours containing also provisions on minority protection (Horn-government: 1994–1998);[78] provided preferential access to Hungarian public services and education institutions for kinspeople living abroad through the Status Law (1st Orbán government: 1998–2002); and granted naturalization on preferential terms, including the right to vote on Hungary's parliamentary elections (2nd Orbán government: 2010–2014).[79]

From Hungary's point of view, their approach ranged from irredentism (1920–1945) and total neglect towards kinspeople abroad (1945–1990) to active kin-state politics (from 1990 onwards) as a means of preserving Hungarian minority communities living behind the state borders, in ever-decreasing numbers (See Tab. 1 and Figs. 4 and 5 in the Annexes for data and illustration). Historical developments on Romania's side show that central governments were never really keen to implement their international commitments in good faith and accepted only temporary limitations on their sovereignty in relation to their treatment of minorities to reach other goals in the process: state recognition, territorial gains, or membership in international organizations.

## 1.7 What and Why

### 1.7.1 Basic Features of the Draft Law on the Autonomy of Szeklerland

Over a dozen statute drafts have been crafted by various organizations since the political transition in Romania, the most salient of which is that of the

78 Article 15 contained these provisions, which included: prohibition of discrimination, prohibition of measures that would alter the ethnic proportions, the right to establish and operate minority organizations, the right to take part effectively in decisions-making, the right to use their mother tongue, and the right to preserve their material and architectural memorials and memorial sites constituting their cultural heritage, history and traditions.

79 Hungary's foreign policy has three basic piers which haven't changed much since the Antall- administration: 1) involvement in the Euro-Atlantic integration, 2) a peaceful and prosperous partnership with adjacent countries, 3) and taking responsibility for Hungarians living abroad. Throughout the years, left-wing administrations tended to emphasize the first pier, while right-wing governments stressed the latter one, leaving the EU integration as a common point of consent.

Szekler National Council.[80] So far this is the only draft which the Romanian legislature has had a formal vote on (four times) and the only one that has been approved by the local citizens in an informal referendum. The first four sections of the General Provisions of the DL adopted by the Szekler National Council resemble the Catalan and Basque statutes in referring to the special identity of the legal subjects of the autonomy. Section 1 (1) begins with stipulating that "in order to express its historical self-identity, to guarantee equal opportunity to its citizens and to safeguard its Hungarian identity, Szeklerland's population will be transformed into a self-governing community". The DL foresees the establishment of an autonomous executive power (The Municipal Committee/*Önkormányzati Bizottság*, hereinafter The Committee)[81] responsible to the autonomous legislature (The Municipal Council/*Önkormányzati Tanács*, hereinafter The Council),[82] whose representatives would be elected by direct and universal suffrage in a free and secret ballot. The legal basis of the autonomy would be provided, among others, by Art. 117 (3) of the Constitution, allowing for the establishment of autonomous administrative authorities. Pursuant to Art. 73 (3) r) of the Constitution, the Statute would be enacted as an organic law,[83] the passing of which requires a majority vote of the members of each Chamber of the Romanian Parliament.[84] Inspired by the Romanian constitutional framework, parallel with the head of the autonomous government, Szeklerland would also have a president,[85] who is directly elected for a term of four years and who can assume this position for two terms of office at most. The president represents the region, appoints the head of The Committee, proposes the date of the Council elections, signs and promulgates legislation of The Council (whose acts are subject to the scrutiny of the Constitutional Court of Romania), and, if asked by the head of the autonomous government, presides over the meetings of The Committee.

---

80 See: Szekler National Council (2009), also available online at the homepage of SzNC: https://www.sznt.org/hu/dokumentumok/statutum/8-szekelyfoeld-autonomia-statutuma, accessed: 2021.07.22.

81 DL Section 30–36.

82 DL Section 19–29.

83 This is a similarity with the Spanish constitutional system, where organic acts are those approving the Statutes of Autonomy (as well as those relating to the implementation of fundamental rights and public liberties: Spanish Constitution Section 81).

84 Art. 76 CR.

85 DL Section 37–46.

With regards to the internal administrative division, the historical Szekler Seats (*Szék*) would be re-established, having the same basic institutions as the whole of the region (council, committee, president).[86] The Council of Szeklerland would have exclusive legislative competencies in the following areas: education and culture, mass communication and media, public welfare, roads and transportation, local commercial and industrial activity, agriculture, forestry, mining and energy production, determining its own municipal system, ownership and management of public property and utilities, levying and collecting own taxes and fees. The autonomous parliament would have its seat in the historical capitol *Marosvásárhely/Târgu-Mureș* (presumably in the building that today serves as the seat of the Council of Maros County).[87] Finally, the annex of the Statute enumerates all 153 municipalities that would be part of an autonomous Szeklerland.

The drafters of the Statute were largely influenced by provisions of existing European autonomy statutes. Similar to South Tyrol, the education system would have linguistically parallel organizational structures. Separate Hungarian and Romanian language education institutions would exist from kindergartens to universities. In Hungarian schools, the teaching language would be Hungarian, and Romanian would be a compulsory taught subject. Hungarian would become an official language of the region together with the Romanian language.[88] To ensure the effective use of both languages in public administration, a quota would be introduced, similar to the one that exists in South Tyrol.[89] According to Sections 97 of the DL, the linguistic composition of employees within public institutions should reflect the proportion between the linguistic groups of the region, as established by the last official census. The financing of the autonomous competencies would not be totally emancipated from state subsidies but would nonetheless be mostly ensured through local taxes and fees. Similar to the Basque fiscal autonomy, all locally generated revenues would be collected and administered by the respective institutions of the autonomous region.[90] A Commissioner

86 DL Section 47–68.

87 After the adoption of the DL, Maros County, as we know it today, would cease to exist, as only some communes of it would form a part of the autonomous Szeklerland. For an enumeration of these communes, see: Appendix No. 1 of the DL.

88 DL Section 82–96.

89 In South Tyrol, this system is often referred to as an "ethnic mirror image"/"*ethnische Spiegelbildlichkeit*".

90 DL Section 103–116.

appointed by the Romanian government would be the highest representative of the central state in Szeklerland, who also mediates in disputes between the state and the region.[91] Lastly, the DL provides a regional entrenchment in stipulating that the amendment of the Statute can only be initiated by the autonomous legislature and that every amendment or the abolishment of the Statute as a whole has to be approved by the local electorate on a referendum.[92]

### 1.7.2 Driving Forces Behind Szekler Autonomy Aspirations

Similar to the case of Tyrol in the Habsburg Monarchy, Szeklerland was a border guard region of the Hungarian Kingdom since the early Middle Ages. As a military class, Szeklers obtained a special status within the social order of the kingdom and developed their special heraldic symbols and flags that symbolized this status.[93] Szeklers were all free men who were exempted from paying taxes to the King in exchange for their military services. As of the 15th century, these various rights and liberties were codified in several acts, constituting a separate Szekler law within the legal system of Hungary.[94] As a consequence of these historical developments, self-governance has been a vital part of their self-identity, which many of them feel currently deprived of, and under modern circumstances could be best re-established in the form of a territorial autonomy. Contrary to

---

91 *Id.* at Section 119. While this office was based on the institution of the prefects, it is noteworthy to mention that a similar way of facilitating connections between state and autonomous entity exists in the Åland islands, where a Governor is appointed by the president of Finland, after having agreed on the matter with the Speaker of the Åland Parliament (see Section 52 of the Act on Autonomy of Åland).

92 *Id.* at Section 13 and 125.

93 Szeklers were not the only ones who received such special "autonomous" status. Consecutive Hungarian rulers granted similar territorial self-governing rights in exchange for military service to Saxons, Romanians, Cumans (*Kun*), Jassic (*Jász*) people and Serbs from the 13th century, the majority of which remained in existence until the second half of the 19th century. Additionally, Croatia formed a part of Hungary from 1102 till 1918 in the framework of a personal union (meaning that the King of Hungary, by virtue of his office, also became the King of Croatia) and was led by the *Bán*, who had widespread exclusive competencies, including the right to mint money and to gather an own army without the consent of the king. For more information about the autonomy arrangements that existed in the Hungarian Kingdom, see: Kocsis (2013), p. 119.

94 From the founding of the Hungarian Kingdom in 1 January 1001 till the adoption of the Stalinist constitution in 20 August 1949, Hungary functioned under a common law system, similar to that of the UK.

the ambitious set of competencies enshrined in the DL, there are numerous deficiencies in the currently existing legal protection afforded to the national minorities of Romania. Below I illustrate some of these deficiencies through the findings of various human rights monitoring bodies of international organizations, showing that there are problems that persist over time, highlighting also some salient cases, and unresolved issues that lay the groundwork for the Szekler community's demand for territorial autonomy.

As a brief introduction to this sub-chapter, it is useful to shed light on the attitudes of Romanians towards minority rights in general (including linguistic rights, education in minority language, and the right to use one's mother tongue in public administration) and the right to effective participation in public life in particular (including attitudes towards territorial autonomy). During the spring of 2019, the Public Policy Institute of Szeklerland (*Székelyföldi Közpolitikai Intézet*) and the Bálványos Institute conducted a survey involving over 2200 participants from across Romania (half of which were ethnic Romanians and the other half ethnic Hungarians living in Transylvania) to gauge their attitudes in a variety of questions, including those related to minority rights and aspirations. When asked about minority rights in general, 29 % of ethnic Romanians replied that national minorities have too many rights, while 45 % of them said that the current level of minority protection is sufficient enough. The same numbers among Transylvanian Hungarians were 3 % and 30 %, respectively. Most minority Hungarians (57 %) said that the level of minority protection in Romania is insufficient. Only 47 % of ethnic Romanian respondents agreed that minority Hungarians should have access to secondary school education in their mother tongue (this number decreases to 43 % in relation to university education), and only 26 % agreed that they should have a separate Hungarian school system.

There is an inverse relationship between support for minority rights and aspirations and the sphere of public administration. The more it appears to empower the Hungarian minority community, the less support has the topic received from ethnic Romanians. In the survey, only 40 % of Romanians thought that members of the Hungarian national community should have the right to be elected as mayors or members of the Romanian parliament. The proportion of respondents who agreed that Hungarians should be able to use their mother tongue in public administration (e.g. at municipalities or before Courts) was limited to 21 %. Finally, only 13 % of Romanian respondents agreed that Hungarians should have autonomy in regions where they represent the majority.[95]

95 For more data, see: Kiss et al. (2020), pp. 133–142.

The above-described negative attitude towards the rights of Hungarians is also echoed in the negative stereotypes surrounding this minority community. The European Commission against Racism and Intolerance (ECRI) presented evidence in their reports of a general social climate pervaded by hostile attitudes towards Hungarians. More specifically, the ECRI noted that Romanian school textbooks contain stereotypes and prejudice about minority groups. Some textbooks, for example, continue to describe the arrival in Romania of "hordes of barbarian nomads who came from the East to spread terror", and the Hungarians are sometimes depicted as foreigners who occupied the Transylvania region. The history course taught to Romanian pupils is entitled "History of the Romanians" rather than "History of Romania".[96]

The ECRI further noted that certain politicians and media have used very harsh discourse targeting Hungarians, which has created tensions between the majority population and this community. More specifically they mentioned that "derogatory public statements have often been expressed in the context of the long-standing tension persisting between the Hungarian national minority and the state authorities, mostly with political overtones arising from the discussion over demands for autonomy and the use of the Szekler flag and symbols in public places".[97]

Layering this picture, the ECRI added that sports events have continued to be a forum for incidents of hate speech: "For example, during a match between the teams Sepsi and Dinamo Bucureşti in Bucharest in 2017, the fans of the host team chanted >>Out with the Hungarians from the country<<. Both parties were condemned to pay a fine of 10,000 RON (2,200 EUR) by the NCCD.[98] The Advisory Committee (AC) of the Framework Convention for the Protection of National Minorities (FCNM) made similar observations as they concluded that "racism and anti-Hungarian sentiment continue to be a negative undercurrent at sports events in Romania". As an example, they mentioned that fans of the basketball team *CSU Atlassib Sibiu* displayed during a game with *BC Târgu Mureş* in 2014 a banner with sexually explicit insults directed at ethnic Hungarians and repeatedly chanted >>Hungarians, out of the country<<)".[99]

96 ECRI (2005), at para. 81.
97 ECRI (2019), at para. 25.
98 *Id.* at para. 32.
99 Source: AC (2017),at para. 62.

### *1.7.2.1 Linguistic Rights, Cultural and Educational Issues*

The European Charter for Regional or Minority Languages (hereinafter, Charter or ECRML) entered into force in Romania on 1 May 2008.[100] The Committee of Experts of the Charter (COMEX) have so far completed two rounds of evaluation on the implementation of the Charter, resulting in reports adopted on 19 June 2012 and 21 December 2017, respectively. Both reports conclude that a significant part of the undertakings[101] were not fully implemented.[102] The first monitoring cycle concluded that out of a total number of 61 undertakings that were relevant from the point of the Hungarian language, only 14 were entirely fulfilled.[103] Eighteen undertakings were only partly fulfilled, including three instances where the undertaking was considered formally fulfilled, but the Committee had concerns about their practical implementation.[104] One undertaking was not fulfilled,[105] while the biggest part of undertakings were those which were not mentioned in the periodical report provided by the Romanian

100 The Language Charter was ratified by Romania through Law No. 282 of 24 October 2007. Available: http://legislatie.just.ro/Public/DetaliiDocument/86674, accessed: 2015.06.23.

101 These undertakings include, among others: availability of education in Hungarian from preschool to Universities; facilitation and/or encouragement of the use of Hungarian, in speech and writing, in private and public life (education, judicial authorities, administrative authorities and public services, media, cultural activities and facilities, economic and social life); guarantee the accused the right to use Hungarian in judicial proceedings; ensure that officers of local branches of the national authorities use Hungarian in their relations with persons applying to them in Hungarian; guarantee freedom of direct reception of radio and television broadcasts from neighbouring countries in Hungarian; encourage production, reproduction, and dissemination of cultural works in Hungarian; or facilitate and/or promote cooperation across borders, in particular between regional or local authorities in whose territory Hungarian is used in identical or similar form.

102 See those parts that are relevant from the Hungarian minorities point of view under: COMEX (2011), pp. 74–91.

103 Fulfilled undertakings were: Art. 8 – Para. 1 a i, b i, c i, e i; Art. 9 – Para. 3; Art. 11 – Para. 1 b i, c i, Para. 2 and 3; Art. 12 – Para. 1 a, b, d, e, f.

104 Partly fulfilled undertakings were: Art. 8 – Para. 1 d i,f i, h; Art. 9 – Para. 1 a ii, b ii, c ii; Art. 10 – Para. 1 a ii, b, c; Para. 2 b, d, g, Para. 4 b; Art. 11 – Para. 1 a ii, d i, g; Art. 13 - Para. 2 e.

105 This was Art. 9 – Para. 3.

authorities.[106] Altogether, there were 28 instances where the Committee was not in a position to conclude on the fulfilment of an undertaking, as the periodical report did not contain any specific information on these. The most "problematic" provision of the Charter proved to be Art. 10 on the use of language by administrative authorities and public services. Here none of the 13 undertakings were entirely fulfilled. Altogether, the COMEX found the following deficiencies: Romanian legislation limits the application of several provisions of Art. 10 to municipalities where 20 % of the population belongs to a national minority.[107] It was recommended to lower the general thresholds in the field of administrative authorities in order to make them compatible with the Charter. Even in localities which meet this very high 20 % threshold, there were severe problems with the implementation of the Charter. To illustrate these problems, the COMEX mentions findings of a shadow report of a locally based NGO called the Civic Engagement Movement (CEMO).[108] The CEMO sent applications in Hungarian to 76 State authorities, local authorities, and public service providers located in *Mureş/Maros* County, where 39.3 % of the population belongs to the Hungarian minority, in order to test whether the right of the Hungarian minority to communicate with public authorities in the minority language is guaranteed, as stipulated by both the Charter, the FCNM, as well as Romanian law on public administration. In its letters, The CEMO asked for replies in Hungarian and made reference to relevant national laws and Art. 10 of the Charter. According to the shadow report, 19 institutions replied bilingually on the substance of the request and 13 in Romanian only, 11 replied in Romanian that the request should be submitted again in the official language, and 33 did not reply at all.[109]

---

106 These were: Art. 8 – Para. 1 fi, g, i, Para. 2; Art. 9 – Para. 1 a iii, b iii, c iii, d, Para. 2; Art. 10 – Para. 2 c, e, f, Para. 4 c, Para. 5; Art. 11 – Para. 1 ei, fi; Art. 12 – Para. 1 b, c, g, h, Para. 2 and 3; Art. 13 – Para. 1 a, b, c, Para. 2 c, d; Art. 14 b.

107 This observation was also mentioned in AC (2017), at para 87-92. The AC further added in para. 91 of this Opinion that, even though article 131 of Law No. 215/2001 expressly states that the provisions of the law remain in effect if the share of a given minority population falls below this 20 % threshold, "in all 15 territorial units where the proportion of persons belonging to the Hungarian minority decreased between censuses of 2001 and 2011 under 20 % the use of the Hungarian language all but ceased in contacts with local public administration in these settlements and none of them translate their official documents, or issue forms in the Hungarian language".

108 The CEMO was preoccupied with advocacy work on behalf of the Hungarian minority community in Romania in general, and those living in Marosvásárhely in particular.

109 See: COMEX (2011), at para. 536.

Similar observations were made in a survey conducted in 2016 by the Democratic Alliance of Hungarians in Romania. All together there are 325 municipalities where persons belonging to the Hungarian national minority constitute more than 20 % of the population. In 102 of these municipalities (located in the Hargita and Kovászna counties), persons belonging to the Hungarian community constitute the majority. The survey found that of all the municipalities contacted, only 130 provided replies on the possibility to use the Hungarian language in relations with the relevant public administration authorities. This is only 40 % of all municipalities that should apply this rule.[110]

The COMEX noted that the use of use of traditional place names in Hungarian in the relevant domains (street names, public transport, and tourist signs or signposts) is not always consistent in areas where the 20 % threshold has been reached and often depends on local initiatives. At times, the Hungarian inscriptions are erroneous or incomplete, for example, in some cases, the Hungarian word for "street" is added to a Romanian name without translating the latter into Hungarian (e.g. "*strada Justiţiei utca*" rather than correct "*strada Justiţiei/Bíróság utca*"). The COMEX reminded that such partial transcription was considered in 2014 by the NCCD (National Council for Combating Discrimination / *Consiliul Naţional pentru Combaterea Discriminării*) to constitute discrimination.[111] Furthermore, the corresponding Romanian legislation does not pertain to place names other than the names of villages/municipalities (e.g. names of streets or geographical features). Romanian counties often fail to use or adopt place names in a minority language, given that they are under no legal obligation to do so, despite being recommended by the COMEX.[112] While the Experts Committee noted some developments in implementation practices during the second monitoring cycle,[113] Art. 10 of the ECRML continued to be the most problematic part. One of the undertakings that was still considered

110 This observation is cited in: AC (2017), at para. 89–90.

111 COMEX (2011), at para. 560.

112 See, for example, COMEX (2017), at para. 18.

113 According to the conclusions of the second monitoring cycle, there were 39 fulfilled undertakings; 21 partly fulfilled (including 3 which was formally fulfilled); 2 not fulfilled; 9 with no conclusion (meaning that the information provided by the state authorities were lacking or insufficient to conclude on the undertaking). The second cycle monitoring procedure grouped these undertakings in a slightly different manner (by including Part II, Art. 7 undertakings in the total count not just the ones under Part III of the Charter), which is why the total count amounted to 71, as opposed to 61 in the first cycle.

unfulfilled was to ensure that Hungarian is used in the provision of public services.[114]

Regarding cultural and educational issues, the COMEX mentions that it is not always possible for children from Hungarian-speaking families to receive Hungarian-medium education from kindergarten to upper secondary school in all the places where Hungarian speakers traditionally reside. There is also no television channel in Hungarian on the national level.

As far as linguistic rights are concerned, the ethnically mixed capital of Szeklerland, *Marosvásárhely*, is the primary "battleground", as the city with the largest Hungarian community (approximately 60,000) that represents nearly half of the total population of the city. Browsing the activity of the above-mentioned advocacy group, the CEMO, the same systemic deficiencies signalled by the COMEX come to the fore also in other spheres of life. The communication used in public (mixed) schools in *Marosvásárhely* is predominantly monolingual (i.e. Romanian),[115] including the general communication with students and parents, the communication relating to public interest information, signs in classrooms, bulletin boards, as well as their homepages. The CEMO made similar observations when analysing the linguistic landscape of the whole city. The language of public road signs, street names, place names, and inscription on local or central government buildings is predominantly monolingual, in a city where almost half of the population belongs to the Hungarian minority community.[116] One of the practical actions of the CEMO included placing bilingual street name signs across the city as their own initiative. This action was not well received by the local police, which fined two volunteers who were "caught in the act" to 1,150 EUR each for "illegal advertising". The CEMO also engaged in strategic litigation – against the Mayor's Offices of three cities where the non-implementation of minority linguistic rights is most conspicuous, namely *Marosvásárhely*, *Nagyvárad/Oradea*, and *Szatmárnémeti/Satu Mare* – to advocate for the implementation of Law No. 215/2001 on local public administration, as well as provisions of the ECRML that were ratified by Romania. In their responses to the complaints sent by the CEMO, these public institutions claimed that the ECRML cannot be applied in the case of bilingual street signs given that

114 The other being the failure to facilitate the creation of at least one public radio station and one public television channel in Hungarian.

115 The CEMO analysed 30 primary and high schools in *Maros/Mureș* county in 2016. See more details in: Civic Engagement Movement (2016), pp. 32–35.

116 *Id.* at pp. 36–40.

domestic legislation does not stipulate any such obligation, and Law No. 215/ 2001 does not allow the placement of bilingual street signs.[117]

This general approach of non-implementation of existing linguistic rights produced some notable cases, resulting in discontent among the Hungarian community of Romania. The most salient of these was that of the University of Medicine and Pharmacy in *Târgu Mureş*, or in Hungarian*: Marosvásárhelyi Gyógyszerészeti és Orvostudományi Egyetem (MOGYE).*[118] Article 363 of the Education Law adopted on 5 January 2011 (*2013 Legea Educatiei Nationale No. 1 din 5 Ianuarie 2011*) enumerates three specific universities that are "multicultural and multilingual".[119] These are: 1.) Babes-Bolyai University in Cluj-Napoca – teaching languages are: Romanian, Hungarian, and German; 2.) University of Medicine and Pharmacy in *Târgu Mureş* – teaching in Romanian and Hungarian; 3.) Arts University in *Târgu Mureş* – teaching in Romanian and Hungarian. The same article also stipulates that the senates of the respective universities must, within six months from the entry into force of the law, adopt their new university charters pursuant to these provisions. In the first and the third cases, the establishment of the minority language department was implemented, in the case of MOGYE, however, the Romanian majority of the Universities Senate denied to follow suit and adopted a Charter that does not foresee the establishment of a Hungarian department.[120] Given that this conduct manifestly violated

---

117 *Id.* at p. 45.

118 The continuous calls of members of the Hungarian minority community for the establishment of an independent Medical Department at MOGYE using the Hungarian language was also noted in: AC (2017), at para. 127. Another education-related case that raised concerns of the AC was the threat of closing of the Rákóczi Ferenc High School in Târgu Mureş established in 2014 with the approval of the local authorities, in a building belonging to the Roman-Catholic Church and providing education in the Hungarian language. The AC noted that in 2015, "the National Anti-corruption Agency filed criminal charges concerning alleged corruption in allocation by the local authorities of funds for the renovation of the building which houses the school. This procedure is still ongoing. Furthermore, in the spring of 2017, the County School Inspectorate did not authorise enrolment of children in the 1st, 5th and 9th grades for the school year 2017–18, arguing that the school has not been properly registered with the Ministry of Education, Research, Youth and Sports" (*Id.* at para. 118).

119 Source: http://www.cdep.ro/proiecte/2010/500/80/7/leg_pl587_10.pdf, accessed: 2021.03.16.

120 See the English translation of the Charter of the University here: https://www.umftgm.ro/fileadmin/documente_oficiale/regulamente/UMFTGM-REG-01_EN.pdf, accessed: 2016.04.11.

the Education Law, the newly elected prime minister at the time, Mihai Răzvan Ungureanu, adopted a governmental decree on 13 March 2012 that established the Hungarian department. As a reaction to this, the opposition, led by social democratic Victor Ponta, lodged a motion of no confidence on 17 April 2012, claiming that the cabinet had violated the universities' autonomy with its decree, that it had been blackmailed to act against Romanian interest, and that a separate Hungarian department would only encourage separatism, and not multiculturalism. On 27 April 2012, 235 representatives voted in favour of the motion (259 of a total of 460 MPs were present at the vote),[121] and Ungureanu fell from power, only 78 days after his inauguration. The separate Hungarian department of the Pharmaceutical University has still not been established. As a matter of fact, the Senate of MOGYE adopted a resolution on 18 April 2018 to merge MOGYE with the Romanian-language Petru Maior University. The new institution was renamed University of Medicine, Pharmacy, Science and Technology of Târgu Mureş.[122] This vote was preceded by continuous protest of local Hungarians and the Hungarian-speaking staff of the University. Hungarian professors of the institution refused to take part in the vote, and Hungarian political forces in Romania have unanimously considered that this step ruins Hungarian medical education in *Marosvásárhely/Târgu Mureş* and eliminates the multicultural nature of the university.[123]

Another prominent case was that of Landman Gábor, an interpreter and a Dutch citizen of Frisian and Hungarian origin, who accompanied a Dutch journalist on 24 December 2013 who wanted to inquire information at the local police station in *Marosvásárhely/Târgu Mureş*.[124] Given that half of the population of the city is Hungarian, the use of the Hungarian language should be guaranteed in all public administration offices. On the contrary, after repeatedly trying to communicate with the local police staff in Hungarian, English, German, French, and

121 The motion also mentioned the clientelism of the administration and that it privatizes public property to cronies of the PDL party. See the original text here: http://legislatie.just.ro/Public/DetaliiDocument/137465, accessed: 2021.03.16.

122 The institution was subsequently renamed in the summer of 2019 again after a Romanian cell biologist, George Emil Palade.

123 Tasi Annabella: *Megszavazták: egyesül a MOGYE és a Petru Maior Egyetem. Magyar Szó Online*, 2018.04.18, available at: https://maszol.ro/belfold/95175-frissitve-megszavaztak-egyesul-a-mogye-es-a-petru-maior-egyetem, accessed: 2021.01.18.

124 Mr. Landman was present in order to liaise between the Dutch journalist and the police authorities. He was a contractor of the journalist as an interpreter authorized by the Court of Amsterdam.

Dutch languages, the police officers got aggravated, handcuffed Mr. Landman, escorted him into an interrogation room, where they pulled down the shades, and one of the officers punched him in the back asking him if he wanted to start a revolution.[125] Mr. Landman later pressed criminal charges against the police officers at the court of *Maros/Mureş* for denial of public services on linguistic grounds. The police reacted to the allegations and stated in a written response that citizens of the EU are not entitled to the same rights as Romanian citizens.[126] They denied that the incident had happened and issued what Mr. Landman says is a falsified report of the events of that day, where the police claims that Mr. Landman and the Dutch journalist entered the police premises illegally (for which Mr. Landman received a fine of 1,500 RON).[127] This report was later on contested by Landman before the competent Court, which ruled in favour of the police on 10 July 2017, a decision that was overruled in the second instance judgement on 29 September 2020.[128] Even so, none of the police officers received any penalty for their actions.

In view of this background, it is not surprising that the DL envisages granting official status to the Hungarian language in Szeklerland.

### *1.7.2.2 Religious Discrimination*

Another contentious issue is the restitution of property that had been confiscated during the communist regime from religious denominations. This restitution process was characterized by the ECRI as extremely slow, having many unsolved cases. As an example, they mention that out of the 2522 restitution requests submitted by Hungarian-minority religious institutions, 1103 remained pending.[129] It was found that the reason for this slowness is that "local authorities have in many cases obstructed the restitution of property, by: not providing information relating to the disputed property; refusing to return certain

---

125 For more information on this incident, visit the advocacy page of Landman Gábor at: http://politialocala.eu/, or view a summary at: http://skypreter.eu/TIRGUMURES_MAROSVASARHELY.pdf, accessed: 2021.02.22.

126 Notably, the ECRML pertains to languages, and not members of minorities using those languages. In this sense, such a restrictive interpretation is not in line with the provisions of the ECRML.

127 See the original document: http://politialocala.eu/ACHTERAF_VERVALST_PROCESVERBAAL_WEB.jpg, accessed: 2021.03.17.

128 Mr. Landman also lodged an application with the European Court of Human Rights on 20 October 2020. The case is still pending.

129 ECRI (2014), at para. 19.

properties; and challenging before court the decisions of the Special Restitution Commission, the section within the National Authority for Property Restitution responsible for returning religious and national/ethnic communal property". As regards, in particular, the return of communal real estate belonging to national/ethnic minorities, between 2006 and May 2011, out of a total of 2,000 claims, only 568 were processed.[130] Concerns about the unresolvedness of the restitution question were also expressed during the second cycle of the Universal Periodic Review (UPR) process of the United Nations Human Rights Council in 2013.[131] In this case, the USA, Italy, and Hungary were particularly keen on encouraging Romania to promptly adopt responsive and non-discriminatory legislation for property restitution seekers and to accelerate the resolution of pending property cases.[132]

For the context, it should be mentioned here that despite the fact that the constitution does not refer to the orthodox church as *de jure* state-church, the state continues *de facto* to treat is as such (raising the issue of possible violation of the provisions of Law No. 489/2006 on Religious Freedom and the General Regime of Denominations) and grants them various concessions that other denominations are deprived of (e.g. donation of land property or real-estate).[133] These concessions are relevant, given that minority Hungarians often point out that the Orthodox Church actively contributes to the assimilation policies of the state, among others, by building churches in Szekler communes where the overwhelming majority of the population belongs to Western Christian denominations (such as Roman Catholic, Reformed, Baptist, or Unitarian), as a means to leave a mark on and to exercise dominance over a given territory, as well as to potentially attract orthodox-Romanian population to these areas.[134]

This desire to dominate public spaces already came to the fore with regards to the previously mentioned cases regarding monolingual public spaces. Another dimension of this phenomena can be observed with respect to the treatment of material heritage linked to the Hungarian national community. In their Fourth Opinion on Romania, the AC of the FCNM made the observation that "some

---

130 *Id.* at para. 20.

131 See Report No. A/HRC/23/5, available at: http://dag.un.org/handle/11176/301681, accessed: 2016.01.27.

132 Similar recommendations were also present in the third cycle UPR of Romania.

133 For more information, see, for example, Andreescu (2007), pp. 451–480.

134 See, for example: Salamon Zoltán: Nem a rendszerben van a hiba, maga a rendszer a hiba! *Krónika Online*, 2014.06.29. Available at: https://kronikaonline.ro/szempont/nem-a-rendszerben-van-a-hiba-maga-a-rendszer-a-hiba, accessed: 2021.07.22

4,500 out of 30,000 listed buildings, constituting material heritage of Romania, are connected with the Hungarian national minority. Regrettably, many such buildings are in poor (or very poor) condition, are left unattended and have not been properly secured due to the state of legal uncertainty surrounding property rights. Long and costly court procedures compound the problem and many buildings have in the meantime been damaged beyond repair".[135] One such protracted legal procedure concerned the Batthyáneum Library and the Astronomy Institute, both belonging originally to the Roman Catholic Archdiocese of *Gyulafehérvár/Alba Iulia,* and resulted in the European Court of Human Rights ruling that it "was unable to discern legitimate justification for the State's prolonged failure to act" and held that "the uncertainty affecting the applicant association for 14 years with regard to the legal status of the property claimed by it was all the more incomprehensible in view of the cultural and historical importance of the assets in question"[136]

### *1.7.2.3 Economic Discrimination*

There are three counties with substantial Szekler–Hungarian populations (Hargita/Harghita—85.2 %—257,707 people; Kovászna/Covasna—73.7 %—150,468 people; and Maros/Mureş—38.1 %—200,858 people),[137] and these are grouped together in the so-called Central-Romanian NUTS II Development Region (hereinafter referred to as CDR) with overwhelmingly Romanian Alba, Sibiu, and Braşov counties. The proportion of Szekler–Hungarians in the CDR altogether is below 30 %,[138] a grievance that came to the fore in case T-529/13 (Izsák and Dabis v. Commission) of the General Court of the EU (concluded on 10 May 2016).[139] The intervention of the council of Kovászna County in this judicial procedure made references to the dramatic divergence in economic development by citing the GDP per capita data of the constituent counties of the CDR.[140]

---

135 Fourth Opinion of the AC on Romania at para. 56.

136 See ECtHR (2012), at para. 97.

137 For the number and percentage of ethnic Hungarians living in Romania by county, see the result of the last general census in Kapitány (2015), p. 230. For a map on demographic trends from 1910 until 2002, see Figs. 4 and 5. For the more recent trends between 1989 and 2011, see Tab. 1.

138 This is particularly important given that earlier plans of the central government included vesting these eight NUTS II regions with administrative competencies.

139 The author of this book was one of the applicants of this lawsuit.

140 For the intervention, see: http://nemzetiregiok.eu/dokumentumok/t-529-13.sz.per-kovaszna-megye-beavatkozasi-kerelme.doc, accessed: 2020.01.06.

They presented data showing that, since Romania's EU accession in 2007, the average per capita GDP of the counties having Hungarian population (Maros, Hargita, Kovászna) has been only 80.5 % of the CDR average, while the same proportion in the counties not having Hungarian inhabitants (Fehér, Brassó, Szeben) has remained well above 110 % (see Tab. 2).

Furthermore, while the average per capita GDP in the two counties having the most substantial Hungarian majority (Hargita and Kovászna) has grown by only 4.6 % and 1.7 % between Romania's EU accession and 2013, counties with Romanian majority have increased multiple times faster. Brassó, for example, has experienced a growth more than eleven times greater in the same period (19.2 %) than that of Kovászna (see Tab. 3, and Fig. 6). This general trend of economic divergence between Szekler and other Romanian counties continues to this day (see Fig. 7), forming what the above stakeholder identified as indirect discrimination targeted against the Szekler community, given that there has been no reasonable justification whatsoever for these disproportionate effects.[141]

An additional aspect of this case was revealed by the expert report attached to the Kovászna Intervention. This material argued that the true economic backlog of the less developed Szekler regions remains hidden within the current NUTS II structure (see Fig. 8). As a matter of fact, measuring the GDP/inhabitant/region data, one can find that the CDR is the third best-performing region, preceded only by the capital (Bucuresti-Ilfov Region) and the westernmost NUTS II region (Vest region).[142] Even though the Romanian Development Plans contain the strategic goal of stopping and preferably reversing the widening trend of regional development disparities,[143] this expert report argues that the present borders of the CDR are economically not efficient to reach that goal due to the manifold differences between the Szekler and the Romanian regions. Furthermore, the boundaries of the CDR violate the provisions of the NUTS Regulation and statistically hide processes that contradict the main goal of the EU's cohesion policy and that of the Romanian Development Plans.[144]

In situations such as the Szekler example, where one deals with multiple identity factors (linguistic, cultural, religious) that can become the source of

141 The data enumerated in the Kovászna intervention is particularly relevant given that it can be quite difficult to identify the disproportionately prejudicial effects of public-policy measures that amount to indirect discrimination. On this topic, see Barelli (2011), pp. 6–8.

142 For data, see, for example, Surd et al. (2011), p. 23 and Otil et al. (2015), p. 42.

143 Government of Romania (2012 and 2014).

144 For more detail, see Dabis (2021).

discrimination, it is particularly important for governments to "recognize and respond to multiple and intersecting deprivations and sources of discrimination that are compounded by one another and make it harder to escape poverty, live with dignity and enjoy human rights".[145]

### 1.7.2.4 Constraints on the Use of Symbols

Restrictions imposed by Romanian authorities on the use of the Szekler flag is another long-standing issue that damages Szekler-Romanian relations.[146] The first regulatory procedure in the case of the Szekler flag occurred in relation to *Makfalva/Ghindari* (north-west Szeklerland), when the municipality decided to place the Szekler flag on the facade of the local council building in December 2009. This event was followed by a police interrogation in January 2010, an investigation of the state prosecution, and another inquiry from the deputy prefect of Maros County, aiming to remove the flag. Even though the deputy prefect was unable to cite a law that forbids the use of the Szekler flag, he added that what is not legally prohibited is not necessarily allowed. The rules applying to this issue (first of all Act No. 75 of 1994)[147] stipulate that it is mandatory to place the Romanian flag on public buildings, but the flags of other countries can only be displayed together with the Romanian flag and only during official state visits, festivities, and international meetings. Accordingly, this regulation contains no orientation point for the use of the Szekler flag. The Judgement that concluded this particular case on 10 August 2010 declared that the Szekler flag is the symbol of a historic community, which does not violate any legislation.[148] In spite of

---

145 Secretary-General of the UN (2019), p. 35.

146 The ECRI mentions this topic in its fourth monitoring report. See: ECRI (2014), at para. 168.

147 The full name of this Act is: "Law no. 75 of 994 regarding the display of the Romanian flag, singing the national anthem and the use of insignia containing the Romanian coat of arms by public authority and institutions"/ *Lege nr.75 din 16 iulie 1994 privind arborarea drapelului României, intonarea imnului național și folosirea sigiliilor cu stema României de către autoritățile și instituțiile publice Textul actului publicatîn M.Of. nr. 237/26 aug. 1994*. Available: http://www.cdep.ro/pls/legis/legis_pck.htp_act_text?idt=14530, accessed: 2019.08.09.

148 Besides the *Makfalva* case, to date there has been only one case where the Judgement came out in favour of hoisting the Szekler-flag on public buildings, namely in the case of *Erdőszentgyörgy/Sângeorgiu de Pădure*. In this latter case the Prefect of Maros county fined the mayor of *Erdőszentgyörgy* for 5,000 RON (1,112 EUR) on 21 January 2015, for refusing to remove the Szekler and the Hungarian flag from the building that serves

this judgement, the then prefect of Kovászna County, Codrin Munteanu, turned to the court in order to remove the Szekler flag from the Mayor's Office of the municipality of *Uzon* and later on called upon all mayors of his county to take off the Szekler flags from all of their public offices. As the prefect had put it: "The flag on the Mayor's Office of *Uzon* symbolizes a non-existing entity and violates the law in the same way as if someone would place the flag of a football team or a car factory on the town hall".[149] Dumitru Marinescu, Munteanus' successor, followed suit with these methods when he ordered the Szekler flag to be removed from the Ceremonial Hall in *Sepsiszentgyörgy/Sfântu Gheorghe*, where his inauguration took place on 2 February 2013. Similar incidents occurred in Hargita (the other county beside Kovászna with a Szekler majority), where prefect Jean Adrian Andrei called upon the mayors of the county to remove all Szekler flags from their public buildings in an official statement on 11 February 2013.

A new line of argument against the Szekler flag emerged later on, when the police of *Târgu Mureş/Marosvásárhely* fined the Hungarian National Council of Transylvania to 30,000 RON for hoisting a Szekler flag on their local headquarters in October 2013. The court ruled against the fine but did not contest the initial argument of the police that the Szekler flag was a commercial banner.[150] This argument later reappeared in August 2014 when the police called upon MEP Tőkés László to remove the Szekler flag from his Central Office in *Nagyvárad/Oradea* envisaging a penalty of up to 50,000 RON in case he would disobey.[151] Tőkés challenged the fine, but the Court of Bihar County ruled in favour of the police.

As a response to these developments, the Romanian legislature codified the use of local symbols by way of Law 141/2015 on the display and use of the flags of administrative-territorial units. Seemingly, this law provides for the

---

as local headquarters of the UDMR party. See: http://www.kronika.ro/erdelyihirek/helyukre-kerulnek-a-zaszlok-erdoszentgyorgyon, accessed: 2017.01.25.

149 See: http://mno.hu/hatarontul/munteanu-figyelmeztetett-ne-tuzzek-ki-a-szekely-zaszlot-1132801, accessed: 2015.06.26.

150 The same approach was present concerning the flag of another historical region of Hungarian majority, the "*Partium*", Judgement of the Court of Bihar County concluded in case No. 284/271/2016 that the flag of *Partium* was a commercial banner, the hoisting of which constitutes a commercial activity, subject to prior authorization processes. See:http://erdely.ma/autonomia.php?id=205813&cim=jogerosen_reklamzaszlonak_%20minositettek_a_partiumi_zaszlot_is, accessed: 2017.02.07.

151 Source: http://index.hu/kulfold/2016/02/01/nem_reklamzaszlo_a_szekely_zaszlo/, accessed: 2016.09.03.

opportunity to gain a *quasi* limited recognition to the Szekler flag as the flag of a county. In practice, however, provisions of the law effectively hinder this process. According to Art. 3, in the framework of the new procedure, the flag-model adopted by the county council should be sent to the Ministry of Regional Development and Public Administration first, which asks for the opinion of the National Committee of Heraldry, Genealogy and Sigillography of the Romanian Academy. Based on the consultative opinion of this Committee, the flag will be adopted by way of a Government Decree. These new provisions effectively strip administrative-territorial units from the right to decide on their own flags and confer this right to the central government, which could delay or even deny the approval of a county decision.

The Fourth Report of the ECRI on Romania mentions that the processes surrounding the Szekler flag cumulated eventually to the point where the hoisting of the flag on official buildings was banned and fines were imposed on municipalities that disobeyed.[152] As the situation was escalating, the ECRI recommend that the authorities appease tensions between the majority population and ethnic minorities by applying the principle of equal treatment concerning the display and use of national and regional symbols and to remedy any violation thereof.[153]

To illustrate the double standards that take place in the treatment of local/Hungarian v. national/Romanian symbols, the ECRI mentions a second case which concerned the wearing of a headband with the national colours of Romania by several pupils in a school in the county of Kovászna on the national day of Hungary (15 March). The teacher of the class asked the pupils to remove the headband, and this led to an escalation of protests in various towns and the burning of the Hungarian flag. Further to this incident, a group on Facebook was formed inciting violence against Hungarians. As a response, the authorities carried out an investigation into the conduct of the school and reprimanded the headmaster and dismissed the teacher who had banned the wearing of the symbol. The ECRI noted that in this respect, there is an inconsistency between the reaction of the authorities in the Szekler case and this latter incident. In the first incident, the authorities banned the display of local symbols, whereas in the second incident, they safeguarded the right to display Romanian national symbols. The ECRI deemed that this incongruence should be remedied in order

152 A specific case the ECRI report mentions was that of *Csikmadaras*, a village where the mayor was fined by the court to 9,000 RON (approximately 2,000 €) for not removing the flag. See ECRI (2014), at para 168.

153 ECRI (2014), at para. 170.

to ensure that there is no discrimination on grounds of ethnic origin in this field.[154]

The intensity and longevity of the dispute surrounding the use of the Szekler flag was demonstrated yet again by an incident mention in the Fifth Report of ECRI on Romania. On 10 January 2018, in reaction to a call for territorial autonomy by ethnic Hungarian parties, the then prime minister, Mihai Tudose, stated in a TV show that "if they fly the Szekler flag on institutions in Szeklerland, all those responsible over there will be flying next to it".[155]

What could be added to the above is that there appears to be a willingness from the Romanian authorities to apply double standards and negative discrimination to the detriment of Hungarians on a regional basis, too. On 4 June 2016, in the centre of *Csíkszereda/Miercurea Ciuc*, local Hungarian civilians and representatives wanted to re-hoist a Szekler flag that had already been on display for a long time but was temporarily removed due to renovation works. The local police, however, intervened, confiscated the flag, took the organizer into custody, and issued a 10,000 RON fine for them on 03 June 2016.[156] By contrast, only a few months earlier on 28 November 2015 in the centre of *Gura Humorului* (a small town in north-eastern Romania, inhabited overwhelmingly by ethnic Romanians), the flag of the historical region of Bucovina was hoisted on the Day of Bucovina, accompanied by police tributes, even though no such administrative unit exists.[157]

Lastly, it is worth mentioning that a similarly restrictive attitude applies to singing the Szekler and Hungarian anthems. One of the most memorable examples occurred in December 2011 when the Romanian ice hockey team – the majority of which consists of Szekler-Hungarian players – played a game against

154 *Id.* at para. 169.

155 Quoted in: ECRI (2019), at para. 25.

156 See: http://www.szekelyhon.ro/aktualis/csikszek/elkoboztak-a-foteri-szekely-zaszlot-csikszeredaban, accessed: 2021.03.16. This certainly was not the first similar case that the city of *Csíkszereda* experienced. There were two other incidents, both of which were brought about by an infamous Romanian NGO (*Asociația Civicăpentru Demnitateîn Europa* / Civic Association for Dignity in Europe) whose leader Dan Tanasă initiated dozens of trials to remove Szekler and Hungarian symbols as well as Hungarian written signs from the facade and the interior of public buildings (see e.g.: http://www.kronika.ro/erdelyihirek/abekemenyitetta-dan-tanasa-a-folytatodik-a-persorozat, accessed: 2017.01.25).

157 See a video of the festivity here: https://www.youtube.com/watch?v=tqa9Oi2k_hQ, accessed: 2021.03.21.

Hungary during the Euro Ice-hockey Challenge in *Csíkszereda*, and the players of the Romanian team sang the Hungarian anthem as well as the Szekler anthem before the game.[158] Romanian news reports were outraged by what was described as a scandalous and preposterous incident. Some news outlets even went as far to speak of high treason.[159] Another memorable incident happened in December 2014, when the prefect of *Kovászna/Covasna* County fined the Hungarian Civic Party because the Hungarian anthem was sung at an event organized by them. The party turned to the court arguing that it is not prohibited to sing the anthem of another country. The court annulled the fine in the end, but not because the singing of the anthem of another county was considered legal, but of procedural flaws committed by the prefect during the procedure.[160]

#### *1.7.2.5 Lack of Dialogue and Insufficient Administrative Practices*

Reports of the COMEX showed that the implementation of provisions pertaining to public administration practices are the most problematic. This issue has also been detected by the AC, as they already made references in their First Report on Romania that the number of persons belonging to national minorities who work as public officials is proportionally low (notably Hungarians and Roma). They, therefore, recommended that the Romanian authorities adopt the necessary measures to promote a fair representation of minorities in the civil service.[161]

Another practical concern of the AC was that certain media outlets report in a manner that strengthens existing negative stereotypes associated with minorities (in particular the Hungarians).[162] They also thought that the persistence of anti-Hungarian sentiment is of considerable concern, in particular, the continuing pernicious language employed by some politicians against persons belonging to the Hungarian minority "perpetuate divisions which are detrimental to finding solutions to problems affecting society".[163] The AC continued by stating that intolerant language has over the years entered mainstream political discourse. As an example, they mention that during a televised debate ahead of the presidential

158 See video footage of the case here: http://erdely.ma/utonomia.php?id=106649&cim=himnuszbotrany_miert_enekeltek_a_magyarok_a_magyar_nemzeti_imat_video, accessed: 2017.01.26.
159 See references in: http://www.origo.hu/sport/jegkorong/20111218-magyarroman-himnuszbotrany-egycsikszeredai-hokimeccsen.html, 2017.01.26.
160 See case no. 5901/305/2014.
161 AC (2001), at p. 22.
162 *Id.* at para. 34
163 AC (2017), at para. 5.

elections in 2014, one of the candidates asked one of the guests not to speak "in horses' language", referring to the Hungarian language.[164]

The AC noted with regret on several occasions that there has only been limited dialogue between the authorities and the representatives of minorities. They specifically mentioned the two counties with Szekler majority (Hargita and Kovászna) where inter-ethnic and inter-cultural dialogue remains problematic,[165] due to which the Szekler community living in these areas faces "particular problems related to preservation of their identity and cultural heritage".[166] As an illustration of this, the fourth cycle opinion mentions two specific examples. The competent courts refused to register associations, such as *Pro Turismo Terrae Siculorum*, on the grounds that "Szeklerland" is not a legally recognized administrative unit, hence this word cannot appear in the name of an association. The AC found this practice particularly surprising given that organizations invoking other historic names such as Bucovina or Banat do not encounter such obstacles. Furthermore, the AC found it regrettable that Romanian authorities, having initiated it in 2015, have subsequently failed to present the documentation required for recognition by UNESCO as non-material heritage of humanity of an annual Whitsunday pilgrimage to *Csíksomlyó/Şumuleu Ciuc* in the Hargita County, practised by a very large number of persons belonging to the Hungarian national community.[167] As a conclusion, the AC recommended to the competent authorities "to engage actively in a dialogue with local representatives of the Hungarian minority from the Covasna, Harghita and Mureş counties on measures to be taken to maintain and develop their culture, and to preserve the essential elements of their identity, namely their religion, language, traditions, and cultural heritage".[168] Romania reacted to these observations of the AC in its fifth cycle report – as well as in their comments to the Fourth Opinion of the AC – by rejecting the presumed intention of the AC to insinuate that any special or "differentiated framework" would be justifiable for the counties having substantial Szekler population. As the state report put it: "The limitation in the text of the draft recommendation to the counties of Covasna, Harghita and Mureş is unjustified and induces the intention to create a differentiated framework for these territorial administrative units in relation to the rest of the regions/localities

164 *Id.* at Para. 61.
165 AC (2005), at para. 92.
166 AC (2017), at para. 51.
167 *Id.* at para 52.
168 *Id.* at para 54.

where persons belonging to the Hungarian minority are living which is inconsistent with the principles of the Framework Convention and is inconsistent with the Constitution and the legislation of Romania in the field".[169]

The AC also noted with regret that the draft law on the Status of National Minorities,[170] which has been under consideration in various forms for a number of years, has still not been adopted and continues to be discussed in parliament.[171] As a matter of fact, Draft Law No. 502/2005 has become the longest-debated bill in the history of post-communist Romania. A legislative process that seems to have no end in sight, as the draft has already been debated in seven Parliamentary Committees (which is also unprecedented, as most legal documents in the country are debated in two or three committees, at most), which resulted in the issue slowly dropping off from the agenda of the Legislature. According to the official homepage of the Chamber of Deputies, Draft Law No. 502/2005 has not been on the parliamentary agenda since 2012 when it was sent back to the Committee for Human Rights, Religions and National Minorities for further analysis.[172]

The Third Report of the AC also makes references to the administrative reform, another process that continues to grow ever longer. Regarding this issue, the AC noted that "the proportion of persons identifying themselves with national minorities is likely to diminish in some of the proposed larger units, which may affect the exercise of a number of rights which are conditional on reaching a certain threshold of persons identifying themselves with a national minority and residing within the territorial unit in question. Such a development, in the opinion of the Advisory Committee, might lead to the weakening of the possibilities for persons belonging to the minorities to influence and participate in local affairs".[173] To remedy the problem, the AC urged the authorities to ensure that "the rights of persons belonging to national minorities are duly taken into account when planning and implementing the reform of territorial administration in Romania and that there is no negative impact on the right of persons belonging to national minorities to participate effectively in public affairs at local

---

169 See p. 16 of the Fifth Report submitted by Romania on the implementation of the FCNM (no. ACFC/SR/V(2019)013), available at: https://rm.coe.int/5th-sr-romania-en/16809943af, accessed: 2021.02.25.

170 The lack of such a legislation means that the rights of minorities are currently scattered in the Romanian legal system in several different sources of law.

171 AC (2012), at para. 38.

172 See: http://www.cdep.ro/pls/proiecte/upl_pck.proiect?idp=6778, accessed: 2021.02.18.

173 AC (2012), at para. 193.

level",[174] in accordance with the principles enshrined in Art. 6 of the Framework Convention.

The topic is also mentioned in the fourth ECRI Monitoring Report, which notes that two issues are at the heart of the growing tensions which have characterized the relations between the majority population and the Hungarian minority. "The first concerns the planned constitutional and administrative reform which aims to reorganize the counties in eight administrative regions. The ECRI has been informed that the Hungarian minority fears that this will dilute their representation in the new regions and that these will not coincide with the cultural 'borders'. The second issue refers to the growing demand from the Covasna and Hargita counties for greater regional autonomy, which has at times been interpreted by the national authorities as a wish to secede from Romania."[175]

It follows from this observation of the ECRI that Romanian public authorities are likely to engage in immediate counteraction to any manifestation that points in the direction of regional autonomy. This approach came to the fore particularly well when the Szekler National Council called upon the 153 municipalities of Szeklerland in 2014 to adopt pro-autonomy municipal resolutions.[176] More specifically, these resolutions stipulated that the Szekler cities and villages wish to be part of a unified Szekler administrative unit in the future, which should be called Szeklerland and should be vested with autonomous competencies as set out in an organic law, and that this autonomy should include granting official status to the Hungarian language, along with the Romanian language.[177] Such resolutions were adopted by 63 municipalities, representing 376,617 inhabitants, amounting to 47.11 % of the total population of Szeklerland (799,340 people).[178]

---

174 *Id.* at para. 194.

175 ECRI (2014), at para. 167.

176 See the text of the call here: http://szekelyfoldert.hu/24-masfelszaz-szekely-onkormanyzat-nyilvanitsa-ki-akaratat-nyilt-level-a-szekely-onkormanyzatokhoz, accessed: 2021.06.10.

177 About the results of this campaign, SzNC informed: The Parliament and the Government of Romania, the Secretary-general of the CoE, the PACE, the Congress of Local and Regional Authorities, the Committee of Regions, the European Parliament, and the Human Rights Council of the UN.

178 See the full list of these municipalities here: http://www.sznt.sic.hu/husic/index.php?option=com_content&view=article&id=752%3Aszekely-oenkormanyzatok-az-autonomszekelyfoeldert&catid=12%3Afolyamodvanyok-valaszlevelek&Itemid=16&lang=fa, accessed: 2019.08.15.

Even though these resolutions pertained to a future preference, and did not contain any tasks to be fulfilled by local authorities, the Prefects of Maros, Hargita, and Kovászna counties challenged all resolutions before the Administrative Courts, which annulled all resolutions through judgements that contained two basic arguments: a) the only administrative units that the constitution recognizes are communes, towns, and counties; b) Romanian language can be the only official language in the country.

The Congress of Local and Regional Authorities (CLRAE) has also condemned some of the institutional practices of Romania. In their Information Report from 2002, the CLRAE noted that the above-described *de jure* suspension of the decisions of local authorities challenged by the Prefect before the administrative courts can have the same effect as annulment and can thus have an adverse effect on the decision-making autonomy of local bodies. Consequently, the provision at issue is contrary to Art. 8.3 of the European Charter of Local Self-Government, which establishes that the intervention by the controlling authority should be kept in proportion to the importance of the interests which it is intended to protect.[179] Finally, Recommendation 300 (2011) of the CLRAE notes with concern the lack of transparency in the allocation of financial resources between the central and local levels of government, which does not allow to address the real needs of local authorities, and points to the insufficient consultation with these local authorities in the decision-making process on all questions directly concerning them.[180]

### *1.7.2.6 Securitization of Autonomy Aspirations*

The securitization of the Szekler-Hungarian community and their autonomy aspirations, as a means to de-legitimize these aspirations, has a robust history in the country, the roots of which go way back to the totalitarian regimes of the 20th century.[181] This is illustrated, among others, by a Memorandum from 1982, which was the only samizdat publication of communist Romania called *Ellenpontok* (Counterpoints). The editorial board consisted of Hungarian intellectuals, and the memorandum was addressed to the second Madrid follow-up meeting of the

---

179 See: CLRAE (2002), at para. 76/a.

180 See: CLRAE (2011), at para. 5/b, c.

181 In this section I draw on Roe's definition of the securitisation of minority issues. In Roe's view, the securitisation of this topic is the process of taking minority issues from "normal politics" to "emergency politics" by framing it as an existential threat that necessitates extraordinary measures. See: Roe (2004), p. 281

Conference on Security and Cooperation in Europe to review compliance with the 1975 Helsinki Accords. The Memorandum points out that: "state powers treat us [the Hungarian community – ed.], especially intellectuals and workers, as if we were the enemies within. Terror on the part of the security forces is the order of the day. If we speak out in defence of our heritage, it is we who are called chauvinistic. We live as second-class citizens in Romania, whose possibilities for career advancement are also limited by the fact that we are Hungarians. We lack any means of self-protection. . . .Thus, our situation is characterized by the denial of not only our individual rights, but our collective rights as well, two sets of rights which are inseparable in our case".[182]

The continuity of these observations is confirmed by the findings of the annual activity reports of the Romanian Secret Service. Autonomy issues are usually mentioned under the sub-chapter dealing with the protection of the Constitution (*Apărarea Constituției*). Here, the "autonomy-discourse" is depicted as "ethnic radicalism" that strives to "internationalize the anti-Hungarian politics of Bucharest" and at the same time aims to "aggressively emphasize Szekler ethno-cultural characteristics".[183]

Furthermore, the National Strategy for Order and Public Safety 2015–2020, elaborated by the Ministry of Internal Affairs of Romania, mentions,[184] among the possible threats to public safety, "manifestations of racism, xenophobia, extremism and other forms of intolerance aimed at achieving autonomy for specific areas/regions based on ethnic criteria". Not only does this paper consider regional autonomy to be a general security threat (such as the deterioration of living standards or the degradation of the education system), it goes further as to characterizing autonomy as an extreme manifestation of intolerance, racism and xenophobia. Even though the quoted part was terminated from the text and is not present in the document that was adopted by the parliament, it demonstrates a securitized approach towards autonomy aspirations.

The most obvious method to securitize the autonomy movement is to label the cause as illegitimate and extremist. This approach can be witnessed with

182 Source: Beszélő online (1982), I. évfolyam, 5. szám: available at: http://beszelo.c3.hu/cikkek/memorandumok-es-programjavaslatok. For the English text of the Memorandum see: http://www.hungarianhistory.com/lib/bors/bors15.htm, accessed: 2016.02.21.

183 SRI (2014), p. 7.

184 Source: http://www.mai.gov.ro/documente/transparenta/SNOSP%202015-2020%20.pdf, p. 6, accessed: 2015.03.26.

regards to the "Day of Szekler Freedom" protests (hereinafter DSF) each year.[185] This event is organized in the historical capital of Szeklerland, *Marosvásárhely/Târgu Mureş*, annually on 10 March by the Szekler National Council and with the participation of Transylvanian-Hungarian political parties as well as foreign politicians and public figures, attracting several thousands of people each year.[186] The main goal of the DSF is to openly display the demand for territorial autonomy for Szeklerland and to protest against the administrative reform plans of the government, discussed above, which in its present format attempts to coalesce the counties with substantial Szekler population into a larger administrative region where the proportion of Szeklers would drop below 30 % of the population.[187] Given the politically sensitive aims of this march, Romanian authorities deployed various tools to hinder the organization of the DSF.

On 10 March 2014, the Gendarmerie of Maros County issued a fine amounting to 12,000 RON / 2,700 EUR for the organizers of the DSF, based on Art. 26 a) of Act 60/1991 on the organization of public meetings. This article aims to penalize those who are "organizing and conducting undeclared, unregistered or prohibited public meetings". This has proved to be the main argument against the event and its organizers and has been continuously invoked by the authorities year after year. The Gendarmerie argued that one would need prior approval from the police to hold any demonstration. On the contrary, the organizers argued that according to the law, one only needs to inform the authorities about a demonstration (which they had done), and not ask for their permission, given that the right to assembly and to free speech are fundamental human rights that are not contingent on the discretion of the police. Consequently, the organizers filed a lawsuit against the Gendarmerie before the Court of *Marosvásárhely/Târgu Mureş*, which transferred the case to the Administrative Court. Three years later, in 2017, it was this latter Court that ruled in favour of the Gendarmerie, and ordered the applicant to pay the 12,000 RON fine.

---

185 The case of the DSF proved to be salient enough to attract the attention of US diplomacy. See the State Secretary's Country Reports on Human Rights Practices for 2015 in Romania, pp. 33-34. Available at: https://2009-2017.state.gov/documents/organization/253103.pdf, accessed: 2017.01.26.

186 *Marosvásárhely/Târgu Mureş* is the multi-ethnic centre of Maros County, where the deliberative and executive branches of the County are seated. According to the last census, 49.17 % of the city's population is Romanian, 42.84 % is Hungarian, and 7.99 % other.

187 According to the last census conducted in 2011: 82.9 % of Hargita, 73.79 % of Kovászna, and 38.09 % of Maros county were composed of Hungarian/Szeklers.

In 2015, the Mayor of Marosvásárhely/Târgu Mureş, Dorin Florea, decided to simply ban the annual DSF in 2015, claiming that it creates "ethnic unrest" and turns the city into a "conflict zone".[188] The organizers contested this decision before the court, which ruled in favour of the Mayor. The court's decision did not consider the merit of the case but instead dismissed it due to procedural reasons, stating that before turning to the court the plaintiffs should have made a prior complaint to the Mayor's Office.

In an attempt to prevent such practices of the authorities, the organizers filed a prior notification, according to the provisions of the law, with the Mayor's Office already on 2 March 2015, announcing that they will hold the DSF in the same usual place both in 2016 and 2017. Even so, the Mayor's Office decided not to acknowledge this notification and argued that the announcement came too early and should rather be made at a later stage, closer to the date of the actual event. Furthermore, the Mayor's Office claimed that organizing the DSF in 2016 will be problematic, given that it falls in election year, and that road construction works were being planned for the trail of the event, due to which public security across the city would be constantly changing (even though they were not able to clarify what kind of construction works they were referring to). The organizers turned again to the court, which ruled in favour of them,[189] concluding that the above-mentioned arguments of the Mayor's Office lacked any kind of legal basis whatsoever to deny the registration of the event and that the organizers fulfilled all prior notification requirements. Additionally, the judge admonished the mayor for refusing to acknowledge the announcement of the organizers, because with this conduct, he deliberately "refused to settle the request of the applicant".[190]

A week after the DSF of 2016 had been held, the Gendarmerie of Maros County started to issue fines amounting to 61,000 RON / 13,700 EUR in 50 cases pursuant to Act 60/1991 for participating in an undeclared, unregistered, or prohibited public meeting and 9,800 RON / 2,200 EUR in 34 cases pursuant to Act 61/1991 for noise disturbance. Moreover, the Gendarmerie started fining not just the organizers but also the participants. In some cases, the fined individuals were not even present in *Tîrgu Mureş/Marosvásárhely* on the day of the demonstration. Given that the event took place without any public disturbance, the organizers believed that the only explanation for penalizing the peaceful exercise

188 See, for example, http://www.evz.ro/marsul-secuilor-naste-tensiuni-inainte-de-organizare.html, accessed: 2016.08.18.

189 See Judgement No. 16/2016 from 8 January 2016.

190 See p. 6, last paragraph of Judgement 16/2016.

of the fundamental right to assembly and free speech was to deter people from participating in the DSF in the future. As a response to these unlawful fines, the organizers lodged a claim for misconduct against the Gendarmerie. The case was transferred to the Office of the Military Prosecutor, where it is still pending. Simultaneously, the Szekler National Council encouraged people to turn to the Court of *Tîrgu Mureş/Marosvásárhely* asking it to annul all fines issued to participants of the DSF.

Not only did Romanian authorities apply punitive measures against citizens peacefully exercising their fundamental rights to assembly and free speech, they did so based on ethnic and political grounds. For example, the far-right, extremist organization, *Noua Dreaptă* (New Right),[191] repeatedly organizes marches in cities inhabited by Hungarians, chanting slogans inciting hatred against Hungarians (e.g. "Harghita and Covasna is Romanian land", "Get Hungarians out of the country!", "Romanian language is the only ruler", or "Romania is for Romanians").[192] On 13 February 2013, *Noua Dreapta* organized a protest in *Kolozsvár/Cluj* at the Hungarian Consulate General and parallel with that a protest in Bucharest at the Hungarian Embassy against the use of the Szekler flag on public buildings. Regardless of the fact that the latter protest was an unregistered event, the police did not intervene or impose any fines afterwards.[193] Even if the DSF is staged without violence, public disturbance, or incendiary messages, the

191 ECRI considers Noua Dreaptă as a movement that engages in the "systematic use of hate discourse against ethnic Hungarians", as well as organising events with "anti-Roma and antisemitic themes". See: ECRI (2019), at para. 28.

192 Sources: Protest in *Sepsiszentgyörgy/Sfântu Gheorghe* on 1 December, 2014 (the national holiday, commemorating the Romanian National Councils declaration from 1918, claiming that Transylvania is part of Romania): http://www.maszol.ro/index.php/belfold/39447-magyarellenes-roman-unnep-sepsiszentgyorgyon, accessed: 2021.03.21. *Noua Dreapta* also marched several times in Arad on 6 October against Hungarian "irredentism" (on this day Hungarians commemorate the downfall of the 1848–1849 revolution and the execution of 13 of their generals in Arad by the Habsburg authorities): http://www.nyugatijelen.com/jelenido/a_magyar_irredentizmus_ellen_tuntetnek_aradon.php, accessed: 2021.03.21. *Noua Dreapta* also prefers to march in *Marosvásárhely*, as they did on 27 March 2015, demanding the unification of Romania with the Republic of Moldova (Bessarabia): http://www.kozpont.ro/hirek/belfold/marosvasarhelyen-tuentetett-az-uj-jobboldal/, accessed: 2016.08.22.

193 Source: http://mno.hu/hatarontul/a-szekelyek-nem-magyarok-tuntettek-a-szelsonacionalistak-1138066, accessed: 2016.08.22. See video on the event at: http://ziuadecj.realitatea.net/eveniment/noua-dreapta-apichetat-consulatul-maghiar-din-cluj-fotovideo--106254.html, accessed: 2016.08.22.

Romanian authorities initiate numerous proceedings against the organizers and, since 2016, also against the participants. Whereas, on the other hand, marches of the Romanian far-right never encountered any bans, fines, or other administrative proceedings, no matter how inflammatory, biased, and disrespectful their messages towards minority communities were. Juxtaposing these examples shows that the authorities in Romania apply the right to assembly in a discriminative and selective way to the detriment of persons belonging to the Hungarian community.

Renewed attempts to hinder the organization of the DSF continued in 2017, when the Mayor's Office argued that the route of the march is in too close proximity to the local hospital, potentially endangering emergency health care, an argument that was contested before and dismissed by the competent Court in the same year.[194] On 9 March 2018, the foreign affairs commissioner of the Szekler National Council, the author of this book, attempted to cross the Romanian border by car at Ártánd to attend the annual DSF, but the Romanian border guards refused to let him pass. While there was no immediate explanation to this behaviour, the Bucharest-based Central Border Police Inspectorate sent a notification on 30 March 2018 that a three-year-long travel ban was issued for the individual that expired on 9 March 2021. The brief letter mentioned that the reason for this entry ban is due to certain acts that constituted a threat to national security.[195] However, the authorities refused to inform in detail about the reasons as they based the claim on classified documents, the content of which was not available for inspection for the accused party.[196] Finally, in the years 2020–2021,

194 On 23 February 2018, UN Special Rapporteurs (SR) David Kaye (SR on the promotion and protection of the right to freedom of opinion and expression), Michel Forst (SR on the situation of human rights defenders) and Fernand de Varennes (SR on minority issues) jointly asked for clarification about these incidents that happened each year. In its reply on 5 July 2018 the Foreign Affairs Ministry tried to defend the decisions of the Mayor's Office of Marosvásárhely, arguing that they were protecting public order, and the safety of the local citizens', and that authorities only fined those participants in relation to the DSF who "acted outside the legal framework" (even though they did not describe these acts in detail). For this letter of the Foreign Affairs Ministry, see: https://spcommreports.ohchr.org/TMResultsBase/DownLoadFile?gId=34199, accessed: 2021.02.03.

195 The applicant won the case at the second instance on 31 March 2021. Accordingly, the Highest Court of Romania annulled the document of the General Inspectorate of the Border Police that introduced the entry ban.

196 Due to the constant hindering of the DSF, the thematic recommendations of the third cycle of the Universal Periodic Review of Romania (adopted by the 38th session of the

the re-centralization of decision-making processes, as a means to tackle the coronavirus outbreak, provided local authorities the opportunity to prohibit the organization of the DSF once again, referring to social distancing measures necessary to protect public health and stop the spread of the Covid-19 virus.

The above-outlined phenomenon indicates that there is a tacit agreement among Romanian authorities that they *de facto* possess the power to effectively ban or allow public protests in case these revolve around politically sensitive subjects, such as territorial autonomy for Szeklerland. This interpretative framework is diametrically opposed to that of the CoE, which was reflected in several cases of the European Court of Human Rights (hereinafter, the ECtHR), most notably in the case of Bukta and Others v. Hungary.[197] In this Judgement, adopted on 17 July 2007, the ECtHR reiterated that "the subjection of public assemblies to a prior-authorization procedure does not normally encroach upon the essence of the right (see also: Rassemblement Jurassien and Unité Jurassienne v. Switzerland, no. 8191/78, Commission decision of 10 October 1979, Decisions and Reports 17)".[198] Furthermore, the ECtHR noted that "where demonstrators do not engage in acts of violence, it is important for the public authorities to show a certain degree of tolerance towards peaceful gatherings if the freedom of assembly guaranteed by Art. 11 of the Convention is not to be deprived of all substance" (see Oya Ataman v. Turkey, no. 74552/01, §§ 41–42, ECHR 2006-XIV).[199]

Further examining the case law of the ECtHR, one can find similarities between reactions of the Romanian authorities to Szeklers and their political events, Turkish reactions to Kurdish political claims, and Bulgarian reactions to activities of Macedonian organizations. One notable example was the Sener v. Turkey case.[200] On 5 September 1993, the Istanbul State Security Court charged the owner and editor of a weekly review (*Haberde Yorumda Gerçek*/The Truth of News and Comments) with having disseminated separatist propaganda against the indivisibility of the State and ordered the seizure of the 23rd edition of the review on that ground. The article at hand spoke of the extermination of a nation, of genocide; used the term "Kurdistan"; and mentioned the right to self-determination of the nations. The Court ruled that Art. 10, 6 (1), and 18 of

Human Rights Council of the UN, 18 June–6 July 2018), included recommendations on guaranteeing the right to freedom of peaceful assembly of minorities without discrimination. See: UN Human Rights Council (2018), p. 33.

197 Available at: www.legislationline.org/documents/id/17932, accessed: 2017.01.29.

198 *Id.* at para. 35.

199 *Id.* at para. 37.

200 Source: http://hudoc.echr.coe.int/eng?i=001-58753, accessed: 2017.01.20.

the European Convention of Human Rights (hereinafter, ECHR or Convention) had been violated and reiterated that freedom of expression constitutes one of the essential foundations of a democratic society, as a consequence of which all exceptions and restrictions to this right should be construed strictly and established convincingly. However, the Court reminded that under the provisions of the Convention, there is little scope for "restrictions on political speech or on debate on questions of public interest" and that the "limits of permissible criticism are wider with regard to the government". In this particular case, the Istanbul State Security Court presented the argument that referring to a specific region of Turkey as "Kurdistan" in itself constituted "dissemination of propaganda". In this connection, the ECtHR noted that Turkish authorities had failed to respect the public's right to be informed of a different perspective on the Kurdish issue, "irrespective of how unpalatable that perspective may be for them". In this respect, the views of the Romanian authorities with regard to Szeklerland are similar to that of Turkish authorities in connection with Kurdistan.[201]

Analogous pro- and counter arguments have emerged with regard to the freedom of assembly and association in the Socialist Party and Others v. Turkey case,[202] where the ECtHR reminded that an organization cannot be excluded from the protection of the Convention irrespective of their political agenda. In this case, "exclusion" took the form of dissolution of the Socialist Party by the Constitutional Court on 10 July 1992, for allegedly undermining the territorial integrity of the state through pro-Kurdish public statements. These statements were in favour of a federalized Turkey where Turks and Kurds would be on an equal footing to the extent that Kurds as a "nation" would have "full and unconditional right to self-determination", including the right to create a separate state should they wish to do so. The ECtHR ruled that Art. 11 of the Convention had been violated, and irrespective of Turkish sentiments towards these ideas, one cannot dissolve an association simply because its activities are regarded by the national authorities as ones undermining the constitutional structures of the State.

Similar findings have been made by the ECtHR in the case of Stankov and the United Macedonian Organisation (UMO) Ilinden v. Bulgaria in 2001.[203] The UMO Ilinden's main political goal was not secession or autonomy, but the recognition of the Macedonian minority in Bulgaria, and the main activity towards

201 For more detail, see section 2.5.

202 Source: http://hudoc.echr.coe.int/eng?i=001-58172, accessed: 2017.01.20.

203 Source: http://hudoc.echr.coe.int/eng?i=001-59689, accessed: 2017.01.20.

this end was the organization of celebrations to commemorate historical events of importance for Macedonians in Bulgaria. Even so, the UMO Ilinden had been refused registration under Bulgarian Law in 1990, 1998–1999, and 2002–2004, on the grounds that its statute and programme were directed against the unity of the Bulgarian nation. Even so, the ECtHR concluded that an automatic reliance on the fact that an organization had been considered anti-constitutional – and refused registration – could not suffice to justify under Art. 11(2) of the Convention a practice of systematic bans on the holding of peaceful assemblies. More importantly, from the Szekler point of view, the ECtHR replied to concerns raised by the Bulgarian government that certain leaders of the UMO Ilinden harboured separatist views and had a political agenda that included autonomy for the region of *Pirin Macedonia* or even secession from Bulgaria. Paragraph 97 of the judgement stated that "the fact that a group of persons calls for autonomy or even requests secession of part of the country's territory. . .cannot automatically justify a prohibition of its assemblies. Demanding political changes in speeches and demonstrations does not automatically amount to a threat to the country's territorial integrity and national security".

The continuous attempt to securitize the Szekler community, and ultimately Szeklerland as a region in itself, came particularly to the fore in a case that had become known to the public as the "Szekler terror trial". On 1 December 2015 and 29 December 2015, respectively, the Romanian Directorate for the Investigation of Organized Crime and Terrorism (*Direcţia de Investigare a Infracţiunilor de Criminalitate Organizată şi Terorism*, DIICOT) arrested two Szeklers, István Beke and Zoltán Szőcs,[204] both members of a right-wing youth organization called *HVIM (Hatvannégy Vármegye Ifjúsági Mozgalom* / Sixty-four Counties Youth Movement, an organization that advocates for the rights of the Hungarian minority community in Romania) on charges that they were planning to explode a remotely controlled home-made bomb at a military parade organized in *Kézdivásárhely/Târgu Secuiesc*, Szeklerland on the Romanian national day (1 December).[205]

The warrant for arrest was based on a house search conducted on 30 November and 29 December 2015, respectively, during which the investigators and prosecutors had seized pyrotechnics, firecrackers, and air-soft sport weaponry

204 Beke was arrested only a few hours prior to the ceremony, which he was allegedly planning to assassinate.

205 The DIICOT indictment is available for the public at: https://issuu.com/lazarlehel/docs/rechizitoriu_structura_centrala, accessed: 2021.02.16.

and equipment. After the arrest, the accused were put under pretrial detention, which was extended several times before they were released from custody into house arrest, the duration of which lasted until 11 November 2016 (when it was mitigated to police supervision). On 18 May 2015, the defendants were charged with attempt of incitement against community, attempt of criminal offense with blazing agent based on Art. 402, 346 of the Criminal Code of Romania, Art. 32 (1) o) (non-compliance with the regime of weapons, ammunition, and explosives), and (attempt of the deeds described under Art. 32 and 33)[206] of Law No. 535/2004 on Preventing and Combating Terrorism.

The indictment ignored the fact that the defendants had ordered the pyrotechnics in 2014, more than a year before the incident, and found, as an aggravating circumstance, that they took part in air-soft games on a regular basis. Together with the personal charges, the Public Prosecutors Office also requested to declare the HVIM and Szent László Serege Egyesület (Association of St. Laszlo's Army), another movement of the Hungarian minority, as racist and fascist organizations. The aim of the criminal process was not just to condemn two individuals, but also to ban and disband these organizations.

What gave birth to most of the concerns that the two Szekler defendants will not be subject to a fair procedure was the attempt of the prosecution to connect both the defendants and their organizations to other Hungarian minority-related cases that had no direct connection whatsoever with the accused individuals. At this point, DIICOT ignored Art. 328 of the Criminal Procedure Code (Law 135/2010), which stipulates that an indictment should be restricted to the deeds and persons that were subjects of the given criminal investigation. Below are a few salient examples to illustrate this phenomenon.[207]

The indictment of the DIICOT mentions a voluntary militia of the far-right Jobbik party of Hungary, called the Hungarian Guard. Without mentioning any direct connection, or solid evidence, DIICOT argues that HVIM in Transylvania aims to use similar methods as the Hungarian Guard to "intimidate and instil fear and insecurity among Romanian ethnic communities in the area of Transylvania".[208] The indictment also mentions a far-right individual, Csibi Barna, who proclaimed himself as the "foreign minister, in exile, of the Republic of Szeklerland", a person who allegedly made efforts with the leaders of the Hungarian Guard in Hungary to establish, on the territory of Romania,

206 This article has been repealed by a subsequent amendment of this law in 2019.

207 The examples included in the indictment are much more abundant.

208 DIICOT indictment, p. 4.

a sub-unit of the Hungarian Guard under the name "Szekler Platoon". The DIICOT, however, fails to draw the connection why this circumstance would be relevant for Beke and Szőcs, who had no known connections to Csibi that would be relevant to the indictment.

The DIICOT also brings up an incident that happened on 16 April 2009 in Bolivia. Following a raid by the Bolivian law enforcement authorities, Magyarosi Árpad, a Romanian citizen of Hungarian ethnicity, born in the Szekler capital city *Marosvásárhely/Târgu-Mureş*, was fatally shot along with Eduardo Rózsa-Flores, a Hungarian-Croatian-Bolivian citizen, and Irish citizen Michael Dwyer by domestic special forces inside Hotel Las Américas in Santa Cruz de la Sierra. The three were suspected of plotting to assassinate Bolivian President Evo Morales. As the DIICOT argued, this information was relevant for the indictment because "according to public data, Magyarosi Árpad had links with the extremist group Hungarian Youth in Transylvania (EMI), a splinter group of HVIM in Romania".[209]

In order to further blur the lines and depict the Szekler community and their aspirations as a security threat, DIICOT uses pictures made at the Day of Szekler Freedom, organized by the Szekler National Council (yet another organization that never had any institutional connections with the suspects or with HVIM) in 2014, to illustrate how "extremists" are trying to generate anti-Romanian sentiment in Szeklerland. Page six of the indictment states the following:

> As you will see, followers of the "policy of small steps", at events organized by these extremist organizations in Romania, wanted to demonstrate strength, power and discipline while they invited prominent members of far-right movements in Catalonia, Northern Ireland,[210] and the Basque Country to attend and to speak, that is from regions with marked extremist/terrorist problems. The aim in organizing such events is to cultivate, maintain and develop among the Hungarian community of Transylvania ultra-nationalist and anti-Romanian sentiments, aimed to put strain on relations among members of the two ethnic communities, and consequently damage the climate of peaceful coexistence, and to intimidate and create fear among ethnic Romanians coming from areas where they are a minority relative to ethnic Hungarians.

The DIICOT expanded its accusation not just geographically but also in time. The indictment recalls an event from 1984, when an improvised explosive device was detonated in the town of *Sepsiszentgyörgy/Sfântu-Gheorghe* at the statue of Mihai Viteazul in the town centre.[211] The hand-made bomb killed a child (of Hungarian

---

209 *Id.* at p. 5.

210 There was never any speaker from Northern Ireland invited to any of the DSF events.

211 Mihai Viteazul, or Michael the Brave, was the prince of Wallachia from 1593 until 1601. For a few months in 1600, he was also the prince of both Moldavia and Transylvania,

ethnicity) who was playing near the premises of the explosion. The indictment says that the perpetrator (a Romanian citizen of Hungarian ethnicity whose name is not mentioned) fled to Hungary and was not extradited to Romania, because he was protected by the dual citizenship he had obtained.[212] At the time of this attack, the defendant Zoltán Szőcs, born in 1986, was not even born yet, and István Beke was only nine years old. Nobody was sentenced for this assault, and public opinion holds that it was organized by the Romanian secret service, in order to prove that "Hungarian danger" is present in Romania.[213] The indictment also refers to the so-called Black March (ethnic clashes in Marosvásárhely in March 1990, already referred to under section 1.1), and baselessly insinuates that Beke and Szőcs attempted to somehow replicate these ethnic clashes.

In addition to the above, the charges were mostly based on a conversation that was recorded by one of the participants of the conversation (possibly an informant of the Romanian secret service)[214] at the office of Beke István on 10 October 2015. However, it was only discovered one and a half years later during one of the hearings on 27 January 2017 that a transcript of the original Hungarian conversation has never been made. Consequently, the defence could not juxtapose it with the Romanian translation. Later on, the Court refused to allow to play the recording in its entirety, only a 25-minute-long excerpt, which, according to trial observers, was largely incoherent and insufficient to prove the charges brought against the accused. This was also confirmed by the Court translator, who refused to verify the authenticity of the Romanian translation given that it was unintelligible for him.

---

territories where Romanian population was present in some proportion at that time. Hence, Mihai Viteazul is considered as a symbol of Romanian unity.

212 In 1984, Communist Hungary did in fact extradite Romanian citizens, irrespective of their ethnicity. This policy changed after 1986 when Hungary stopped extraditing political refugees (the best know example is Nadia Comăneci fleeing to Hungary). A common criminal, a terrorist who murdered a child, would have been extradited even in 1984. There is no publicly known record, however, that an extradition request for the perpetrator of the said terrorist act ever existed. Additionally, the institution of dual citizenship was introduced by the Hungarian state only on 20 August 2010, so it couldn't have been applied in 1984.

213 For more details, see the summary of lawyer Kincses Előd (2017): Vádirat vagy politikai pamflet? *Erdélyi Napló*, 2017.06.23. Available at: https://erdelyinaplo.ro/aktualis/osszeallitasok/vadirat-vagy-politikai-pamflet, accessed: 2021.02.17.

214 See more at: https://atlatszo.ro/kozpenzek/perek/bunvadi-eljarasok/atnyalaztuk-beke-istvan-es-szocs-zoltan-dossziejat/, accessed: 2021.02.17.

As part of the trial, a simulation was carried out on 19 February 2016 at one of the training yards of the Romanian military. According to the defendants, the experts responsible for conducting this simulation used materials that had not been found in the defendant's houses, like, for example, nails or detonating cords.[215] On the request of the prosecution, the classification of the charges was changed to crimes against the constitutional order and illegal use of pyrotechnical devices on 24 March 2017. Hence, the first instance judgement, delivered on 7 April 2017 (Judgement no. 67/2017), pertained to these new charges. This judgement declared that the applicant was not guilty of instigating or attempting crime against the constitutional order, but was guilty of illegal use of pyrotechnical devices, and therefore sentenced them for the exact same amount of imprisonment (11 months for Beke, 10 months for Szőcs) that they had already served during their pretrial detention and house arrest, meaning that there was no need for further imprisonment.

The appeal procedure initiated by both the prosecution (as they thought the sentence was too mild) as well as the accused parties (pleading for absolution from both charges) resulted in a judgement the circumstances of which further substantiated the foundations of the defendant's application to the European Court of Human Rights in Strasbourg.[216] Criminal verdict no. 172/2018, issued on 04 July 2018 by the Court of Appeal of Bucharest, manifestly infringed the defendants' right to defence. This verdict amended the first-instance judgement, altering the legal qualification of the charges and declaring Beke and Szőcs guilty in attempt of incitement against community, one of the original charges. Accordingly, the defendants were sentenced to five years of imprisonment. The second-level court carried out this alteration without requesting the opinion of the parties, and the defence-attorney was not given any opportunity, not even orally, to respond to this alternation, despite that these "new" charges were more severe from the point of view of the defendants. The two convicts were immediately transferred to a high-security prison in Codlea, Brasov County, where they were placed under solitary confinement, with strictly limited possibilities to communicate with the outside world. They were later on transferred to a lower-security penitentiary, but even there the conditions of imprisonment

---

215 *Id.*

216 The application with the ECtHR was lodged on 12 July 2018 with the assistance of the Institute for the Protection of Minority Rights. The core information used here to present the case of István Beke and Szőcs Zoltán came from these applications, with the consent of the family members of the affected parties.

were still inhumane: the prison cell is over-crowded and not properly sanitized (there are bed bugs across the facility); access to some medicine is withheld; at times they were denied access to books, newspapers, and fresh information that family members wanted to share; and they have only one hour/day outside on the fresh air.

It is due to the unusual abundance of irregularities, the lack of the presumption of innocence and the principle of good administration, paired with rights violations, including the right for a fair trial and the right to defence, that the general public viewed the "Szekler terror trial" as a politically motivated show trial that served the purpose of intimidating the Szekler community.[217]

The above cases represent proactive attempts of Romanian state institutions and agencies to influence public perception and shape public policy decisions to create a hostile environment towards Szeklerland and its autonomy aspirations. The essence of such state attempts to securitize Szekler autonomy claims was summarized by the president of the Szekler National Council, Izsák Balázs, at a conference in the European Parliament on 19 April 2016 in the following way:

> Various regulatory institutions of Romania function as political police that implement retribution targeted against those Hungarians who protest against the violation of their rights and who speak out in favour of more autonomy for their community. The practices of the Ceausescu regime`s secret service, the Securitate, are present to date and can be carried out by any of the regulatory bodies of the central state in pursuit of intimidating Hungarians who try to exercise their rights.[218]

From the Szekler community's point of view, the discrimination and rights violations outlined in this sub-chapter are so widespread and multifaceted that it supports the argument that the overall situation can only be redressed and remedied in its complexity through a territorial autonomy arrangement.

---

217 The Brasov County Court approved the release on parole of the two Szekler convicts on 19 July 2021.

218 Source: http://tokeslaszlo.eu/cikk/a_brusszeli_autonomiakonferenciarol, accessed: 2021.02.17.

# 2 Autonomy and the Constitution of a Nation State

## 2.1 Romanian Constitutional Traditions

For a better understanding of the contemporary constitutional design, it is helpful to take a historical overview on Romanian constitutional traditions. The three periods that can be distinguished are the liberal constitutionalism of the 19th century and the early 20th century, followed by the communist period and the current post-communist period.

### 2.1.1 Liberal Constitutionalism

At the beginning of the 19th century, most Romanians lived in two separate autonomous entities: Wallachia and Moldavia, both having been under Ottoman suzerainty for centuries. While the Ottoman Empire recognized the political, administrative fiscal, and judicial autonomy of these two Principalities, as of the beginning of the Phanariot rule (1711–1821), it was the prerogative of the Porte to directly appoint the Princes to both thrones. As a consequence of the Russo-Turkish War (1828–29), the Treaty of Adrianople was concluded on 14 September 1829, giving Russia most of the western shores of the Black Sea along with the estuary of the Danube. Moldavia and Wallachia came under Russian protectorate until the Crimean War, which facilitated freedom of trade for Russia in these territories. To govern the local administration, the Russians adopted a series of Organic Regulations (*Regulamentele Organice*), which entered into force in 1831–1832 and lasted until 1858. They were a mixture of constitutional and administrative regulations inspired by the monarchy enshrined in the French Constitutional Charter of 1814. The holder of sovereignty by divine right was the Prince (*Hospodar*), who was elected for life from among the aristocracy. The parliament (*Adunarea Electiva*) was composed of members of the nobility and had legislative competencies only to the extent to which the Prince was ready to cede the exercise of power. The regulations did not contain provisions on an independent judiciary and ignored the idea of fundamental rights of citizens, moving the Principalities toward neo-absolutism. The regime of the Organic Regulations ended with the Treaty of Paris from 1856, which settled the Crimean War. As a result, Moldavia and Wallachia remained under nominal Ottoman rule but were granted independent constitutions and national assemblies, which were to be monitored by the victorious European powers. These Ad

Hoc Assemblies (*Ad hoc Divans*) were established in 1857 on the basis of popular vote. The main topic of these Assemblies was the unification of the two principalities into one state. Even so, the Ad Hoc Assemblies specifically voiced their desire to have a foreign Prince as the ruler. This preference accrued from previous experiences, as the fourteenth to nineteenth centuries were coined by intense power struggles between competing local ruling houses and short reigning periods for rulers interrupted by protracted fights among the potential successors. This was a result of historical lack of established rules of succession: while the male-preference principle was clearly present, the rule of primogeniture was absent. Thus, all legitimate and illegitimate sons of deceased rulers fought to accede to the throne. A return to such affairs was seen as a threat to the national unitary state project; therefore, the idea of a foreign Prince within a hereditary monarchy was considered the best solution. The Paris Convention of 1858 largely neglected these preferences and instead established a constitutional order that was more favourable for the European Great Powers. This entailed the imposition of two separate states led by separate princes with only a limited degree of integration on the level of some secondary institutions. Furthermore, it meant the establishment of a French-inspired authoritarian regime, led by an elected Romanian prince who disposed over excessive powers and had the jurisdiction of absolute veto right over decisions of the parliament. This constitutional design was also to the detriment of the principles of liberal constitutionalism, such as separation of powers or individual rights and freedoms. The two states attempted to bypass the decision of the Great Powers by electing the same candidate, Alexandru Ioan Cuza in 1859 as *Domnitor* (ruler) for both countries. On 5 February 1862, the parliaments of the Principality of Moldavia and the Principality of Wallachia formally united to create the Romanian United Principalities. As an admirer of Napoleon III, Cuza started to develop an "authoritarian appetite" for more power. On 2 May 1864, he initiated the adoption of Developing Statues of the Paris Convention (*Statutul Dezvoltător al Convenției de la Paris*), which directly transplanted the constitutional model of the Second French Empire. New laws on suffrage were enacted, which extended the right to vote to the bourgeoisie and to peasants.[219] Nevertheless, Cuza launched electoral manipulation through his extensive executive powers; one could thus conclude that the "Romanian unitary state was not founded on parliamentarianism, but against it".[220] Since the Greater Powers did only recognize the association of

219 Before this new regulation, active and passive suffrage established a census of sex and relatively high wealth, which led to the domination of parliament by great landowners.
220 Selejan-Gutan (2016), p. 10.

Moldova and Wallachia for the duration of Cuza`s reign, the challenge arose in 1866 (after he had been forced to abdicate the throne) as to how to maintain the *status quo* afterwards. This reignited the request to elect a foreign Prince, which in the end came from the Swabian Hohenzollern-Sigmaringen House. Carol I of that family was the ruler of Romania from 1866 to 1914. It was also in the year 1866 when the first Romanian Constituent Assembly began to elaborate the first modern Constitution of Romania, based on massive amounts of direct transplant of provisions from the 1831 Constitution of Belgium. Consequently, the Constitution of 1866 established the Senate as the second chamber of the parliament and stipulated the irresponsibility of the Monarch. This constitution also took steps to consolidate an "ethnocentric constitutionalism, with strong religious accents",[221] that was concerned with the national unity of ethnic Romanians. These views were reflected in Art. 7, which refused to grant citizenship to non-Christians. This regulation in fact made it nearly impossible for Jews to obtain citizenship, while, on the other hand, the Romanian Orthodox Church was elevated to a superior status as the embodiment of the dominant religion of the Romanian state. The institutions, procedural mechanism, and principles that were transplanted from the Belgian constitution fell on less fertile soil, given that the great majority of the population at the time (about 80 per cent) was still composed of illiterate peasants.[222] The small number of intellectuals, on the other hand, studied to a large extent in France, which is one of the main reasons why government meetings were held in French from the 1820s up to the beginning of the First World War, despite the Monarch himself being German.[223] It was also during this period that Romanians started using the Latin alphabet, as opposed to Cyrillic, which was in use until the language reform of 1860. This language reform was the first step in a series of planned language reforms aimed to bring the grammar and the vocabulary of the Romanian language closer to the Romance languages, not the least in pursuit of supporting politically motivated ambitions to recreate the origins of the Romanian peoples.[224] Following successful military campaigns of the Russo-Turkish War of 1877–78, fighting on the Russian side, Romania gained independence from the Ottoman Empire in 1877 and was transformed into a kingdom four years later in 1881. This recognition,

221 *Id.* at p. 11.
222 *Id.* at p. 12.
223 *Id.* at p. 31.
224 According to the theory of Daco-Roman continuity, Romanians descend from the romanized inhabitants of an eastern province of the Roman Empire (*Dacia Traiana*), where the native Dacian people mixed with Roman colonists.

however, was contingent on the amendment of the constitution of 1866, pursuant to Art. XLIV of the Treaty of Berlin, which stipulated that "the difference of religious creeds and confessions shall not be alleged against any person as a ground for exclusion or incapacity in matters relating to the enjoyment of civil and political rights, admission to public employments, functions, and honours, or the exercise of the various professions and industries in any locality whatsoever".[225] This was the first attempt of the international community to place restraints on Romania's conduct towards its minorities. The unsuccessfulness of this attempt was vividly demonstrated by the fact that despite the required constitutional amendment, the Romanian legislature had placed additional administrative obstacles in the way of access to citizenship, which resulted in only 200 Jewish residents obtaining citizenship, from a Jewish community that counted around 270,000 members at that time.[226]

The next important step after independence was to expand the territory of the state with neighbouring regions that had Romanian populations to varying extent (Transylvania, Banat, Bukovina, and Bessarabia), which happened under the auspices of the Versailles Peace Conference after the First World War. This also meant the incorporation of extensive minority communities: Hungarians, Saxons, Russians, and Jews. While the Romanian National Council, which professed to represent the Romanian community of the Austro-Hungarian Monarchy, promised to respect the administrative autonomy as well as the cultural and linguistic identity of these communities through the Declaration of Alba Iulia, adopted on 1 December 1918, aspects of minority protection were marginalized in comparison with the aim to consolidate a unitary national state. Consequently, the minority political movements of the newly absorbed territories could not bring about a shift in the ethno-centric approach of the pre–First World War era Romania. Against this backdrop, the newly adopted constitution of 1923 contained no provisions regarding administrative autonomy or linguistic identity of minorities. In 1938, the "New Royal Constitution" replaced the short-lived Constitution of 1923 and created what is now referred to as the "royal dictatorship" of King Carol II, only to be suspended two years later when Marshall Ion Antonescu seized power. As "Leader of the State", Antonescu assumed all

225 Full text of Treaty between Great Britain, Germany, Austria, France, Italy, Russia, and Turkey for the Settlement of Affairs in the East: Signed at Berlin, July 13, 1878 is available at: https://archive.org/stream/jstor-2212670/2212670_djvu.txt, accessed: 2019.08.09.

226 Bölöny (1940), p. 5.

legislative and executive power in the framework of the National Legionary State (*Statul Naţional Legionar*) from 6 September 1940 to 23 January 1941. It was a right-wing, one-party dictatorship based on the German Führer model of the time, dominated by the fascist paramilitary Iron Guard in conjunction with Prime Minister Ion Antonescu. This jurisdiction did not extend to Northern-Transylvania after that territory came under the rule of Hungary again as a result of the second Vienna Arbitration signed on 30 August 1940.

### 2.1.2 Communist Period

After the Second World War, it was Petru Groza who presided over the consolidation of communist dictatorship as of 6 March 1945. The Senate was dissolved in 1946, and King Michael I was forced to abdicate in 1947 as the country officially became the "People's Republic of Romania" under a new interim law that was meant to be in force until the adoption of a new Constitution. This law established a Soviet-like collective organ as the bearer of executive power (the Presidium of the Republic). A new unicameral parliament called the Great National Assembly (*Marea Adunare Nationala*) was elected and entrusted with the task to prepare a new constitution for the "new order". This Constitution was adopted in 1952, according to which power lied with the working class, who exercised it through the Great National Assembly. While a set of freedoms and liberties was formally enshrined in the text of this constitution, in practice this period was characterized by confiscation of private property, installation of a single-party political system with heavily manipulated elections, and pervasive terror of the political police, who persecuted, incarcerated, or even executed the "enemies of the state" who were accused of acting against the socialist order. As mentioned before, it was this constitution which established the Hungarian Autonomous Province due to Soviet pressure. Under the auspices of a totalitarian regime, this autonomy, however, was largely in lack of true substance regarding decentralization. It also contradicted the ethnocentric mentality of the political elite, which did not cease to exist even under a theoretically internationalistic ideology. Proletarian internationalism was nowhere to be found in Romanian communism. Thus, the boarders of this autonomous region were changed in 1960 to make its ethnic composition more Romanian, and then eight years later it was abolished altogether.

The last communist constitution was enacted in 1965. The state organization was similar to that of 1952: "the supreme organ of state power and sole legislator" was the Great National Assembly, and "the supreme organ of the state with permanent activity" was the Council of State. These were complemented in 1974 by the "President of the Republic", which was a formality, given that in practice state power rested with the General Secretary of the Romanian Communist Party, a position that was filled by Nicolae Ceauşescu from 1965 to 1989 after his predecessor Gheorghe Gheorghiu-Dej died. The reign of Ceauşescu can accurately be characterized as one of the most oppressive totalitarian regimes of the 20th century. In the framework of an extreme cult of personality, Ceauşescu gave himself titles such as "The Genius of the Carpathians" (*Geniul din Carpaţi*). He asserted political persecution through arbitrary arrest, fabricated trials, and introduced an atmosphere of fear, paranoia, distrust, and terror through the political police, the infamous *Securitate*.

### 2.1.3 Post-communist Period

As mentioned earlier, the Romanian political transition was ignited by the harassment of Hungarian clergyman Tőkés László in the winter of 1989. New electoral legislation was adopted by Decree-Law No. 92/1990, according to which the first democratic and free elections were held in May 1990. Between 22 December 1989 (the adoption of the revolutionary declaration of the National Salvation Front, NSF)[227] and 8 December 1991, Romania did not have a constitution. There were no roundtable discussions on the matter; instead, the newly elected legislature established a Drafting Committee having delegates from all parties but being dominated by the NSF. The most controversial issues of the drafting procedure were: the form of government, the structure of the parliament, the powers of the president and other institutions of checks and balances. Among the contentious issues there was also the request of representatives of the Hungarian community to include autonomy rights in the text. The proposal was rejected as it was seen by the majority of the parties as something that was contrary to the national and unitary character of the state. The Draft Articles were finally sent to the legislature in November 1990, where it was adopted on 21 November with an overwhelming majority of 81%. The constitution was revised in 2003, adding, among others, an important third paragraph to Art. 1,

227 *Frontului Salvării Naţionale* was the name of the *ad hoc* political umbrella organization that was the governing body of Romania in the first weeks after the Romanian Revolution in 1989 and which subsequently became a political party and won the 1990 election under the leadership of then-President Ion Iliescu. An unusual result from this aspect is that Iliescu himself was a communist who became member of the Central Committee of the Romanian Communist Party in 1965 but fell from grace gradually as Ceauşescu saw an adversary in him.

which states that: "Romania is a democratic and social state, governed by the rule of law, in which human dignity, the citizens' rights and freedoms, the free development of human personality, justice and political pluralism represent supreme values, in the spirit of the democratic traditions of the Romanian people and the ideals of the Revolution of December 1989, and shall be guaranteed." This means that the complete legal system of the country as of that point should be interpreted in the spirit of democracy, rule of law, and fundamental civil liberties.

There was a subsequent attempt to amend the constitution in 2013.[228] The main issues of constitutional reform were inter-institutional relations, electoral laws, as well as the administrative reform (or regionalization process), which is of particular relevance for the autonomy discourse. This failed attempt would have conferred administrative competencies to the NUTS II regions of the country.[229] Instead of bringing about an administrative reform that pays attention to geographic-cultural-and historical circumstances, this reform plan would have had an adverse effect on the counties with substantial Szekler population, as these would have lost their majority position, by means of being incorporated into a larger administrative region, together with overwhelmingly Romanian counties (Alba, Brasov, and Sibiu).

Overall, we can say that the constitutional history of Romania was characterized by the failure to successfully transplant provisions of western European constitutions into the Romanian legal system due to discrepancies in the political culture and social structure. Strong personalization of power and constant dominance of the executive branch were present as opposed to more parliamentarianism, which was perceived as a threat to the national unitary state and its political stability. Human rights, including minority rights, were only formally consecrated, and they "never succeeded to become a true state of mind in the Romanian society".[230] Constitutional ethnocentrism was an overarching feature, providing a perpetual guideline for various political systems. The lack of democratic constitutional traditions and a track-record of having manipulated and fabricated elections were also pervasive features. As Selejan-Gutan summarized the Romanian constitutional history, "interest in limiting political power and in the separation of powers decreased in favour of the idea of building a strong

228 For more insight on this failed amendment, see, for example, Blokker (2013), pp. 187–204.

229 The Nomenclature of Territorial Units for Statistics or NUTS is a geocode standard for referencing the subdivisions of member states of the EU for statistical purposes.

230 Guțan (2013a), p. 251.

nation state; the interest in rights and freedoms diminished in favour of the idea of national unity; the idea of a political community was replaced by the idea of a community united by blood, language, history and (especially) religion".[231]

### 2.1.4 Constitution in Force

Romania is a Republic, with a bicameral legislature that is elected for four years by universal, equal, direct, secret, and free suffrage.[232] Bicameralism is symmetrical, which means that both the House of Deputies and the Senate have equal powers to discuss and enact laws within their respective spheres of competence,[233] while none of the Chambers have the jurisdiction to override vetoes or amendments adopted by the other house. The two Chambers are congruent in the sense that they are directly elected and, at the same time, use a similar electoral system, resulting in similarity of their partisan composition. The dual executive branch consists of the president, directly elected for a term of five years, and a prime minister with an equally long term, elected by the House of Deputies.

Differences in election often produce political *cohabitation*,[234] a phenomenon well known in similar semi-presidential political systems, most notably in France. In an attempt to deviate from past abuses experienced by an indirectly elected president during Communism, the democratic constitution followed the framework of the 1958 French Constitution in having a directly elected president but with narrower powers than its French counterpart.

Another provision where the Romanian constitution shows similarities with the 1958 French constitution is the so-called eternity clause, which limits the scope of constitutional revision. Article 152 (1) CR states that the national, independent, unitary, and indivisible character of the Romanian State, as well as the republican form of government, territorial integrity, the independence of justice, political pluralism, and the official language, shall not be subject to revision. (The same part of the French constitution, Art. 89, stipulates that "no amendment procedure shall be commenced or continued where the integrity of national

---

231 Selejan-Gutan (2016) *Supra note*, p. 26.

232 Article 62 (1) CR.

233 Enumerated under Art. 75 CR.

234 Cohabitation occurs when the president and the majority of the members of parliament come from opposing parties. The most memorable example of cohabitation in Romania happened in 2012 between Romania's Prime Minister Victor Ponta and President Traian Băsescu over the issue of who should represent the country at the European Council. After weeks of clashes, eventually Ponta prevailed.

territory is placed in jeopardy" and that "the republican form of government shall not be the object of any amendment".)[235]

The constitution is on top of the hierarchy of norms, followed by three types of state legislation. The parliament can pass constitutional, organic, and ordinary laws.[236] While constitutional laws pertain to the revision of the Constitution, organic laws regulate some of the most relevant institutions of the constitutional fabric, such as the functioning of parties, the organization of referendums, state of emergency, rules of local autonomy, and the status of national minorities.[237] Due to the more salient nature of the fields covered by organic laws, the passing of such legislation requires the majority vote of all the members of each Chamber.[238] In contrast, the third type of legislation, ordinary laws, is passed by the majority vote of the members present in each Chamber.[239] Even with this distinction, there are no clear procedural requirements for introducing organic laws to the legislature. Other sources of law contain government decrees and resolutions of local governments.

The CR adopts the monist approach in incorporating international treaties, which means that Treaties ratified by the parliament shall become part of national law. Article 20 (1) CR states that Constitutional provisions concerning the citizens' rights and liberties shall be interpreted and enforced in conformity with the Universal Declaration of Human Rights, with the covenants and other treaties Romania is a party to. Furthermore, where any inconsistencies exist between the covenants and treaties on fundamental human rights Romania is a party to and the national laws, the international regulations shall take precedence unless the Constitution or national laws contain provisions that are more favourable.[240] Consequently, irrespective of any presumed ethno-centric intention of the drafters of the Constitution of 1991,[241] Romanian authorities are not free in

235 There are only a handful of European countries with similar provisions, including Ukraine, Norway, Portugal, and Turkey. Such eternity clauses are more common in third world countries, see full list in Beauséjour (2018), p. 52.

236 Art. 73 (1) CR.

237 *Id.* Art. 73 (3).

238 *Id.* Art. 76 (1).

239 *Id.* Art. 76 (2).

240 *Id.* Art. 20 (2). This follows the Spanish model, where Section 10 (2) contains similar provisions.

241 Selejan-Gutan reminds that during the constitutional drafting process fears concerning threats to the unity and integrity of the state came to the fore, which triggered the desire to add an "identity mark" to the text of the constitution and emphasize the national character of the state and to carve it in stone for future generations through

interpreting the regulations pertaining to fundamental rights and freedoms, as the above provisions put a restraint upon them to align their interpretation with the corresponding international covenants. Article 4 (2) CR further strengthens these restraints by stating that Romania is the common and indivisible homeland of all its citizens, without any discrimination on account of race, nationality, ethnic origin, language, religion, sex, opinion, political adherence, property, or social origin.

Finally, an important aspect of the constitution for the subject matter of this book is the fact that it refers to several forms of autonomy. Article 29 (5) pertains to personal autonomy in the form of freedom of conscience by stipulating that religious cults shall be autonomous from the State and shall enjoy support from it. Article 32 (6) guarantees the functional autonomy of universities, while Art. 120 sets out the principles of local autonomy for territorial administrative units. Article 117 (3), which we discuss in later chapters, provides a special form of administrative autonomy.

## 2.2 Opinion No. 405/2004 – the Essential Summary of All Arguments

Having outlined the core features of the constitutional system of Romania, we can now turn more specifically to the question of how territorial autonomy fits in this legal framework. Opinion no. 405/2004, adopted by the Legislative Council of the Romanian Parliament on 11 March 2004, is the single most important document that summarizes the legal arguments against the territorial autonomy of Szeklerland.[242] The main assertions of this Opinion were subsequently reaffirmed in the three other instances when the DL was submitted to the Romanian legislature, without adding any new arguments to it. Below I present both the substantive and procedural objections contained in this document.

---

limitations on constitutional amendment, hence the eternity clause mentioned earlier. See Selejan-Gutan (2016) *Supra note*, p. 41.

242 This Opinion responded to proposal no. Pl-x no. 87/2004 (Legislative provisions of the Statute of Autonomy of Szeklerland) submitted to Parliemant on 1 March 2004 by six members of the DAHR fraction: Birtalan Ákos, Kovács Zoltán, Pécsi Ferenc, Szilágyi Zsolt, Toró Tibor, Vekov Károly-János. See: http://www.cdep.ro/pls/proiecte/upl_pck2015.proiect?cam=2&idp=5343, accessed: 2021.03.23.

### 2.2.1 Substantive Objections

I. The DL aims to create a separate state entity, parallel with the unitary, national Romanian State.[243]

II. As the DL refers to several international legal documents, Opinion 405/2004 reminds that the territorial organization of a state is not subject to community law and falls exclusively under the scope of the authorities of the member states of the European Union. It also adds that European organizations do not promote the creation of "asymmetrical, non-uniform or simply just separate, exclusively ethnicity-based intrastate entities, such as autonomous regions"[244] and that persons belonging to minorities do not have collective rights under international law.[245]

III. Territorial autonomy would result in the positive discrimination of an ethnic minority to the detriment of persons belonging to the majority.[246] More specifically, Art. 94 of the DL (on the use of mother tongue in cultural life) would violate Art. 16 of the Constitution on the principle of equality of rights among citizens.[247] These provisions also contradict Art. 6 of the Constitution (the right to identity) as well as the provisions of international law. The Opinion specifically quotes Art. 16 and 17 of Resolution 1334/2003 of the CoE, stipulating that "the granting of autonomy must never give a community the impression that local government is a matter for that community alone. Successful autonomy depends on balanced relationships within a state between majorities and minorities, but also between minorities themselves. Autonomous status must always respect the principles of equality and non-discrimination and be based on the territorial integrity and sovereignty of states". Accordingly, granting special rights to administrative entities that are not recognized by the constitution and are organized exclusively along ethnic lines would violate the principle of equality between citizens of the State.

IV. The DL manifestly contradicts the constitutional order as it foresees the creation of an administrative-territorial institution different from the administrative territorial units enshrined in the constitution in terms of both its organization and its special powers. The Opinion cites Art 1 (1) and Art. 2 of the Constitution. The former contains the "classic Westphalian" method

---

243 Paragraph 1 of Opinion No. 405/2004.
244 *Id.* at Paragraph 2.
245 *Id.* at Paragraph 3.
246 *Id.* at Paragraphs 3 and 6.
247 *Id.* at Paragraph 12.

of guaranteeing integrity by means of an indivisibility clause, stipulating that Romania is "a sovereign, independent, unitary and indivisible National State". The latter one states that "national sovereignty shall reside with the Romanian people" . . .and that "no group or person may exercise sovereignty in one's own name". The Opinion argues that the DL violates these provisions and infringes on the sovereignty as well as the unity and indivisibility of the State in the following manner:

a) *Unity* is understood by the Legislative Council as a single state formation that "assumes a legal order based on a single constitution and a single system of organization, through which the three basic powers are being exercised, and whose population has one single citizenship. This and only this formation is a subject of international law".[248]
b) *Indivisibility* is described in the sense that Romania "cannot be segmented, nor can it be subject to total or partial division into different legal regimes".[249]
c) *Sovereignty* is violated through the delegation of special – and sometimes exclusive – competencies to the autonomous region whose exercise would eliminate the primacy of state sovereignty within Szeklerland. With the adoption of the DL, the population of Romania would no longer belong under one political and legal organizational structure nor would it have a single state apparatus or a unified state structure, and this territorial division would prejudice the fullness of the sovereignty of the state.[250] Furthermore, the formation of the autonomous region would make it impossible to implement laws and other legal acts adopted by the Government all over the country.[251]

   Altogether, territorial autonomy would mean giving powers to an autonomous region that is detached from state sovereignty as that is the nature of territorial autonomy in the understanding of the Legislative Council.[252]

V. Art. 11 (3) of the DL guarantees the free use of Hungarian national symbols, which contradicts Art. 12 of the Constitution on the national symbols of Romania.[253]

---

248 *Id.* at Paragraphs 4 and 7.
249 *Id.* at Paragraph 4.
250 *Id.* at Paragraph 7.
251 *Id.* at Paragraph 8.
252 *Id.* at Paragraph 5.
253 *Id.* at Paragraph 9.

VI. Art. 10 of the DL stipulates that the Hungarian language would become equal to the state language within Szeklerland. This provision violates Art. 13 of the Constitution on the official language of Romania. The rights of persons belonging to minorities to use their mother tongue is not the same as granting equal status to a minority language with the official language of the state.[254]

### 2.2.2 Procedural Objections

I. According to Art. 3 (3) of the Constitution, the country's territory is organized administratively into communes, towns, and counties. Only these levels have administrative and financial competencies, which raises two issues. On the one hand, no such unit as a "region" or a "seat" exists within the current constitutional framework of the country, while both of these are present in the DL. Consequently, no such unit could receive any kind of administrative or fiscal competencies, whatsoever. On the other hand, Szeklerland would have three administrative levels (municipal, regional, and that of the Seats), whereas the rest of the country would be organized into two of these levels only (municipal and county level). This would generate impediments and dysfunctionality with regard to both internal and external cooperation.[255]

II. According to Art. 12 (3) of the DL, the legal basis of the establishment of the autonomous region is Art. 117 (3) of the Constitution, which stipulates that autonomous administrative authorities may be established by organic law. In the interpretation of the Legislative Council, however, this article refers to the central public administration as opposed to the local public administration regulated under Art. 121, which provides an exhaustive list of local authorities that cannot be further expanded.

III. The DL violates the provisions of Law No. 215 of 2001 on Local Public Administration, according to which "the territorial delimitation of the communes, towns and counties shall be established by law. Any change in their territorial limits may be made only by law and only after prior consultation of the citizens in the respective territorial-administrative units by referendum, to be organised according to law".[256] The Opinion notes that no

254 *Id.* at Paragraph 10.

255 *Id.* at Paragraphs 6 and 15.

256 See Art. 20, and 22 of law 215/2001.

such referendum was organized prior to the submission of the Draft to the Parliament.

## 2.3 Decision No. 80/2014 of the Constitutional Court of Romania Rejecting the Constitutional Amendments Proposed by the Special Committee of the Parliament – the Constitutional Court and the Recognition of the National Ideal

During the second Ponta administration, the government pushed forward with a constitutional reform package, which included plans on reforming the administrative division of the country by granting administrative competencies to the NUTS II regions. Such an administrative reorganization would have been detrimental for Szeklers, as it foresaw to incorporate Szeklerland into a region where the Hungarian-speaking community represented less than 30 % of the population. Trying to react to these developments, the dominant Hungarian party (DAHR), aimed to turn the situation to their advantage by elaborating a draft on amendments to the constitution. These included an additional paragraph (para 3.) to Art. 3 of the constitution. Bearing in mind the example of the South Tyrolean province, which blends into a greater region (Trentino – Alto-Adige), this proposed amendment foresaw that "organic laws may recognize traditional areas as administrative subdivisions of regions".[257] The same draft also proposed an amendment to Art. 6 of the constitution (on the right to identity), stipulating that "legal representatives of national minorities may establish their own decision-making and executive bodies according to the Statute on National Minorities adopted through legislation,[258] that are vested with the powers to preserve, develop and express their identity".[259] Furthermore, this draft foresaw that "decisions of central and local authorities on the preservation, development and expression of ethnic, cultural, linguistic and religious identity are taken after consultation with the organizations of national minorities".[260] Besides the territorial division and the competencies exercised by them, a third relevant issue was expressed in the government proposal, namely that of the symbols. In pursuit to

257 CCR (2014), p. 18.

258 This phrasing refers to the need to codify a single statute summarizing all the minority rights, as these are currently dispersed in various laws of the legal system.

259 CCR (2014), *Supra note*, p. 19.

260 *Id.* at, p. 19.

amend Art. 12 of the constitution (on national symbols), the proposal stated that "national minorities can freely use in public and in private, their own symbols that represent their ethnic, cultural, linguistic and religious identity".[261]

Against these proposals, the Constitutional Court of Romania (CCR) raised already familiar objections in its decision of 16 February 2014. On national symbols, the CCR concluded that such amendment could not be realized under Art. 12 of the Constitution as that would entail accepting the idea that the symbols of national minorities are "national symbols", indicating that national minorities have the right to opt for the use of their own symbols as opposed to symbols of the Romanian national state. If such a paragraph did have any place in the constitution in the first place, then it would come under Art. 6 on identity, and only on the condition that minority symbols can be used together with symbols of the Romanian national state.

On the proposals regarding the right to identity, the CCR announced that the amendment would create collective political autonomy based on ethnic criteria and would thus contradict the principle of equality among citizens and infringe upon the unitary nature of the state, given that "the essence of the unitary state is the existence of an exclusive set of institutions with political and legal powers (one legislative body, one executive authority, one judicial authority)".[262]

Finally, when it came to the question of the administrative subdivisions, the CCR pronounced something that up until that point has only been insinuated by political actors. They stated that granting administrative competencies to "traditional areas" would not only violate the unitary nature of the state, but they would also "call into question the national character of the Romanian state".[263] As such, they would also infringe upon Art. 152 (1) of the constitution, stipulating that the "national, independent, unitary and indivisible character of the Romanian State, the republican form of government, territorial integrity, independence of justice, political pluralism and official language shall not be subject to revision".

## 2.4 Political Assertions

Even though the DL was rejected by the parliament, the procedural objection of the Legislative Council on the lack of a local referendum gave momentum to a referendum campaign, whereby voluntaries of the Szekler National Council

261 *Id.* at, p. 20.
262 *Id.* at, p. 19.
263 *Id.* at, p. 18.

went from one municipality to another with self-made ballots asking local citizens residing in the municipalities of Szeklerland if they agreed with the establishment of an autonomous Szekler administrative unit in Romania. The process lasted from December 2006 until February 2008. Approximately 395,000 citizens were contacted, out of which 210,000 cast their votes. 99.31 % of these ballots were in favour of creating an autonomous Szeklerland.[264] This process spanned through two parliamentary terms and three governments, igniting heated reaction from Romanian Members of Parliament (MP). In order to provide the political context behind the debate on legal reforms pertaining to power-sharing, it is important to refer to salient political assertions regarding the idea of an autonomous Szeklerland.

In his interpellation from 19 December 2005, right-wing (Democratic Party, *Partidul Democrat*, PD) politician Bogdan Cantaragiu asked the then Minister of Public Administration (Vasile Blaga) if his ministry was prepared to cope with possible separatist activities and actions aimed to undermine the authority of the state, which could take place in the "so-called Szeklerland" due to the fact that the Szekler National Council had repeatedly requested to adopt a Statute of Autonomy for this area. In his response, Blaga agreed that the activities of the SzNC affect the climate of public order in the areas inhabited by Szeklers and that the Ministry of Administration and Internal Affairs will have an eye on such activities and make the necessary legal steps if required.[265] In 14 February 2007, Gabriel Sandu, MP of the centre-right National Liberal Party (*Partidul Național Liberal*, PNL), demanded answers from the prime minister about the measures his administration intends to take against the self-proclaimed referendum on the autonomy of Szeklerland, given that such an illegal referendum can be a real threat to the territorial integrity of the State and can trigger a series of grave problems.[266] In his response, Prime Minister Călin Popescu-Tăriceanu noted that the municipal resolutions aiming to organize local autonomy-referendums were either annulled by the courts or are in the process of being nullified. He also mentioned that several complaints were recorded by the DIICOT coming from parliamentarians invoking Art. 166 of the Criminal Code[267] and Art 19 of

264 See Appendix No. 2 in: Szekler National Council (2009), p. 102.

265 See: *Interpelarea* no. 952B/20-12-2005. All questions and interpellations cited in this chapter are available at the homepage of the Chamber of Deputies of Romania: http://www.cdep.ro/pls/parlam/interpelari.home, accessed: 2015.05.09.

266 See: *Interpelarea* no. 2386B/14-02-2007.

267 The mentioned article of the Criminal Code in force at that time stipulated that any illegal or violent action that aimed to change the constitutional order or the national,

Law No. 51/ 1991 on the National Security of Romania.[268] While the prime minister reminded that the initiators of the referendum established no illegal intelligence structures nor did they engage in any violent actions, he also expresses his disapproval of the idea of autonomy on ethnic grounds as he did many times before. Socialist MP Ion Stan initiated a similar inquiry on 3 March 2008 addressed among others to the Director of the Romanian Intelligence Service (*Serviciul Român de Informaţii*, SRI).[269] In his interpellation, Stan asked about the consequences of the "so-called referendum" that was initiated by the "so-called Szekler National Council", which the MP considered an incitement to discrimination and territorial separatism under Art. 30 (7) of the Constitution. Additionally, the Interpellator also demanded a scrutiny of the legality of the financial sources used for "autonomist-separatist activities". In his written response, George Cristian Maoir, Director of SRI, made it clear that the Intelligence Service monitors and investigates every activity that affects the rule of law, the constitutional order, and the social stability, including those relating to the illegal promotion of autonomist-separatist projects based on ethnic criteria. As Maoir further added, if they encountered cases where the obtained information revealed the existence of threats and risks to national security and whose realization would be likely to endanger sovereignty, unity, and indivisibility of the Romanian national state, the corresponding authorities were notified so that they could take the necessary measures to prevent or counteract such developments. Regarding the legality of financial resources, the SRI Chief notes that in many cases the representatives of foreign NGOs performing propaganda in favour of autonomist-separatist goals in Romania are acting as individuals and are consequently not subject to Romanian laws on financial control.

Leading politicians made an abundance of like-minded assertions outside the parliament as well. On 12 August 2013, the then Head of the State Traian Băsescu said during a Summer University in *Izvoru Mureşului/Marosfő* that he guarantees: "…one will never make an administrative reorganization of the country along ethnic lines. Those who think they can do that confuse us with

sovereign, independent, unitary, and indivisible character of the Romanian state shall be punished by a term of imprisonment of between 5 and 15 years. This provision has been removed from the Law during its revision in 2009.

268 The initiation, organization, establishment, or support of intelligence structures that might affect national security is punishable by imprisonment for a term of 2–7 years. For this version of the Act, no longer in force, see: http://legislatie.resurse-pentru-democratie.org/legea/51-1991.php, accessed: 2015.05.09.

269 See: *Interpelare* no. 3600B/03-03-2008.

the Stalinists. Only Stalin organized a Hungarian Autonomous Region".[270] Next year, on 13 April 2014, *Realitatea* TV made an exclusive interview with Băsescu where the president made it clear that: "Romania defines herself as a unitary state and anyone who wants autonomy will confront the Romanian constitution and logically also the Romanian state".[271] On 25 May 2013, at a conference on the administrative reform of the country, Crin Antonescu, president of the centre-right PNL Party at that time, mentioned that regionalization in Romania will not mean the establishment of "enclaves based on ethnic criteria".

These views of right-wing politicians are unequivocally shared by their left-wing counterparts. Regarding the regionalization process, social-democratic prime minister Victor Ponta mentioned that a region composed of *Covasna, Harghita*, and *Mures* was never on the table, "because that would mean a region along ethnic lines, which does not happen in the EU".[272] Foreign affairs minister of the Ponta cabinet Bogdan Aurescu reminded after a meeting with his Hungarian counterpart in Budapest that "territorial autonomy based on ethnic criteria is incompatible with the Romanian Constitution, its support is not a part of European norms and is therefore unacceptable".[273] At a conference that took place on 31 April 2015 at the Babeş–Bolyai University, in *Cluj Napoca/Kolozsvár*, Aurescu also highlighted that "Romania has developed its own minority protection model, based on the inclusion of minorities into political decision-making, which is not perfect. . .but is still better than other models". Aurescu also noted that "only the dialogue of the cultures can lead to social development", adding that "cultures which isolate themselves are not able to develop, henceforth territorial autonomy based on ethnic criteria cannot be a good solution within minority protection".[274] A week later, he reasserted these views in an interview with the Romanian news agency, Agerpres, claiming that "Minority protection in Romanian is guided by interculturality, which is the philosophy of the

---

270 Source: http://www.mediafax.ro/social/basescu-doar-stalin-a-facut-regiunea-autonoma-maghiara-inromania-nu-se-va-mai-intampla-11247073, accessed: 2016.08.12.

271 Source: http://www.3szek.ro/load/cikk/69492/b%C3%84%C2%83sescu:_az_autonomia_alkotmany ellenes, accessed: 2016.01.28.

272 Source: http://www.reporterntv.ro/stire/ponta-despre-regionalizare-singura-formula-posibila-e-cu-8regiuni-altfel-deschizi-cutia-pandorei, accessed: 2016.08.12.

273 Source: http://www.szekelyhon.ro/vilag/ujabb-nem-az-autonomiara, accessed: 2016.02.03.

274 Source: http://www.3szek.ro/load/cikk/80249/konferencia_ellentmondasok_kereszttuzeben_kisebbsegvedelem_kisebbsegek_nelkul, accessed: 2016.01.28.

Framework Convention for the Protection of National Minorities of the Council of Europe. Therefore, we support the merging of cultures and reject separation including autonomy based on ethnic criteria".[275] Finally, foreign affairs minister of Romania Titus Corlățean said in 2013 that "autonomy based on ethnic criteria blatantly violates European standards". In his point of view, there should be "no segregation, no conflicts and ethnic tensions"; however, these would be generated by the acceptance of autonomy aspirations that aim to create "islands in a country" based on ethnic criteria. He added that Romania is not going to follow these proposals that come from "very hot minds" of some Hungarian politicians with an "extremist nationalist rhetoric".[276]

Characterizing the maintenance of a minority culture as an undesirable enclave and linking this form of "separation" with undesirable economic developments came also to the fore during the T-529/13 Izsák & Dabis v. European Commission case. The initial request of the plaintiffs in this case revolved around a European Citizens' Initiative aimed at the reform of the cohesion policy of the EU, which – according to the initiators – should pay special attention to regions that differentiate themselves from the surrounding regions through national, ethnic, cultural, religious, or linguistic characteristics (a.k.a. national regions).[277] The government of Romania joined this lawsuit and argued that the plaintiffs' proposals on the reform of the cohesion policy would have the result that the national, ethnic, cultural, religious, or linguistic characteristics of the given national region remain unchanged. As the government pointed out, the proposal would cause the "enclavisation" of these regions leading to detrimental economic developments.[278]

As a closing part of this sub-chapter, it is also worthy to recall political assertions and developments that commenced after the fourth submission of the DL on 18 December 2019. There was a peculiar circumstance that affected the process this time, the Covid-19 pandemic. The public discourse in Romania has become increasingly hostile towards the Hungarian minority community in a

275 Source: http://www.kronika.ro/belfold/aurescu-veszelyeztetett-a-magyarorszagi-romanok-kulturalisidentitasa, accessed: 2016.01.28.

276 Source: https://www.mediafax.ro/social/corlatean-romania-mentine-modelul-european-privind-minoritatile-fara-insule-pe-teritoriul-tarii-11516450, accessed: 2021.02.26.

277 For more information on this European Citizens' Initiative visit: http://www.nationalregions.eu/, accessed: 2021.03.17.

278 See the relevant documents of this lawsuit at: https://curia.europa.eu/juris/documents.jsf?num=T-529/13, accessed: 2021.03.17.

very short period of time during the state of emergency, introduced by Decree no. 195/2020 on 16 March 2020 in order to tackle the coronavirus outbreak. What ignited this escalation was an announcement of the president of Romania on 29 April 2020 that came as a response to an unusual event that occurred in the Romanian legislature a few days earlier.

On 23 April 2020, the Statute of Autonomy for Szeklerland, put forward by Hungarian MPs József Kulcsár-Terza and Zsolt Bíró, acquired "automatic approval" in the Chamber of Deputies. This peculiar event occurred due to Art. 75 (2) of the Romanian Constitution, which stipulates that after a certain period of time, legislative proposals which were not subject of a plenary debate are automatically adopted. Under the extraordinary circumstances introduced by the coronavirus outbreak in all spheres of public life, deputies of the lower Chamber, who were adamantly opposed to the idea of an autonomous Szeklerland in three previous votes, apparently lost track of bill no. 670/2019 on the Statute of Autonomy of Szeklerland, which eventually resulted in its procedural adoption.[279] Even though the Senate quashed the bill six days later in a decisive vote (126 against, 9 in favour), the political response to this situation was overwhelming.

In a video message broadcasted on 29 April 2020,[280] the president of Romania, Klaus Iohannis, made references to the adoption of the autonomy-statute by accusing his political opponent, the Social Democratic Party (PSD, *Partidul Social Democrat*), that while the government and the authorities combat the coronavirus pandemic, "PSD works in the Parliament's secret offices to cede Transylvania to Hungarians".[281]

This securitization of minority aspirations has ignited a race to the bottom in domestic politics.[282] On 6 May 2020, PSD announced that the party proposed

279 See the adopted text of the bill and all relating legislative documents at: Pl-x no. 670/ 2019 Propunere legislativă privind Statutul de autonomie al Ținutului Secuiesc. Available at: http://www.cdep.ro/pls/proiecte/upl_pck2015.proiect?idp=18286, accessed: 2021.02.25.

280 Source: Declarație de presă susținută de Președintele României, domnul Klaus Iohannis - 29 aprilie 2020. *Facebook*. Available at: https://www.facebook.com/watch/live/?v=658820878240744&ref=external, accessed: 2021.02.25.

281 Due to these assertions, the NCCD of Romania decided to sanction President Iohannis to a fine of 5,000 Lei (around 1,000 EUR, or 1,150 USD) for discrimination and violation of the right to dignity on the basis of ethnic and national affiliation.

282 The president doubled down on this assertion on 4 May 2020, claiming that the PSD supports another unacceptable bill that was proposed by the leading Hungarian political party, RMDSZ (*Romániai Magyar Demokrata Szövetség* – Democratic Alliance

amending the house rules of both Chambers of Parliament so as to disable it in the future for MPs to submit bills that concern the independent, unitary and indivisible nature of the Romanian state.[283] On 8 May 2020, a Senator of the small, right-wing party PMP (*Partidul Mişcarea Populară* – People's Movement Party), Cătălin Lucian Iliescu, announced on social media that he is thinking about drafting a bill whereby "any person who speaks about territorial autonomy in Romania, will be expelled wherever they want to continue their lives".[284] On 13 May 2020, the Romanian Chamber of Deputies adopted a law with an overwhelming majority (235 in favour, 21 against, and 25 abstained)[285] to declare 4 June as the Day of the "Treaty of Trianon". The legislative proposal, which was initiated by senators Titus Corlăţean and Nicolae Şerban of the PSD, aimed to regulate the measures for the "proper marking" of this day at national and local level, as in other instances of "celebration of symbolic moments".[286] Proper celebration in this case includes, among others, that central and local administrative bodies shall "take the necessary measures for the Romanian flag to be hoisted on this day".[287] As one of the initiators, MP Corlăţean, further elaborated for the press, this law was needed because it marks "with national dignity" an important moment in the history of the Romanian nation, "which has been subject to

---

of Hungarians in Romania) on public administration. This proposal contained several new provisions that would have been favourable for minorities, including the opportunity to use languages in public administration in settlements where the proportion of minority speakers was under 20 % (the current threshold stipulated by law for the use of a minority language in local public administration). The president was of the opinion that this bill would "make the Hungarian language compulsory in certain parts of Transylvania" Source: https://kronikaonline.ro/erdelyi-hirek/az-rmdsz-a-kozigazgatasi-torvenyrol-iohannis-ismet-elohuzta-a-magyar-kartyat, accessed: 2021.07.26.

283 Source: https://www.agerpres.ro/magyar/2020/05/06/h-zszab-ly-m-dos-t-st-kezdem-nyez-a-psd-ezut-n-ne-fogadja-be-a-parlament-a-rom-nia-nemzet-llam-jelleg-t-rint-tervezeteket--499822, accessed: 2021.02.25.

284 Source: https://www.facebook.com/iliescu.c.lucian/posts/10217105650702402, accessed: 2021.02.25.

285 Only the Hungarian-speaking MPs of the legislature voted against this bill.

286 Sorce: Corlăţean, Titus & Şerban, Nicolae (2020): *Expunere de Motive pentru declararea zilei de 4 Iuinie Ziua Tratatului de la Trianon, p. 2.* Available at: https://www.senat.ro/Legis/PDF/2019/19L459EM.pdf, accessed: 2021.03.21.

287 Art. 4. (1) of the Law on the declaration of June 4 as the Day of the Treaty of Trianon 2019 (Lege pentru zilei de 4 Iunie Ziua Trataului de la Trianon). Available at: http://www.cdep.ro/proiecte/2019/500/20/1/se792.pdf, accessed: 2021.02.25.

attempts to be rewritten, by the revisionist positions that have been promoted over the years in Budapest by various political forces".[288]

These political manifestations had a spillover effect that was tangible in the social climate of Szeklerland, a region where, as mentioned earlier, inter-ethnic and inter-cultural dialogue has always been problematic.[289] For example, a far-right NGO (*Calea Neamului* – The Way of the Nation) organized a rally on 4 June 2020 in the town of Sepsiszentgyörgy, a town where the population (56,000 citizens) is overwhelmingly ethnic Hungarian (74 %, according to the census of 2011), where they emphasized that Szeklerland is a part of the Romanian nation state and that Romanian is the only official language of the country.[290] The organization justified their selection of location with the argument that due to the autonomy aspirations of the region, the "presence of the Romanian flag is necessary here".[291] It happened in the same town on 8 May that a Romanian employee of a local shop of the supermarket chain Lidl yelled at a 70-year-old consumer for trying to communicate in Hungarian at the counter. As this employee put it: "*Trăiți în România! Trebuie învățat limba statului!*" meaning that "You live in Romania! The language of the state must be learned!"[292]

---

288 Source: https://www.agerpres.ro/politic/2020/05/13/corlatean-4-iunie-declarata-ziua-tratatului-de-la-trianon-legea-necesara-pentru-marcarea-unei-simbolistici-nationale--504759, accessed: 2021.02.25.

289 These examples also show how the coronavirus crisis amplified existing problems and was instrumentalized for political ends by significant fragments of the Romanian political elite, allowing the president of the country the opportunity to play the "Hungarian card" in a political battle between government and opposition.

290 See the online video of Erdély TV: *Román nacionalisták Sepsiszentgyörgyön*. Available at: https://www.youtube.com/watch?v=bsg9cU9XbJk, accessed: 2021.02.25.

291 The instrumentalization of 4 June and the Treaty of Trianon is a novelty in Romanian politics. When it comes to the question of Transylvania's incorporation into Romania, the political class usually makes references to an *ad hoc* gathering of the Romanian-speaking citizens of the Hungarian Kingdom that occurred on 1 December 1918 in Gyulafehérvár/Alba Iulia as opposed to the conclusion of the Treaty of Trianon. From a political point of view, highlighting the former event provides the framing that Transylvania became a part of Romania as a genuine manifestation of the popular will of Romanians, whereas the latter frames this event as part of a reward that was granted by the victorious *entente* powers as a means to irrevocably weaken one of the loosing powers of the First World War.

292 Source: https://www.3szek.ro/load/cikk/132826/raszoltak-hogy-beszeljen-romanul-panasz-a-lidl-aruhazra, accessed: 2021.02.25.

The above-quoted declarations of politicians illustrate some of the long-standing characteristics of Romanian politics. Suspicions towards and full rejection of autonomy in general is present regardless of ideological affiliation or the structure of government coalitions. In practice, the presence or absence of a Hungarian party within the government does not alter this basic characteristic. Romanian politicians tend to challenge the existence of Szeklerland by referring to it only as the "so-called Szeklerland" (*aşa-zisului Ţinutul Secuiesc*) and/or by putting it between quotation marks ("*Ţinutul Secuiesc*"). Autonomy aspirations are being perceived as an imminent threat to public order, national security, and state sovereignty, which is why state authorities need to monitor the organizations engaged in such "subversive" activities. Furthermore, in the interpretation of the Romanian political elite, territorial autonomy equals self-isolation and the maintenance of ethnic enclaves and would further exacerbate the social and economic backlog witnessed in regions inhabited by minorities. The solution to these non-desirable effects in the "Romanian-model" is interculturality and the merging of cultures, understood as the process of minority assimilation, which in turn contributes to economic development and provides social peace and adequate mobilization channels for persons belonging to national minorities, while it also eliminates the root causes of the problem: cultural, linguistic, and ethnic diversity.

## 2.5 Similar Approaches

Conceiving autonomy as a potential threat to the unity of the state is a thought that is shared by many states across Europe. While the study concentrates on the Romanian case, it is noteworthy to mention some of the similar approaches to deepen the understanding of this phenomenon, in particular the cases of France and Estonia. While there are some countries where governments tend to treat whole minority communities as potential threats for various reasons (this is the case with Macedonians and Turks in Greece and Bulgaria; the Russian minority communities in the Baltic states; Kurds in Turkey; or Hungarians in Ukraine), the two examples presented below are salient due to the fact that they represent cases where institutions of central states provided legal arguments against autonomy *per se*.

As far as France is concerned, an interestingly different approach is present between the Overseas Departments and Territories (*départements et territoiresd'outremer*, DOM-TOM) and Metropolitan France (including not just the mainland but also the surrounding Mediterranean Islands). Within the DOM-TOM regions, a large variety of institutional arrangements exists,[293] out

293 See Art. 72 - 75–1 of the French Constitution.

of which the ones possessed by New Caledonia are the widest in scale.[294] As a result of the 1998 Nouméa Accord, the archipelago gained a special status in 1999, which also included the launch of a public consultation on the independence of New Caledonia from France between 2014 and 2018. Based on these developments, two referendums were held on the independence of New Caledonia from France. The first on 4 November 2018 and the second 4 October 2020. (The local population rejected the idea of "full sovereignty" both times with a narrow margin: 56.67 % and 53.26 %, respectively.) A New Caledonian citizenship was also established, and a gradual transfer of exclusive legislative and executive powers from the French state to New Caledonian institutions commenced.[295] The constitution of France clarifies that this unique status is based on the principle of the self-determination of peoples and is due to the former colonial status of these territories.[296] Due to this post-colonial context, the comparative value of these examples is largely confined. Nonetheless, they are interesting if one compares this "cordial" approach to the more restrictive one exhibited in relation to Metropolitan areas, among others, in the case of Corsica. The issue of Corsica has been on the agenda of consecutive governments for decades, the modern phase of which can be traced back to the mid-1960s, an era characterized by violent actions of the National Liberation Front (FLNC). There were several attempts in various forms to address the issue. Right-wing administrations (1986–1988; 1993–1995; 1995; 1997) generally applied tactics of repression and "double diplomacy": negotiating with Corsican political actors while also dealing with separatists and playing one against the other. Left-wing governments (1981–1986; 1988–1993; 1997–2002) sought to propose institutional solutions

294 See Title XII of the French Constitution.

295 Under section 99 of Organic Law No. 99–2009 enacted pursuant to Art. 76 and 77 of the French Constitution, the jurisdiction of New Caledonia pertains to: rules on base and methods of local tax collection, own identity symbols, fundamental principles of labour law, trade union law, social security law, ownership, civil and commercial obligations, rules on access to employment, environmental issues, the electoral system, and the internal municipal system.

296 As the preamble of the French Constitution puts it, by virtue of the principles enshrined in the Declaration of 1789 – confirmed and complemented by the Preamble to the Constitution of 1946, and the rights and duties as defined in the Charter for the Environment of 2004 – and that of the self-determination of peoples, the Republic offers to the overseas territories which have expressed the will to adhere to them new institutions founded on the common ideal of liberty, equality, and fraternity and conceived for the purpose of their democratic development.

instead.[297] There are two relevant rulings of the Constitutional Court of France on Corsica: Decision 91–290 DC of 9 May 1991 and decision 2001–454 of 17 January 2002. The first one is more often referred to because it declared unconstitutional Section 1 of the so-called Joxe Statute (a Law on Corsican competencies adopted in 1991), which stipulated that "the French Republic guarantees to the Corsican people, a living historical and cultural community and part of the French people, the rights to the preservation of its cultural identity and the defence of its economic and social specific interest". The Court declared this provision unconstitutional on several grounds. It infringes upon the unity of the French people (as set out by the Preamble of the French Constitution), the indivisibility of the republic (Art. 1) and, finally, it violates Art. 3, which designates the people as the sole possessor of national sovereignty. The Court argues that the French people regardless of their origin constitute a whole unit incapable of any subdivision by statute. The concept of the French peoples perceived in this manner is invoked by the 1789 Declaration of Rights, the Constitution of 1946, and the Constitution of 1958 and is therefore a legal concept of constitutional status. The only exemption is the overseas peoples, which is why the Court has also ruled unconstitutional Section 2 (1) of the Joxe Statute, which stipulated that Corsica constitutes a territorial unit of the Republic within the meaning of Art. 72 of the Constitution on the Territorial communities. The court reminded that Art. 72 and 74 are reserved for overseas territories as opposed to metropolitan France, but noted that devolution of responsibilities that are normally regulated by statute (i.e. by the central legislature) is not foreseen by Corsica and so cannot be declared unconstitutional. This part argues in favour of the legitimate nature of granting administrative competencies to Corsica, as opposed to legislative ones, but it also sets further boundaries to this type of administrative autonomy. The right of the Corsican Assembly to be consulted on bills

---

297 These included: 1) Law No. 82–214 of 2 March 1982, *Statut de la collectivité territoriale de Corse* that established the Corsican Assembly which was vested with the special power to communicate directly with the government and to be consulted by it on all matters concerning Corsica, even though their opinion was of a non-binding nature. 2) Law of 13 May 1991 (a.k.a. the "Joxe Statute") that established a special constitutional status for Corsica (like the overseas territories of Saint-Pierre-et-Miquelon, or Mayotte). 3) the Matignon Process of 1999–2000 that resulted in a third autonomy statute in January 2001 (granting for the first time the opportunity to teach Corsican language in kindergartens and elementary schools) and constitutional reforms in 2003 that redefined the unitary republican model of the state. See more in Daftary (2004), pp. 24–27, and Henders (2010), 89–123.

containing provisions specific to Corsica are not unconstitutional, as they do not restrict the power of the Government to take legislative initiatives. This is not the case with the power to make proposal for legal acts in Corsican matters in a way that obliges the prime minister to respond to these proposals, nor is the establishment of a special financial arrangement (regarding, among others, transfer of tax revenues and the allocation of budget resources). Lastly, the Court argued that inserting the Corsican language into school curricula is only constitutional provided that it does not become a compulsory subject. This line of thinking also insinuates that if Corsican would become a mandatory subject in schools, it would violate the constitutional status of the French language as the only official language of the state.

The second decision came 11 years later in response to the third autonomy statute, adopted in January 2001 (for simplicity hereinafter, the "Matignon statute"). Decision 2001–454 covers mainly the same issues that were brought before the Court in 1991. It reaffirms the reservations regarding the right of Corsica to propose the amendment or adaptation of legal acts and the compulsory education of the Corsican language. Apart from these, the Matignon statute wished to expand the autonomous competencies of Corsica in a very delicate manner. According to the proposed provision, where the Corsican Assembly considers that legislative provisions in force or in the process of elaboration as regards the powers of the territorial unit raise difficulties of application related to the specific circumstances of the island, it may ask the Government to have the legislature to give it possibility of conducting experiments possibly involving exceptions from the rules in force, for the subsequent adoption by the Parliament of appropriate legislative provisions. Even to this "moderate" proposition, the Court reacts restrictively, stating that "by giving the legislature, even for a derogatory experiment with limited duration, the possibility of empowering the territorial unit of Corsica to take measures on matters that fall to be regulated by statute, the Act referred has intervened in a matter that is for the Constitution" and which Act would delegate the powers of the legislature in a manner not provided for by the Constitution.

All in all, the French thinking differentiates between overseas people who have the right to self-determination as separate entities from the French people of the mainland. Due to this basic difference, the former can be granted an increased share of public powers, even exclusive legislative and executive ones, or be vested with powers to secede from France (as in the case of New Caledonia), while the latter, which is composed of every *citoyen* regardless of their language or culture, exercises their sovereignty as an indissoluble whole. In theory, this approach would ensure *de jure* equality among the citizens, whether they are members of the majority or a minority. In practice, however, the interpretation of the constitutional court shows that the majority and its culture enjoy *de facto* dominance. For the minorities of metropolitan France (including not just Corsicans but Bretons, Basques, Alsatians, etc.), this means that they are only entitled to a narrower sense of self-government, which is subject to the better judgement of the majority (as seen with the arguments on the power to propose legislation) and which thus excludes legislative and executive competencies (and includes administrative ones only), limiting also their opportunities of consultation with the centre (allowed only to the extent to which it does not bind the actions of the central government in any way) and marginalizing their mother language relative to French (through non-compulsory teaching of minority language).

Another notable example is that of Estonia. In reaction to certain historic events,[298] as well to Russian policies in the mid-1990s,[299] Estonia did not automatically grant citizenship to migrants who originated from the former USSR and required naturalization instead under the Nationality Law, effective as of 1 April 1995.[300] Because of this policy, even by the end of the 1990s, there were around 150,000 to 200,000 stateless persons present in the country,[301] as not all residents were able or willing to apply for a citizenship or opt to leave the country instead (even today there are still about 77,000 people (5.7 % of the population) with undetermined citizenship (who are mostly of Russian origin).[302] Reacting

298 Throughout the course of the Soviet occupation (1940–1991), the demographics of Estonia were dramatically altered as a result of Sovietization policies. Several tens of thousands of Estonians were either killed or deported, while at the same time a large number of Soviet immigrants was sent to Estonia as a result of forced migration policies.

299 Russia declared that persons of a "post-Soviet" kind who resided outside Russia may apply for Russian dual citizenship.

300 For more information on the issue, see, for example, Thompson (1998) and Suksi (1999).

301 Suksi (1999), p. 44.

302 In order to address the problem, the Estonian Government began to issue special identity documents as of 1996 (known as "alien's passport" or *välismaalase pass*) to persons of undetermined citizenship who had previously held Soviet passports, thus granting those persons the opportunity to have an official identification within Estonia with which they are also allowed to travel abroad. Due to naturalization laws adopted on this issue, the number of people with undetermined citizenship decreased from 500,000 in 1992 (32 % of the population of Estonia) to 77,268 by 1 January 2018 (5.7 %). Source: https://www.ohchr.org/Documents/Issues/Racism/SR/Nationality Immigration/Estonia.pdf, accessed: 2021.03.17.

to the discriminative nature of this situation, the overwhelmingly Russian-populated Narva City Council adopted a resolution on 28 June 1993 to organize a local referendum posing the following question: "Do you want Narva to have the status of a national-territorial autonomy within the Republic of Estonia?"[303] The City Council of Sillamäe followed suit and adopted a similar resolution on 6 July 1993. The Constitutional Review Chamber of the Supreme Court of Estonia declared the unconstitutionality of these resolutions through decision No. III4/A-2 of 11 August 1993 and III-4/A-3 of 6 September 1993, respectively. In a brief conclusion, the Court raised the substantive legal objection that the constitution does not refer to national-territorial autonomy but only to cultural autonomy, as stipulated by Art. 50 of the Constitution. Consequently, the national-territorial form of autonomy is in conflict with the spirit of the constitution. Furthermore, the Court Decision also mentions that the absence of an act concerning the division of territory of Estonia into administrative units does not constitute a ground for a local government council to determine its own status or to change the Constitutional order of the Republic of Estonia. The Court also alluded to two procedural problems: Due to the fact that the Constitution makes no reference to local referendums, such referenda can only be interpreted as a means to decide on issues that fall within the competence of a local government. In relation to this argument, the Court mentioned that the formation of a national-territorial autonomy falls outside the scope of the local authority's jurisdiction (stipulated under § 154 (1) of the Constitution), as it represents a national issue to be resolved pursuant to the procedure for deciding national issues. Even given these circumstances, one has to note that Estonia does not rigidly reject every form of autonomy. The Law on Cultural Autonomy for National Minorities adopted on 26 October 1993 ensures non-territorial self-government over cultural affairs and education in the minority's mother tongue.

---

303 According to the last census conducted in 2011, the total population of Estonia was slightly above 1.3 million, 25 % of which had Russian origins (about 325,000 persons) with other ethnic nationalities adding up to 64. 000 (consisting mostly of Ukrainians, Belarusians, and Finns). For census data, visit the homepage of the Statistical Office of Estonia: http://pub.stat.ee/px-web.2001/Dialog/statfile1.asp, accessed: 2015.04.27.

# 3 Deconstructing the Constitutional Barrier

## 3.1 Counterarguments to Opinion No. 405/2004

### 3.1.1 Counterarguments to Substantive Objections

I. The territorial autonomy envisaged by the DL would not result in the creation of a separate state entity parallel with the Romanian state. According to Art. 2 of the DL, Szeklerland is an autonomous region having legal personality within Romania. The DL further adds that "the autonomy of the region does not infringe on the territorial integrity and sovereignty of the Romanian state"[304] and that the exercise of autonomous rights has to be "in harmony with the laws of the State".[305]

Parallel competencies are to be found mostly in federal states which have, for example, law enforcement or judicial proceedings on both federal and member state level. Such "duplications" would not accrue from the entry into force of the DL. Although exclusive jurisdiction to adopt legislation on devolved issues is the very essence of autonomy, the entry into force of the particular set of shared and exclusive competencies present in the DL would not infringe upon the jurisdiction of the central state to exercise the exclusive jurisdiction it would still retain over foreign policy, monetary policy, social security, and judicial powers. Decisions of the central state in these issues would continue to be compulsory even for an autonomous Szeklerland.

II. The territorial, administrative organization of a state is in fact an exclusive competence of the respective national authorities; the DL does not contain any provisions that contest this fact, neither did those who drafted or submitted the DL to the parliament ever made assertions that questioned this. The very reason why promoters of territorial autonomy keep submitting the DL to the Parliament of Romania is because they themselves are well aware that it would require the reorganization of the administrative system of the country and would touch upon the competencies exercised by the newly established autonomous administrative entity. Both of these questions require the approval of the legislature according to the Constitution, bearing also in mind that any administrative reorganization should reflect the preferences of the concerned local citizens (Art. 13 (3) of Law 3/2000 on the Organization

304 Art. 3 DL.

305 *Id.* at Art. 23.

of Referendums stipulates that changes in the territorial boundaries of administrative units can only be made after prior consultation with the affected citizens) and take into account the socio-political, ethnic, cultural, and traditional ties of the local population (pursuant to Art. 3 of Law 2/ 1968).[306]

While Opinion no. 405/2004 of the Legislative Council argues that European organizations do not promote the creation of autonomous regions, there is an abundance of documents falsifying this claim, including, for example: Recommendation 1201 (1993), Resolution 1334 (2003), Resolution 1985 (2014) of the PACE; Resolution 361 (2013) of the CLRAE; Paragraph 35 of the Document of the Copenhagen Meeting of the Conference on the Human Dimension of the CSCE (5–29 June 1990); and Paragraph 7 of part IV of the Report of the CSCE Meeting (Geneva) of Experts on National Minorities; as well as the Lund Recommendations of the OSCE.

III. The argument made by the Legislative Council in stating that the special status of Szeklerland would discriminate against the majority, and violate the principle of equality, by granting privileges to a minority that the majority is deprived of, is a "typical" misconception that often emerges with respect to minority rights in general. As Minority Rights Group, an international human rights organization puts it,[307] measures protecting minorities, including those aiming at improving their participation in public life, result in equality in society, not discrimination against majorities. The very aim of policies and programmes that aim to ensure implementation of minority rights is to make the playing field level so that everyone has the same opportunities. Majority communities participate in society and promote their identity automatically because they are the dominant group. Minority rights create the conditions whereby minority groups can also participate effectively in society and promote their identity. Minority rights thus enable minority groups to enjoy their human rights equally with the rest of the population.

The desired level of minority protection may vary from community to community, showing diversity in minority claims. In the Szekler case, there is an openly exhibited desire to improve a pivotal aspect of minority protection, the effective participation in public life, through an autonomy arrangement. Therefore, what could lead to the lack of equality, referred to

306 In this sense, the Romanian legal system promotes subsidiarity.

307 See: Minority Rights Group (2012), Topic 1, Section 4.

by the Legislative Council, along with increased division in society, or even conflict between majority and minority groups, is not the autonomy claim of a minority community but the persisting practice of central governments to neglect these aspirations. As Kardos noted, perceiving minority rights as an existential threat or arguing that regional autonomy would infringe upon the rights of the majority citizens or disadvantage them in any way is a form of nationalistic thinking, which proves that the political identity of the majority is based on culture rather than civic equality.[308]

Furthermore, there is an aspect of the DL that needs to be emphasized here, the one pertaining to the protection of "new minorities" within an autonomous Szeklerland as per the recommendations of Resolution 1334/2003. Andreas Gross, rapporteur of this Resolution, listed nine recommendations to respect when granting an autonomous status.[309] The last one of these states that the devolution of powers to autonomous entities must imperatively protect the rights of minorities living in them. The DL does actually foresee the establishment of such an inherent minority protection scheme. Accordingly, the language of persons belonging to a national-ethnic-linguistic community, whose numbers exceed one hundred in villages, one thousand in towns, five thousand in municipalities, and ten thousand in the territory of the Seats, will also have the same status as the official language of the state.[310]

IV. "Nation state" is not a term of constitutional law, which is why it is difficult to attribute any constitutional legal content to it. No wonder that it does not appear in constitutions very often. As a matter of fact, Doc. 10762 of the Committee on Legal Affairs and Human Rights of the PACE on the concept of "nation" shows that while the term "nation" appears in most of the constitutions, Romania is the only European country whose constitution enshrines the concept of the "nation state".[311] The same report concludes that "the constitution of Romania enshrines clearly the concept of the

---

308 Kardos (2015), pp. 38- 39.

309 See Art. 22.9 of Resolution 1334/2003.

310 Art. 10 (3) DL. This provision of course does not pertain to the state language. Based on the same article, Romanian would continue to be an official language in all municipalities of an autonomous Szeklerland.

311 In 2003, the Parliamentary Assembly of the Council of Europe (PACE) debated the question of preferential treatment of national minorities by their kin-states in the light of the Hungarian "status law" of 19 June 2001 concerning Hungarians living in neighbouring countries. Among other provisions, this law has defined the concept of "nation" in its preamble. It was not until this debate that the Assembly had

civic nation, composed of all Romanian citizens", without any discrimination on account of race, nationality, ethnic origin, language, religion, sex, opinion, political adherence, property, or social origin as set out by Art. 4 (2) CR. Moreover, as the comprehensive constitutional analysis conducted by Beauséjour shows,[312] Romania is one in only five countries around the world (the others being Azerbaijan, Moldova, Spain, and Turkey), where the indivisibility clause of the constitution is *expressis verbis*, unequivocally an attribute of the country, understood as the common homeland of all citizens. Finally, bearing in mind that the fundamental principle of non-discrimination, enshrined in numerous international documents ratified by Romania – including among others Art. 21 of the Charter of Fundamental Rights of the European Union, or Art. 14 of the European Convention on Human Rights – is a peremptory norm (*jus cogens*) of international law, from which no derogation is permitted,[313] references to the national character of the Romanian state cannot result in conceptualizing Romania as the national state of ethnic Romanians. Art. 1 of the CR cannot have the legal effect that citizens of the titular nation enjoy more rights than citizens possessing different national identities. Looking at it from this perspective, we can make the following remarks on the unity, indivisibility, and sovereignty of the Romanian state:

a) *Unity* would remain intact even after the entry into force of the DL. No separate constitutional order would come into being. The population of an autonomous Szeklerland would remain citizens of Romania. The autonomous region would be entrenched in the Romanian legal system based on Art. 117 (3) CR. The Constitution of Romania would remain the highest legal norm for an autonomous Szeklerland. It is exactly for this reason that the DL stipulates that in case the legal acts of the autonomous authorities contradict the constitution, the CCR shall annul

---

realized that to date there had been "no common European legal definition of the concept of 'nation'" (quote from Resolution 1335/2003 adopted after the mentioned debate). Consequently, the Assembly called on the Committee on Legal Affairs and Human Rights to analyse the various forms in which the concept of "nation" is being interpreted in the constitutions of CoE member states in order to clarify this so often used terminology. The results are shown in Doc. 10762 and the Recommendation adopted by the Assembly accordingly (Recommendation 1735 (2006) The concept of "nation").

312 Beauséjour (2018), p. 47.

313 See, for example, Bianchi (2008), p. 506.

them.[314] This legal restraint safeguards that the autonomous sub-unit would not be granted disproportionate leverage against the central state and that the DL would not transform the constitution into a "suicide pact".[315]

Surprisingly, the Legislative Council of the Romanian parliament argued that "unity" also entails that the population has one single citizenship. This would render Law No. 21/1991 on Romanian citizenship (containing provisions on dual citizenship), as well as provisions on the preferential naturalization of kinspeople living in Moldova unconstitutional. However, no such objections were ever raised against this domestic legal regime. The constitution of most EU member states allows for dual citizenship (15 to be exact),[316] the vast majority of which are unitary states (12, with the exception of Belgium, Germany, and Austria). In fact, as the Research Service of the European Parliament noted, the increasing tolerance of dual citizenship is a "major contemporary citizenship trend" in the EU.[317] While it is difficult to see how single citizenship could be a prerequisite of unitary statehood, what's important for the subject matter is that the DL contains no provisions that would create a separate citizenship for residents of the autonomous entity.

Not only does autonomy not threaten the unity, it is, on the contrary, an instrument to strengthen the integrity of the state. As Paragraph I/5 of the Explanatory Memorandum of CLRAE on Resolution 361 (2013) states: "Special status arrangements for sub-national units not only are consistent with the overarching public international law principle of territorial integrity of states: they also help preserve such integrity by addressing specific claims without challenging the unity of the state". Similarly, Paragraph B. 19) of Part III of the Explanatory note to the Lund Recommendations of the OSCE reminds that "territorial

314 Article 120 DL.

315 "The Constitution is not a suicide pact" is a phrase used in the political and legal discourse of the USA. It refers to the viewpoint that constitutional restrictions on the power of the central governmental should be balanced against the need for the survival of the state. The phrase was referenced in some notable cases, for example, Terminiello v. City of Chicago, 337 U.S. 1 (1949), or Kennedy v. Mendoza-Martinez, 372 U.S. 144 (1963).

316 These are: Belgium, Cyprus, Finland, France, Greece, Hungary, Ireland, Italy, Luxembourg, Malta, Poland, Portugal, Romania, Slovakia, and Sweden.

317 Mentzelopoulo & Dumbrava (2018), p. 4.

self-government can help preserve the unity of States while increasing the level of participation and involvement of minorities by giving them a greater role in a level of government that reflects their population concentration". More broadly, the United Nations former Working Group on Minorities observed that "the promotion and protection of the rights of minorities contribute to the political and social stability of the States in which minorities live and contribute to the strengthening of friendship and cooperation among peoples and States".[318]

Furthermore, there appears to be an academic consensus that autonomy arrangements strengthen the unity of a state instead of weakening it. Wolff considers territorial self-governance arrangements as a tool of statecraft and a mechanism of conflict management in divided societies - specifically when compact ethnic groups make demands for self-determination - that provide "institutional solutions that allow the different segments of diverse societies to realize their aspirations for self-determination while simultaneously preserving the overall social and territorial integrity of existing states".[319] Åkermark notes that in essence autonomy is a security arrangement, in the sense that it "helps to fit the idea of a unitary state in the multiplicity of the nation and vice versa to fit the factual and inevitable multiplicity of the nation into the idea of a unitary state". Parallel with this, autonomy consolidates not only territorial integrity but also the democratic political system of states due to the "participatory paradigm" thereof.[320] Comparing secessionist movements in Canada, Spain, and the UK, Guibernau concludes that if devolution is founded upon mutual trust, recognition, and a sound financial arrangement, then it stands as an antidote against secession for the following reasons: 1) The creation of devolved institutions contributes to the dynamism of civil society by reallocating resources of decision-making and by promoting regional businesses as well as the preservation of regional cultural heritage. 2) Devolution tends to foster a sense of common regional identity where it did not previously exist and strengthen it where a pre-existing sense of identity was already in place (while not excluding the possibility of an overall national identity). 3) A substantial degree of devolution when accompanied by sufficient – or even moderately generous – resources automatically raise the profile

318 UN Working Group on Minorities (2005), at para. II/3.
319 Wolff (2013), p. 7.
320 Åkermark (2013), p. 24.

of regional political elites, which elites in turn will be reluctant to make a "radical move of unpredictable consequences towards independence". 4) Devolution tends to strengthen democracy through introducing more subsidiarity in public policy decision-making.[321]

In fact, even in cases where an autonomous region has seceded from its host country,[322] it is quite difficult, to argue that the autonomous arrangement was to blame for that result. On the contrary, scholars argue that secessionist ideas tend to arise in those minority communities who are precluded from playing a decisive role in their own future and who are not dealt with "fairly and sympathetically".[323] As Beauséjour sarcastically notes, "pretending that opportunity makes the thief would be something of a shortcut".[324] Finally, in practical terms, it is also important to note that secession is an option for border regions. Szeklerland, however, lies in the heart of Romania, which provides further explanation as to why there aren't any secessionist parties here, such as the ones existing in Flanders, Scotland, or Catalonia.

b) According to Art. 12 of Resolution 1334 (2003) of the CoE, "*indivisibility* must not be confused with the concept of the unitary state, and the indivisibility of the state is thus compatible with autonomy, regionalism and federalism". The term "indivisibility" itself is primarily a signpost for external forces, mediating the message that the territory of the country should remain intact and that borders should be respected.[325] In this context, indivisibility clauses of national constitutions are pivotal parts of inter-state affairs that help to reinforce the overarching international legal principle of prohibition of threat or use of force in international

321 Guibernau (2006), pp. 70–73.

322 See the Caucasian examples in Cornell (2002), where the geographic proximity to Russia and Russian aspirations in the region are more likely to be behind the results seen among others in Abkhazia or South Osetia. One could add the Crimean-peninsula to this list.

323 See, for example, Beran (1984), p. 30.

324 Beauséjour (2018), p. 10.

325 This interpretation is also mirrored in the CR. While the president of Romania represents the unity and integrity of the state (Art. 80 CR) and elected representatives of the parliament are obliged to take an oath to protect Romania's sovereignty, independence, unity, and territorial integrity (Art. 82 CR), in practice, Art. 118 of the CR confers the duty to guarantee the country's territorial integrity on the armed forces of Romania.

relations and promote international peace and security (insofar as wars are most often started due to territorial disputes).

The affirmation of the indivisibility of the state also implies outlawing of secession by internal forces.[326] The DL, however, clearly stipulates in its second and third sections that it aims to establish regional autonomy for Szeklerland within Romania. Consequently, devolving more competencies from the centre to local authorities cannot be understood as a means of secession, or external self-determination, or as a way of segmenting the country into a patchwork of different legal regimes, but as a way to improve the right of minorities to effective participation in public life. This is also how the Lund recommendations of the OSCE as well as the Documents of the Geneva and Copenhagen meetings of the CSCE interpret such autonomy arrangements. More specifically, when the question of Romania's administrative reform first reached the agenda of the Congress of Local and Regional Authorities in 2002, rapporteurs Jean-Claude Frecon and Lambert van Nistelrooij pointed out in their report that there is no constitutional provision in Romania whatsoever that prohibits considerable devolution of state powers to the counties.[327] As Weller warned, denying any form of dialogue and labelling groups pushing for more home rule as "secessionist and rebels" could have the counterproductive effect of radicalizing self-determination demands.[328] Similar views were expressed by the Minority Rights Group, which reminded that "experience shows that accommodating the concerns of minorities and promoting their rights within the state results in members of the minority becoming more willing to identify with the state. Reducing grievances makes state-breakup less likely".[329]

For this reason, it is important to view the territorial autonomy of Szeklerland, as foreseen by the DL, for what it actually is. A legal proposal

326 Art. 40 (2) of the CR explicitly alludes to the possibility of declaring political parties or organizations unconstitutional provided that their aims or activity, militate against political pluralism, the principles of a State governed by the rule of law, or against the sovereignty, integrity, or independence of Romania. This also means that from the point of view of the state, safeguarding territorial integrity, and indivisibility from internal forces allow of restrictions to fundamental rights, in this case, the right to association.

327 See: CLRAE (2002), at paragraph 83.

328 Weller (2005), p. 4.

329 Minority Rights Group (2012) *Supra note*, Topic 1, Section 4.

for the internal self-determination of the population of a historical region that wishes to achieve a more effective participation in public life within the constitutional framework of Romania, through a democratically elected autonomous legislature without prejudice to the territorial integrity and indivisibility of the state.

c) *Sovereignty* would not cease to exist in an autonomous Szeklerland; it would simply be exercised through a democratically elected body other than the parliament in Bucharest. According to Art 2 (1) of the Constitution, sovereignty lies not with the state but with the citizens of the state, who shall exercise this sovereignty by means of their representative bodies as well as by referendum. In democratic polities, sovereignty is not a zero-sum game, as it can be shared, devolved, or delegated. Furthermore, as Krasner noted, sovereignty in issues regarding minorities have never been an exclusive jurisdiction of the states.[330] In this question, the distance between the views of the "majority" and the "minority" is quite visible. While the DL presents a bottom-up process, presupposing the voluntary consent of the local citizens in establishing the autonomy arrangement, the Opinion of the Legislative Council is of a hierarchical, top-down nature, in which popular sovereignty is being confusingly supplemented with state sovereignty.

V. While there is legislation on the use of state symbols, and the use and adoption of municipal symbols, there are no specific laws on the symbols of national minorities or historical regions with no administrative competences, such as Szeklerland. On the international level, there is no direct reference to the use of symbols in the FCNM, however, the case law of the ECtHR shows that the free use of symbols (e.g. flags) is protected under art. 10 of the ECHR, as a manifestation of the freedom of expression.[331] As such the use of both the Szekler and the Hungarian flags should not be subject to any restrictions, in conformity with Art. 20 (2) CR, which stipulates that international regulations shall take precedence where any inconsistencies exist between the covenants and treaties on the fundamental human rights Romania is a party to, and national laws.

In practice, however, the lack of clear legal provisions enables dissenting interpretations on what is permitted and what is prohibited, resulting in debates and court cases on what the lawful conduct is with respect to the use of various symbols. While there is a scholarly debate on the possibility

330 Krasner (1999) *Supra note*, pp. 220–239.

331 See: European Court of Human Rights (2021), p. 23.

of an open legal system and the absence of law (*non liquet*),[332] as opposed to conceptualizing a universal and, by extension, closed legal order where the negative law is an inherent part of the legal system,[333] the concept of "residual principle" is used and commonly referred to in legal practice and legal theory as well. As Stone notes, most legal orders lay down some kind of residual principle, "the effect of which is to occupy the space which would otherwise be devoid of law".[334] One of the most well-known of these is the "residual negative principle", which refers to the idea that everything that is not legally prohibited is legally permitted. This idea stems from the understanding that certain areas of life that are not positively regulated by law are not devoid of law but rather regulated in a residual or negative manner by precluding legal effects in those specific areas. Consequently, in the absence of a norm limiting specific behaviours, the legal system is neutral as to the legal consequences, which grants citizens the freedom to exercise activities of their choice within that framework, including, as in our case, the free use of minority symbols.

VI. Similarly, to views on the exclusivity of sovereignty, a zero-sum mentality is present in the case of linguistic issues. Even though the DL only suggested recognizing Hungarian as a regional-official language in addition to the Romanian language, the Legislative Council thought that in a unified state there could only be one official language. The regional-official status of the Hungarian language is without prejudice to the provisions of Art. 152 of the Constitution, which stipulates, among others, that the official language of the state is not subject to revision. The DL does not seek to revise the official language of the state; it merely foresees to complement the official Romanian state language with Hungarian in a specific region. From a comparative point of view, one could find numerous examples similar to the system envisaged in the DL, where multilingualism contributed to social peace and mutual understanding among different cultures. Such positive examples include, above all, the linguistic quota system of South Tyrol, where all public office positions are assumed by local residents in a proportion that reflects the proportion of linguistic groups as per the last official census, while also

332 Lauterpacht (1958), pp. 196–221.
333 Radbruch (1956), p. 298.
334 Stone (1964), pp. 188–192.

requiring fluency in both German and Italian languages.[335] Another best practice example is the official status of the Swedish language in Finland. This example is particularly relevant due to some common features between Finland and Romania. Finland is an equally "young" state (even younger than Romania) which, due to its geographic position, had its fair share of foreign occupations (just as Romania). The Swedish community is equally large relative to Finns, just like Hungarians relative to Romanians (about 6–7 % of the total population), and their distribution within the country is similar (having in both cases significant areas where they represent the majority). The constitutional design has or had similarities, as both countries are unitary states, led by a semi-presidential form of government (though Finland has shifted towards a parliamentary system by adopting a new constitution in 2000). Yet, Finland takes a diametrically opposite approach in linguistic issues. Language Act no. 423/2003 stipulates that Swedish is the second national language in Finland. This means that as far as state communication with citizens is concerned, the officially used language of the new-born citizen will be the one that was requested by the parents upon birth. It is a declaration that can be changed by the individual later on if so desired. As far as local administration is concerned, a municipality is either unilingual or bilingual – a status which is determined every 10 years based on official statistics. A municipality is designated bilingual if the population includes both Finnish and Swedish speakers and the minority comprises at least eight percent of the population or at least 3,000 persons. A bilingual municipality is designated unilingual if the minority comprises less than 3,000 persons and its proportion has decreased below six percent.[336] While there are some considerable challenges in the implementation of this model of bilingualism, surveys show an overall satisfaction of Swedish-speaking citizens with regard to state services in Swedish language.[337] Notably, bilingualism did not "tear apart" the political and social fabric of Finland but rather contributed to the preservation thereof.

335 For more information on the functioning of the South Tyrolean linguistic quota system, see, for example, Dabis (2013), pp. 43–95.

336 Section 5 (2) of Law 423/2003.

337 The quality of state services in Swedish language received an average of 7.6 points (out of a total of 10 points) from the Swedish-speaking citizens, based on the availability of services in Swedish. Source: Government of Finland (2009), p. 25.

### 3.1.2 Counterarguments to Procedural Objections

I. The fact that an administrative unit is not listed in the constitution of a country does not mean that it automatically becomes unconstitutional. Comarques, for example, exist in all 17 self-governing communities of Spain, even though they are not mentioned in the constitution.[338] Similarly, NUTS regions are not mentioned in the constitution of Romania, yet they still function and have an important statistical purpose.

An autonomous Szeklerland could fit in the present administrative system of Romania as an autonomous county, not affecting the first-level territorial division of the State into counties, whose internal administrative division could be regulated by the Statute of Autonomy. Unique internal divisions of autonomous administrations, which revitalize historic administrative units can be found, among others, in the terçons of Aran, Catalonia's comarca system, which to a large extent follows the historical comarques of the *Principat de Catalunya* (an administrative structure that was already revived for a short period of time in 1936),[339] or in the Basque Country, where the historical provinces (Bizkaia, Araba, and Gipuzkoa), are pivotal elements in the exercise of the fiscal autonomy of the region. The re-establishment of the historical administrative units of the Szekler Seats would be in line with Art. 3 of Law 2/1968, as it would take into account socio-political, ethnic, cultural, and traditional ties of the population. Hence, the establishment of these Seats would not violate the legal system of Romania, nor cause any practical administrative issues, insofar as they are capable of exercising the duties that accrue form the statute of autonomy, while also not hindering Szekler municipalities from carrying out their duties enshrined in the constitution as well as other sources of law.

II. The fact that the DL makes reference to Art. 117 (3) CR might seem somewhat misplaced at first, given that this article appears in the section on "specialized central public administration", whereas local public administrations are being dealt with under the following section (Art. 120–123). The scope of the activities of specialized central public administrative authorities is national, which would certainly not be true to the institutions of an autonomous Szeklerland. Even so, invoking this article is relevant insofar as it would be central public authorities conferring competencies to the

338 According to art. 137 CS, the Spanish state is organized territorially into municipalities, provinces and self-governing communities.

339 The Principality of Catalonia was a medieval and early modern state that existed between the 13th and the 18th centuries.

autonomous region, authorizing it to make decisions for Szeklerland in matters which otherwise would fall under the jurisdiction of the central public administration. From the point of view of the state, this would mean that as of the entry into force of the organic law on the status of Szeklerland, the legislative and executive competencies would no longer be carried out by the central administrative authorities but by decision-making bodies of the autonomous region, to the extent that the statute of autonomy allows for it. In other words, in relation to Szeklerland, a set of nationwide competencies of central administration bodies would be taken over fully or partially by the autonomous authorities of Szeklerland. As Stanomir notes, the very essence of autonomous administrative authorities is that they are not subordinated to the government, but they share relations with the parliament in varying forms. Autonomy clearly alludes to the lack of central governmental coercion and the capability to act freely within the boundaries set out by law.[340] The shear fact that the constitution refers to various forms of autonomy as instruments that can be established through legislation is in itself a valid argument that autonomy *per se* does not contradict the constitution, given the assumption that provisions of the constitution do not contradict one another. This interpretation is also in line with the basic principles laid down in Art. 120 (1) CR, according to which public administration in territorial-administrative units shall be based on the principles of decentralization, local autonomy, and deconcentration of public services.

The legislature of France, which is a constitutional "model country", also inserted a similar provision into the constitution as a means to accommodate increasing regional demands for larger self-rule within a unitary state structure. Since the constitutional amendment of 28 March 2003, Art. 1 of the constitution now stipulates that France shall be organized on a decentralized basis. The same amendment introduced more specific regulations on how to transfer powers from the central government to the territorial communities (Art. 72-1 to 72-4).[341] Lastly, the analogy of devolution in the UK is worth mentioning, given that the predecessors of the devolved parliaments, the Scottish and Welsh Offices, were ordinary Whitehall departments in the beginning,[342] whose competencies were gradually assumed by the respective regional legislative assemblies when these were re-established in the late 1990s.

340 Stanomir et al. (2010), p. 50.

341 For a more detailed description on local governance in France, see: Boyron (2013), pp. 206–235.

342 Whitehall department is short for British government departments.

III. Pursuant to the Legislative Councils conclusions on the necessity to hold a referendum, Szekler Communes started to adopt municipal resolutions to organize local referendums. Thirty-four municipalities adopted such resolutions, posing the question whether or not the citizens agree that by modifying the current county borders, Szeklerland should become an autonomous territorial administrative unit, which the given municipality should form a part of.[343] In line with Opinion 405/2004, these resolutions based their legality on Law No. 215/2001 on Local Public Administration and also on Law 3/2000 on the Organization of the Referendum, Art. 13 (1) of which stipulates that "issues of particular interest for an administrative-territorial unit may be subject, under this law, to the approval of the population by local referendum". Moreover, paragraph 3 of the same article states that "legislative proposals on amending the territorial delineation of municipalities, cities and counties, shall be submitted to the Parliament only after consultation with the citizens of these administrative-territorial units by referendum. In this case the referendum is binding". The constitutionality of these resolutions was contested by the Prefects of Kovászna and Hargita Counties before the Administrative Courts on the following grounds: Art 12 (1) b) of Law 3/2000 stipulates that the adoption of a special policy decision on the organization of local public administration, territory, and general rules on local autonomy is a question of national interest and subject, therefore, to nationwide referendums. In this sense, the territorial distribution of a country surpasses local interest and constitutes a national level of interest. The courts also reaffirmed the most common counter-argument that the referendum would result in the establishment of an administrative unit not foreseen by Art 3 (3) of the Constitution and is therefore unconstitutional. Consequently, the court declared all eleven resolutions null and void. The phrasing of Act 3/2000 is vague enough to give birth to dissenting interpretations (especially when comparing Art. 12 and 13). Still, it is fair enough to suggest that the adoption

343 These municipalities were: From Bardóc-Miklósvár-seat: Barót, Nagybacon, Vargyas; from Csík-seat: Csíkszentdomokos, Csíkszereda, Gyimesközéplok; from Gyergyó-seat: Borszék, Gyergyóalfalu, Gyergyócsomafalva, Gyergyószentmiklós, Gyergyóújfalu; from Kézdi-seat: Kézdivásárhely; from Maros-seat: Makfalva; from Orbai-seat: Nagyborosnyó, Zabola; from Sepsi-seat: Árkos, Illyefalva, Kökös, Mikóújfalu, Réty, Sepsibükszád, Sepsiszentgyörgy, Uzon; from Udvarhely-seat: Farkaslaka, Fenyéd, Kápolnás, Lövéte, Székelyderzs, Székelykeresztúr, Székelyudvarhely, Szentábrahám, Szentegyháza, Újszékely, Zetelaka. Some of the plaints of the Prefects against these resolutions can be found under: http://sznt.sic.hu/husic/index.php?option=com_content&view=category&id=20&Itemid=26 &lang=hu, accessed: 2019.08.16.

of special policy decisions on local administration that is binding for the whole country, and is thus subject to referendums on the national level (Art. 12), should not be confused with referendums on issues of particular interest for an administrative territorial unit and with referendums on the delimitation of the borders of the administrative units (Art. 13), in which local citizens have to be invited to the polls even if the final decision might be taken on a higher level by the national parliament. As mentioned earlier, after these proceedings, the Szekler National Council organized an informal referendum with the use of their own mobile ballot boxes and ballots between December 2006 and February 2008. Of the collected 210,000 ballots, 99.31 % were in favour of creating an autonomous Szeklerland.[344] The case of the local referendums shows that in practice the approval or disapproval of the legality of a referendum on the borders and status of Szeklerland is contingent on discrepant interpretations of different state institutions on the same legal texts.

## 3.2 Counterarguments to Decision No. 80/2014

In his Dissenting Opinion, Judge Puskás Bálint Zoltán claimed that the CCR refused to consider both the existing national and international legal framework and the elements of comparative law. By ignoring those grounds, the Court pronounced a wrong solution, based on an artificial argumentation.[345] Puskás notes that the state is yet to deliver on pledges enshrined in the Declaration of *Alba Iulia/Gyulafehérvár*. In spite of not being explicitly referred to in the constitution, this declaration has a constitutional legal value. It represents such a direct and genuine manifestation of popular will that it must be respected, recognized, and developed at all times, because it lays down the foundations of the Romanian state, as a result of which these values and principles remain immune to the passing of years.[346] Given that national minorities are members of the national state as equal citizens of the country, the acknowledgement of an administrative-territorial organization which recognizes the historical realities does not in any way affect the legal relationship between the state and its citizens. Moreover, the initial proposals did not intend to alter or limit the unitary and indivisible character of the state; on the contrary, they organically blend into the said provisions of the Constitution. Declaring the analysed legal solution unconstitutional calls

344 See Appendix No. 2 in: Szekler National Council (2009), p. 102.

345 CCR (2014) *Supra note*, p. 74.

346 *Id.* at, p. 77.

into question the good faith of the CCR`s interpretation.[347] Underpinning this argument, Puskás referred to: the wording of Art. 3 of Law 2/1968; the constitutional setting of unitary states like Spain, Italy, and Serbia, whose unity was not affected by granting autonomy to their minorities; as well as to the relevant literature of Romanian constitutionalists. Lastly, the dissenting opinion notes the contradiction embedded in the CCR`s viewpoint regarding the establishment of decision-making bodies under Art. 6 of the Constitution. If the right of persons belonging to national minorities to their identity is truly recognized and guaranteed, but they are not allowed to establish their own bodies to implement this right, that would mean that the majority is entitled to impose on the minority the appropriate way they can maintain, express, and develop their identity.[348] A similar critique is expressed regarding the use of minority symbols. If a national minority cannot use its symbols, not even in areas where it represents the overwhelming majority that is equivalent to denying the right of national minorities to identity.[349]

The thoughts of Puskás on identity do not stand alone. A few years earlier, similar views were echoed in the Stanomir-report.[350] As the report concludes, one of the basic principles that has to govern every constitutional amendment process is the protection of the identity of national minorities.[351] The report characterizes the Romanian Constitution as one of the most rigid ones due to Art. 152 (1), which lists a number of provisions not subject for revision at all. This approach stems from fears that coined the 1991 constitutional process (like separatism and isolation based on ethnic criteria), and which should be surpassed in a new constitutionalization process, as these inhibit the possibilities of legal development by generating artificial conflicts.[352]

347 *Id.* at, p. 78.

348 *Id.* at, p. 77.

349 *Id.* at, p. 78.

350 In 2008, the president of Romania initiated the establishment of a Commission made up of constitutional law experts chaired by Ioan Stanomir Professor at the University of Bucharest in order to investigate the possibilities of revising the constitutional structure of the country. For the full report, see: http://www.jakabffy.ro/magyarkisebbseg/pdf/02stanomir.pdf, accessed: 2015.04.19.

351 Stanomir et al. (2010), p. 89.

352 *Id.* at pp. 31–32.

## 3.3 Legal Entrenchment – Flexible Solutions to Accommodate Autonomy Arrangements

Now that we have presented the pros and cons and outlined the different views of the majority and the minority on autonomy, we can address the core of the subject matter. When it comes to legal arguments about the constitutionality of an autonomy arrangement, this core is the legal entrenchment, that is, the practical way to anchor an autonomous legal regime within the constitutional system of a given state. When elaborating this chapter, I took into consideration the type of entrenchment that the DL envisages, not excluding, however, some examples that might be of relevance, bearing in mind that the DL is not carved in stone but is open for changes as part of a dialogue between the state authorities and representatives of the Szekler community. In order to identify and differentiate between certain forms of legal entrenchment, I used the six-tier typology of Markku Suksi, which includes regional-, special-, general-, semi-general-, international-, and self-determination-based entrenchment (as outlined in more detail under section 1.4). As a relevant factor, I will also make references to the importance of how the legal entrenchment and the constitutional framework in some cases were interpreted by state institutions.

Much favourable for national communities who are in pursuit of more self-governance and for states willing to address such aspirations, a broad selection of examples is available to draw inspiration from. The autonomous republic of Tatarstan, for example, fits into the constitutional system of the Russian Federation through a special bilateral treaty (signed on 15 February 1994), as opposed to other sub-state units of the federation which signed the multilateral Russian Federal Treaty. Another unique example would be that of Puerto Rico, ceded to the USA by Spain as the consequence of the Spanish-American War in 1898. The autonomy of the Commonwealth of Puerto Rico originated in its status as an "unincorporated territory" of the USA, which meant that its residents did not enjoy certain constitutional rights but were also exempted from certain obligations (most importantly tax-related ones).

The entrenchment of devolution in the UK is peculiar in the sense that it takes place within a common law system, which lacks a written constitution. Even so, the UK example is valuable given that before the reestablishment of the Scottish Parliament and the Welsh Assembly in the late 1990s, the country used to be as centralized as contemporary Romania. These slowly evolving devolution processes gained new impetus with the BREXIT referendum,[353] after which both

353 BREXIT is a portmanteau word that combines the words "British" and "Exit" to refer to the UK leaving the European Union following the EU membership referendum held on 23 June 2016.

the federalization of the country and the breakaway of Scotland and/or the unification of Ireland and Northern Ireland are considered as potential scenarios. Even if Scotland seceded from the UK in the future, the type of devolution it had enjoyed from the adoption of the Scotland Act in 1998 until the construction of a separate state is worth studying.

With respect to Scotland, there are no *de jure* special rights regarding the amendment of the Scotland Act that enumerates the competencies of the autonomous legislature.[354] The Parliament of Scotland may make laws within its area of competence, known as the Acts of the Scottish Parliament, notwithstanding, however, the power of the Parliament of the United Kingdom to make laws for Scotland, as set out by Section 28 (7) of the Scotland Act. Deducting its logic from the doctrine of parliamentary sovereignty,[355] this section provides a clear residual power for Westminster to legislate for Scotland in devolved areas without the consent of Scotland. This provision, however, has never yet been invoked due to the so-called Sewel Convention.[356] Later on, a Memorandum of Understanding from 2002 between Westminster and the devolved administrations expressed the same position with regard to all of the devolved legislatures, as the Memorandum stipulates that "the United Kingdom Parliament retains authority to legislate on any issue, whether devolved or not. It is ultimately for Parliament to decide what use to make of that power. However, the UK Government will proceed in accordance with the convention that the UK Parliament would not normally legislate with regard to devolved matters except with the agreement of the devolved

---

354 While some scientists refer to the Scotland Act as the "Constitution" of Scotland (see, e.g. Himsworth (2013), p. 359.), from a legal point of view this Act can be seen as a functional equivalent to the autonomy statutes discussed in this book.

355 According to the so called "Diceyan Orthodoxy" (referring to British Albert Venn Dicey constitutional theorist and his influential work from 1885: "Introduction to the Study of the Law of the Constitution"), the parliament is vested with the power to make or unmake any law and no person or body has the right to set aside or override an Act of Parliament.

356 The Sewel convention is named after Lord John Sewel, who was the Minister of State in the Scottish Office responsible for the conduct of the Scotland Bill in 1998. He was the MP who first stated during the Lords Committee stage of the Scotland Bill on 21 July 1998 that the Government expected a convention to be established that Westminster would not normally legislate with regard to devolved matters in Scotland without the consent of the Scottish Parliament.

legislature".[357] In practice, the convention requires a Legislative Consent Motion (LCM) to be put forward by the UK Government, according to which Holyrood has to agree that the provisions of the given Bill should be considered by the UK Parliament,[358] insofar as the matters fall within the competence of the Scottish Parliament. Since the first session of the Scottish Parliament in 1999 to date, there have been well over 150 LCMs.[359] Even though the option of withholding consent exists, Holyrood is yet to test the Sewel Convention in that manner as so far all of the LCMs were passed by the autonomous legislature.[360] An LCM procedure was also required when the UK government wanted to enact amendments to the Scotland Act. Due to some concerns of the Scottish government, this procedure spanned through two legislative cycles between its initiation by the Labour government in 2010 and its adoption by the following Conservative-Liberal Coalition in 2012. In spite of this protracted procedure, there was no effort from the British government to override Scottish opposition by passing the Bill without an LCM. In other words, as long as the Sewel convention remains in place, the Scottish autonomy will have a protection under the political conventions of the UK from unilateral amendment of its competencies.

The Faroe Islands enjoy a remarkably wide scope of competencies, including also the jurisdiction to conclude international treaties despite the fact that this autonomy lacks a general constitutional entrenchment and was enacted through an ordinary law instead which can be unilaterally amended by the Danish Parliament through a majority vote whenever they so decide.[361] However, not

---

357 Paragraph 13 of the Memorandum of Understanding, as laid before the Scottish Parliament by the Scottish Ministers, January 2002: http://www.scotland.gov.uk/Publications/1999/10/MofU, accessed: 2015.07.13.

358 Holyrood is an Anglicisation of the Gaelic word *halyruid* (holy cross), which functions as a metonym for the Scottish legislature located near Holyrood Palace that has served as the residence of Scottish Monarchs since the 16th century.

359 See: https://www.parliament.scot/parliamentarybusiness/Bills/31313.aspx, accessed: 2021.03.19.

360 For Legislative Consent Memorandums and Motions by Session, see: http://www.gov.scot/About/Government/Sewel, accessed: 2015.07.13.

361 There are opposing opinions as to the status of Greenland relative to the Faroe Islands. One argument would say that ever since the Greenland Home Rule Act (577/1978) was replaced by the Act on Greenland Self-Government (473/2009), Denmark has agreed to recognize that "the people of Greenland is a people pursuant to international law with the right of self-determination" (Preamble of Act 473/2009). This right includes the right to secession under chapter 8 of the Act. The unilateral amendment of this statute would violate the principles of self-determination as set out by international law, which thus grants a higher protection for the Greenlandic autonomy

once has it happened since the enactment of Act No. 137 of March 23rd 1948 on Home Rule of the Faroe Islands that the Danish Parliament has amended this statute or repealed parts of it without the consent of the Faroese Parliament. This practice is still present decades later and is reflected *expressis verbis* in Danish Act no. 578 of 24 June 2005, relating to the Takeover of Affairs and Fields of Affairs by the Faeroe Islands Public Authorities (shortly, Assumptions Act). The preamble of the Assumptions Act stipulates that "this Act is based on an agreement between the Faeroe Islands Home Rule Government and the Danish Government as equivalent parties". One could thus argue that this favourable mindset of the Danish political culture represents a type of political entrenchment, insofar as the central state power compels itself to seek agreement as opposed to adopt unilateral measures, "in acknowledgement of the special position held by the Faroe Islands within the Kingdom in national, historical and geographical respects".[362]

---

compared to the Faroese one (even though the Greenland Self Government Act is still an ordinary law as far as the hierarchy of norms of the Danish legal system is concerned). On the other hand, however, this argument can be contested by the fact that in the Reports of Denmark on the implementation of the ICCPR, both the Faroe Islands and Greenland are considered as peoples under Art. 1 of the Covenant. Additionally, a circular note of the Danish government from 7 November 2005 – to all heads of diplomatic missions accredited to Denmark – makes it clear that though Denmark has granted powers to both Faroe and Greenland to conclude agreements under international law, such agreements can solely pertain to matters for which internal powers have been transferred to the respective autonomous entities. Prior to the exercise of this power, the Danish Foreign Ministry must be consulted in both cases. These sources allude to the fact that there is no substantial difference between the legal statuses of the two autonomous regions and that it is indeed the internal form of self-determination that is the available option for both communities. Finally, Art. 21 (3) of the Act on Greenland Self Government stipulates that independence is contingent on the consent of the Danish legislature as part of an agreement between Greenland and Denmark. Unilateral form of external self-determination is therefore precluded from the Act, and secession is only possible in the framework of a negotiated process. But then again, a negotiated secession is possible in the case of Faroe as well (or in the case of any other region elsewhere for that matter) irrespective of the fact that the Faroese statute does not explicitly mention a Faroese right to secession.

362 Preamble of the Home Rule Act of the Faroe Islands.

The cases of the Faroe-islands and Scotland prove that conventions can constitute an effective political entrenchment even in the absence of a constitutional one.[363]

Similar to the Faroese model, the 1994 organic law on the special legal status of Gagauzia provides exclusive legislative and executive competencies in various matters, from culture and education to economy and environment, but given that the law was enacted after the new constitution of Moldova was adopted, the Gagauz autonomy had functioned without a general constitutional footing for almost 10 years. It was only through the amendment of the constitution in 2003 that Art. 110 and 111 were inserted providing a general constitutional entrenchment for the autonomy of Gagauzia.[364]

Another special example was that of the Åland Island prior to 1994. Between the entry into force of the initial autonomy act (Law No. 124/1920 adopted on 6 May 1920), and the amendment of the constitution in 1994, Åland enjoyed a unique form of entrenchment as an "act of exception".[365] The legal structure of Finland comprised, and still does, of the constitution (whose amendment requires a two-thirds majority in two consecutive legislative cycles),[366] ordinary laws (whose adoption requires the majority votes of the MPs) and decrees adopted by the central or local-municipal governments. The lack of organic laws in this system disabled a semi-general constitutional entrenchment, while a general entrenchment was hindered by the fact that the 1920 Autonomy Act was adopted after Finland had already enacted its constitution as a newly independent state on 17 July 1919. Consequently, the autonomy of Åland functioned for almost seven and a half decades without a general or semi-general constitutional entrenchment. Unlike Faroe, Greenland, or Gagauzia before 2003,

363 For more information on the similarities between the Danish "theory of delegation" and the British doctrine on "sovereignty of Parliament", see: Larsen & Rógvi (2012), pp. 348–350.

364 See Weller et al. (2010), p. 242.

365 Suksi (2011), p. 145.

366 An important difference between the current constitution and the one that was in force during the adoption of the Åland Autonomy Act is that after Finland gained independence, the country functioned under a multi-documentary constitutional system consisting of 4 Constitutional Acts: the 1772 Form of Government Act, the 1789 Union and Security Act, the 1906 Parliament Act, and the 1906 Act on Freedom of Speech, Assembly and Association. The new constitution that merged these documents into one unified constitutional text was adopted on 1 March 2000. For more information on the evolution of the Finnish constitution, see chapter 5 of Dawn (ed.) (2011), pp. 87–115.

however, this *sui generis* position did not mean that the Finnish governments would have been able to unilaterally amend the statute of autonomy. The ålandic autonomy was firmly entrenched as an act of exception,[367] which means that Law No. 124/1920 was adopted by the parliament under the same procedure that was otherwise exclusively reserved for the amendment of the constitution but without making the Autonomy Act a part of the formal constitution of Finland or without declaring the Act constitutional.[368] As far as the doctrine of the acts of exception is concerned, when a political community encounters an exceptional political situation that produces compelling reasons, the parliament may adopt an ordinary act of law using the procedure prescribed for constitutional legislation. The "exceptional political situation" in the case of Åland came in the face of a secessionist movement. Under the leadership of Julius Sundblom, the Swedes established their own parliament and brought forth a petition addressed to the Swedish government fostering the merger of Åland and Sweden, invoking the principle of self-determination of the peoples.[369] The petition campaign was completed on 29 June 1919 and was signed by 9735 people who supported the Union with Sweden, while 461 persons refused to sign the petition (the total population of the islands was approximately 21,000 at that time). The situation also had its international resonances, as there were attempts already in 1919 to refer the case of Åland to the Versailles Peace Conference, which ultimately failed, given that Sweden was not a belligerent party and remained neutral throughout the course of the First World War. Some authors also claim that the granting of autonomy was much more influenced by external rather than internal factors. According to this theory, after the Ålandic issue was referred to the Council of the League of Nations, the Finnish government anticipated that the decision might not be in favour of Finland and they adopted Law 124/1920 only to improve their chances before the Council.[370] Nonetheless, the times were exceptional for Finland, which gave enough incentive to legislate in an extraordinary manner. Normally, one would have needed a two-thirds majority in the Finnish legislature, the *Eduskunta*, for a constitutional amendment to take place, precluding those instances where the legislature votes for an amendment to be

367 The Autonomy Act was completed by a special Act on the Acquisition of Land on the Åland Islands, which had the same *sui generis* legal entrenchment and amendment procedure as the Autonomy Act.

368 The lack of such a declaration is relevant because of the multi-documentary nature of the constitutional structure of Finland at that time.

369 See more in: Suksi (1993), p. 220.

370 See: Hannikainen (1997), p. 58.

adopted under expedited order. In that case, the *Eduskunta* would first have to vote for an expedited order with 5/6 of its members and have a following vote on the amendment itself requiring this time a 2/3 majority. This was exactly the case with the Åland Autonomy Act, where the *Eduskunta* first approved the expedited order with a 5/6 majority (158 in favour and 21 against), and then voted for the Act itself with 152 in favour, 27 against and 1 abstention on 6 May 1920. Such extraordinary legislation happened quite a lot during the often chaotic first years of the Finnish state. What was so special with Åland, however, was that the Islands received the additional insurance that the Autonomy Act could only be amended in the same manner as the Constitution and with the consent of the Legislative Assembly of Åland, while other acts of exception could have been repealed by the Finnish legislature with a simple majority through an ordinary act. The Constitutional self-limitation that Finland imposed on itself was quite robust here in spite of the lack of a general constitutional entrenchment. The Ålandic case provides a vivid example that in the presence of political will a specific minority issue can be resolved, even if the resolution requires the central state to resort to extraordinary constitutional-legal means.[371]

Similar to the case of Åland, the Paris Agreement (also known as the Gruber-de Gasperi Agreement, named after Italian Prime Minister Alcide de Gasperi and Austrian Foreign Minister Karl Gruber, who signed the treaty on 5 September 1946) sought to "safeguard the ethnic character and the cultural and economic development of the German language group" of South Tyrol.[372] This Agreement was annexed to the Peace Treaty of Paris, published in the Gazette of the Italian Republic on 24 September 1947, becoming a part of the Italian legal system. Unlike the Agreement between Sweden and Finland on Åland, the Paris Agreement took the form of a treaty and ensured leverage for Austria as a party to the treaty that could appeal against non-implementation. The obligation of Italy to grant special status to South Tyrol was thus already part of the domestic legal system when the Italian Constituent Assembly adopted the new constitution on 22 December 1947. Consequently, this constitution referred to the special status of South Tyrol. This general constitutional entrenchment has remained in place since then. The satisfying implementation of the Paris Agreement, however, only commenced after several decades and a wave of bomb attacks aimed

---

371 A detailed summary of the procedure pursuant to which the Statute of Åland was adopted can be found in: Finlands Riksdag (1920), pp. 86–87.

372 Article 1, Paris Agreement.

at the secession or South Tyrol from Italy orchestrated by the South Tyrolean Liberation Committee (*Befreiungsausschuss Südtirol*).[373]

Art. 116 of the Constitution of Italy (CI) enumerate the five special regions of the country that exist beside the 15 ordinary regions (the special regions are: Sicily, Sardinia, the Aosta valley, Friuli-Venezia-Giulia, and Trentino-Alto Adige/Südtirol). Since the amendment of the Constitution in 2001, Art. 117 has listed the exclusive competencies of the state, which include national questions such as foreign policy, defence, judicial powers, social security, citizenship, or currency. Other competences that fall outside this exclusive enumeration were passed to the regions (with the difference that ordinary regions have to follow state guidelines in concurrent competencies), the resolutions of which can only be contested by the government through the Constitutional Court (whereas before the 2001 amendment, the government was able to refer regional laws back to the regional government).[374] On the other hand, special regions have exclusive or shared powers in the fields of economics (including the disposal over locally generated tax revenues), education, culture, environmental issues, etc., enumerated by their respective special statutes. The case of South Tyrol is peculiar even within the five special regions not just because of the international entrenchment but also because South Tyrol, as a province within Trentino-Alto Adige region, exercises competencies that in the other four cases are allocated to the regional level. Thus, there is a complex eight-level system of power-sharing: exclusive legislative powers of the State;[375] concurring legislative powers shared by the State and its Regions;[376] exclusive legislative competencies of Trentino–Alto Adige

---

373 The discord of the South Tyroleans was due to the fact that the first autonomy statute adopted in 1948 gave autonomous competencies to the Italian majority region of *Trentino-Alto-Adige*, instead of the overwhelmingly German-speaking *Südtirol* Province, and the neighbouring bilingual townships, as foreseen by the Paris Agreement. Invoking the non-implementation of the Gruber-de Gasperi Agreement, Austria raised the South Tyrolean question before the UN General Assembly, which adopted two resolutions on the issue in 1960 and 1961, respectively. Pursuant to these resolutions, Italy then set up a commission of inquiry with the mandate to find solutions to the South Tyrolean question. This organization, called Commission of Nineteen, was the one that adopted the "Package" consisting of 137 measures to alter the existing legal regulations on the autonomy of Tyrol, which resulted in the revised autonomy statute that entered into force in 1972. See the elements of this package in: Ferrari (2009a) pp. 63-124.

374 See: Peterlini (2013), p. 130.

375 Article 117, Paragraph 2, points a) to s) CI.

376 *Id.* Art. 117, Paragraph 3.

region;[377] exclusive competencies of the autonomous provinces of Trento and Bolzano[378] (previously referred to as primary jurisdiction from the autonomous entities point of view);[379] concurring legislative powers shared by the State and Trentino–Alto Adige Region;[380] concurring legislative powers shared by the State and the Province (secondary jurisdiction);[381] powers to enact the provisions of national laws (tertiary jurisdiction);[382] and competencies delegated from the State to either the region or the province.[383]

Since Constitutional Law No. 1/1999 entered into force, the autonomy statutes of both the special and the ordinary regions must be adopted by the national parliament with a constitutional law.[384] Thus, the autonomy statute of South-Tyrol lies between ordinary laws and the Constitution in the hierarchy of norms, meaning that simple majority legislation of the Italian Parliament cannot repeal nor amend the statute. Accordingly, Regional Statutes are adopted and amended by the Regional Council with a law approved by an absolute majority of its members, with two subsequent deliberations at an interval of not less than two months.[385] The constitutionality of these statutes can be contested before the Constitutional Court by the central government within 30 days of their publication. The statute is submitted to popular referendum if one-fiftieth of the electors of the Region or one-fifth of the members of the Regional Council so request

377 Article 4 of the Special Statute of Trentino-Alto Adige Region – Decree No. 670 of the President of the Republic from 31 August 1972 (hereinafter, ASt).

378 Article 8. ASt and Art. 117. Paragraph 4 CI regarding regional involvement in EU decision-making processes.

379 Before the constitutional amendments in 2001 the jurisdiction of the autonomous entity could be categorized into primary (or exclusive), secondary (or shared), and tertiary (or complementary) competencies, while all other powers remained with the central state. As of the amendment of the CI in 2001 it's the other way around. The constitution enumerates the exclusive state competencies in art. 117, and all other residual powers are vested with the regions, or in the case of South Tyrol, the province, notwithstanding relevant limitations enshrined e.g. in community law. See more in: Ferrari (2009b), p. 198.

380 Article 5. ASt, which adds some specific competencies (like organization of public welfare and charitable institutions, local savings banks and credit institutions) that are not present in the general framework as set out by Art. 117 CI.

381 Article 9. ASt.

382 *Id.* Art. 10.

383 *Id.* Art. 16, Paragraphs 3 and 4, and article 17.

384 Article 116, Paragraph 1 CI.

385 *Id.* Art. 123.

within three months from its publication. The statute that is submitted to referendum is not promulgated if it is not approved by the majority of valid votes.[386]

These provisions provide a firm general constitutional entrenchment of the autonomous statutes, but they also make the statutes quite hard to amend. Consequently, in the case of regions with special statutes, there is a peculiar institutional mechanism enabling a more flexible adjustment of the autonomous legal system to eventual new challenges. "All special regions can negotiate with the state the concrete developments of their autonomy, bilaterally and on an equal footing. For each of the five special regions, a joint body of state and regional representatives (in equal number) has been established, with the crucial task of drafting the enactment decrees implementing the regional autonomy statues. These drafts are submitted to the national government, which approves them in the form of governmental decrees. The decrees are by-laws of the autonomy statute and cannot therefore be abrogated or amended by the laws of the national parliament.[387] This is due to the so-called >>principle of specialty<<, according to which special regions have a privileged status with particular regard to negotiations with the state,[388] which are carried out in a way that is similar to international relations: either there is consensus among the parties involved or the agreement cannot be reached. In other words, the relations between the state and the special regions are not based on hierarchy but, in principle, on parity. Put differently, the existence of two categories of regions cannot be abolished even by means of a constitutional reform".[389] In South-Tyrol, these enactment decrees (*Durchführungsbestimmungen*) are adopted by the so-called Commission of Six (*Sechser-Kommission*), consisting of three Italian members (appointed by the Italian Parliament) and three German-speaking members (appointed by the South-Tyrolean *Landtag*).

The case of Italy shows that the constitution of a unitary state can flexibly accommodate a "federalist-like" division of powers (where the state is "only" vested with enumerated powers, and all other legislative and administrative competencies are transferred to the regions), as well as asymmetrical regionalism

386 A similar procedure applies to constitutional laws on the national level under Art. 138 CI.

387 This means that enactment decrees in practice lie between constitutional laws and ordinary legislation in the hierarchy of norms.

388 This principle has been recurringly affirmed in the case law of the Constitutional Court of Italy. See, among others, Judgements No. 20/1956; 22/1961; 151/1972; 180/1980; 237/1983; 212/1984; and 160/1985.

389 Woelk et al. (2008), pp. 39–40.

(whit different levels of competencies even among the special regions) open to further devolution of powers from state to regional or provincial levels. While the Romanian constitution safeguards the unitary indivisible and unilingual character of the state to the extent that these features may not be subject to a constitutional amendment,[390] the Italian Constitution rather safeguards the special status of its autonomous entities, as their competencies cannot be unilaterally abrogated or amended by the national parliament, not even by means of a constitutional reform. Furthermore, the involvement of the kin-state (Austria) and the UN as mediators in the South Tyrolean conflict from the late 1960s onwards makes the case of South Tyrol one of the most salient examples to analyse from the Szekler point of view.

The Constitution of Spain (CS) is unique in the sense that Section 2 recognizes and guarantees the right to self-government of the nationalities and regions of which it is composed. Under the auspices of this "right to autonomy", the administrative structure is decided by the Self-governing Communities (*Comunidades Autónomas*),[391] who are free to decide whether or not they would like to form a common province or accede to an existing one.[392] This so-called dispositive principle (*principio dispositivo*)[393] allows for a structure that is permanently open, at the disposal of the autonomous communities.[394] The scope of the competencies they can assume is equally flexible. Section 149.1 enumerates the exclusive competencies of the central state, such as international relations;[395] immigration;

390 Article 152 (1) CR.

391 These communities are defined by Art. 143 CS as provinces with common historic, cultural, and economic characteristics, insular territories and provinces with a historic regional status. Currently there are 17 Autonomous Communities: Andalusia, Aragon, Asturias, Balearic Islands, Basque Country, Canary Islands, Cantabria, Castile-La Mancha, Castile and León, Catalonia, Extremadura, Galicia, La Rioja, Madrid, Murcia, Navarre, Valencia. In addition to these, there are two autonomous cities on the northern coast of Africa: Ceuta and Melilla.

392 Section 143 CS.

393 For a broader explanation of this principle, see among others Constitutional Court Decision 247/2007 from December 12.

394 The constitution also differentiates between a fast-track (Art. 151 CS) and a slow assumption of powers (Art. 143 CS). In most cases, the latter one was chosen.

395 Notwithstanding the exclusive competencies over foreign affairs, there is an institution called the Conference on Issues Related to the European Union (*Conferencia para Asuntos Relacionados con la Unión Europea, CARUE*), aimed to channel the views and interests of the Autonomous Communities regarding EU decision-making before Madrid adopts a position on various EU policy issues. A similar parity-based organ was established through organic law 8/1980 called the Council of Fiscal and

defence; administration of justice;[396] commercial, criminal, civic, or labour legislation; regulations on customs, tariff, and foreign trade; basic legislation on the financial system, health-, and on social security; etc.[397] But matters not expressly assigned to the State by the Constitution may fall under the jurisdiction of the Self-governing Communities by virtue of their Statutes of Autonomy, while jurisdiction on matters not claimed by Statutes of Autonomy shall fall with the State.[398] The competencies that the Communities can assume are enumerated under section 148 CS and include fields such as: organization of own institutions; urban planning and housing; public transportation; woodlands and forestry; agriculture and fisheries in accordance with general economic planning; and administration of local cultural institutions (schools, museums, and libraries). The precise enumeration of competencies is particularly important, given that state law and regional legislation enjoy the same legal value, meaning that in case provisions of these two forms of legislation clash, the law will prevail that was adopted by the legislature, which possesses jurisdiction over the given subject. Due to this legal equality, it is the Constitutional Court alone that can decide in such cases which law prevails over the other.[399] Ordinary judges cannot perform such scrutiny. Theoretically, this system allows for the gradual development of asymmetric regionalism by providing the self-governing communities the opportunity to fine-tune the scope of their jurisdiction. However, such attempts have their own limits, some of which came particularly well to the fore when the Catalan Parliament adopted a new Statute of Autonomy on 30 September 2005, which aimed to widen the powers of the *Generalitat de Catalunya*.[400]

---

Financial Policy (*Consejo de Política Fiscal y Financiera*), in order to adapt the coordination between the financial activities of the Autonomous Communities of the State Treasury.

396 While the legislative and executive branches are decentralized, the judicial power remains an exclusive power of the State.

397 The CS also allows the state to lay down the basics of a field to be regulated while leaving it to the Communities to enact the detailed regulations or to ensure the regional administrative enforcement of state level legislation.

398 Section 149.3 CS.

399 The Constitutional Court`s scrutiny, however, is a point where there is a difference between national and regional legislation, as the CCS can suspend the application of regional laws but not national ones.

400 The term *Generalitat* refers to the three main decision-making institutions of, including the Parliament of Catalonia, the president of the *Generalitat de Catalunya* and the Government of Catalonia.

In general, the text of the Statutes of autonomy is adopted by the respective regional legislatures but is subject to the approval of the Spanish Parliament (*Cortes Generales*),[401] which in practice means a political veto, and not just a constitutional one, as we saw in Italy (as Arzoz characterizes this system: "the autonomy statutes were denied a constitutional role in the process of developing the decentralisation model").[402] The text then has to be approved on a referendum, after which the Constitutional Court can still exercise scrutiny over the statutes' compliance with the Constitution and can overrule provisions or define the interpretation thereof. However, once enacted, the autonomy statute cannot be unilaterally amended by the central government.[403]

It was against this backdrop that the mentioned amendment of the 1979 statute of autonomy of Catalonia took place. After the overwhelming majority of the Catalan Parliament voted in favour of the text (125 in favour, 15 against out of a total 135 representatives), the statute was submitted to the Spanish legislature where about half of the provisions were already repealed as part of a deal with the then governing socialist party (PSOE) in January 2006. The Congress and the Senate both approved the new Statute on 10 May 2006 when the amended text was passed with the support of all parties, except for the Spanish main opposition party, the conservative People's Party (PP), and the Catalan separatist party *Esquerra Republicana de Catalunya*. On 18 June 2006, the new statute was approved in a referendum, gaining the support of 73.9 % of the participating electorate. In early 2006, PP members of the *Cortes* filed an appeal against the new Statute with the Constitutional Court of Spain (CCS) arguing that 126 articles were unconstitutional and that the French model of popular sovereignty applies also to Spain: "It can be said, with reason, that the centralism

401 Section 147.3 CS.

402 Arzoz (2012), p. 187.

403 In theory, the only way for the central government to unilaterally encroach upon autonomous competencies is to adopt "laws of harmonization". As Art. 150.3 CS stipulates, the State may enact laws laying down the necessary principles for harmonizing the rulemaking provisions of the Self-governing Communities, if general interest so requires. However, the Constitutional Court has been restrictive in the interpretation of this rule, and has annulled the only harmonizing law that has so far been adopted (See ruling STC 76/1983). Another, more severe option is the suspension of autonomous competencies under 155 of the CS, a measure that has only been invoked once since the entry into force of the constitution in 1978, namely after the Catalan independence referendum, after which the Spanish Senate voted in favour of invoking Art. 155 on 27 October 2017.

characteristic of French constitutionalism is not comparable to the Spanish constitution of 1978. But what is without doubt identical to it [in our constitution] is the concept of the people. The question is of enormous constitutional relevance because the concept of the people is used for nothing less than to attribute to it national sovereignty. National sovereignty is not fragmentable and still less, consequently, is the Spanish people. This is not a federative concept, formed by grouping the peoples of the different Spanish communities. The individual components of this sovereign people . . . are the citizens. All of them belong to a single category, not to be differentiated territorially".[404] The appeal dragged on for four years. In the meantime, the terms of four judges expired in late 2007 (and one place was vacant since 2008 due to the death of one judge), who were not replaced immediately at that time. Finally, in late June 2010, after four years of deliberation, a divided court rendered 14 articles of the statute unconstitutional and 27 others subject to further legal opinion (while also criticizing much of the PP appeal as inaccurate and badly argued).[405] In light of Decision 80/2014 of the Constitutional Court of Romania, this latter group of provisions are particularly relevant given that they shows the impact of how one interprets provisions of the constitution.

Instead of rendering some of the provisions that were deemed by PP critics as unconstitutional, Decision no. 31/2010 of the CCS provided an interpretation which allows for these provisions to remain in place,[406] given that they are interpreted in a specific manner (much to the dismay of the Catalan Parliament, these interpretations were unacceptable for them in many ways).[407] For this reason, it is worth mentioning some of the findings of this ruling.

Some of the contested provisions of the New Statute of Autonomy of Catalonia (NSAC) alluded to symbolic issues. The Preamble stipulated that the Parliament of Catalonia defined Catalonia "as a nation by an ample majority" and that "The Spanish Constitution, in its second Article, recognizes the national reality of Catalonia as a nationality". Accordingly, Art. 8 of the NSAC described the flag,

---

404 Introduction of PP`s appeal to the Constitutional Court as quoted by: Friend (2012), p. 105.

405 Rejection applied to articles concerning judicial powers of the Council of Justice of Catalonia, some financial powers of the Taxation Agency of Catalonia, and some linguistic competencies.

406 For the English translation of this Decision see: Constitutional Court of Spain (2010).

407 See Legal Report of experts commissioned by the president of the *Generalitat* as a response to CCS Decision 31/2010: http://premsa.gencat.cat/pres_fsvp/docs/2010/07/21/12/11/76d06239-427f-48da-a5335cf2492b43ea.pdf, accessed: 2016.07.13.

the holiday and the anthem of Catalonia as "the national symbols of Catalonia". These articles have been challenged for classifying as "national" the symbols of Catalonia, which were believed to contradict the concepts of unity and indivisibility as set out by Section 2 of the CS. The CCS mentions that "it is indeed possible to speak of nation as a cultural, historic, linguistic, sociological and even religious reality. But the nation of importance here is solely and exclusively the nation in its legal and constitutional sense".[408] This means that, as far as constitutional law is concerned, the term "nation" can only be interpreted as a civic bond between all citizens of Spain irrespective of their cultural identity. Consequently, the interpretation of the references to "Catalonia as a nation" and to "the national reality of Catalonia" in the preamble of the NSAC have no legal effect. In other words, while the communities of Spain have the right to self-government, the exercise of this right can only happen within the indissoluble Spanish nation, where the concept of the "nation" connotes the civic understanding of a political community composed of all citizens of the Spanish state and can only be used by a sub-state entity for self-identification within these constitutional boundaries. Finally, as far as "national symbols of Catalonia" are concerned, this wording can allude to a manifestation of the right recognized under Section 2 CS with "no intention to challenge the competency or counteract the symbols of the Spanish nation".

With regard to linguistic issues, the *Generalitat* attempted to place Catalan on equal footing with Castilian by stating under Art. 6 (2) NSAC that "all persons have the right to use the two official languages and citizens of Catalonia have the right and the duty to know them". These provisions were inspired by Section 3.1 CS, which lays down the duty of all Spaniards to know Castilian. In the CCS's opinion, these provisions would be unconstitutional and null if their intention was to impose a duty to know Catalan, equivalent in meaning to the constitutional duty to know Spanish. However, the CCS noted that there is a different possible interpretation, according to which the "the duty to know Catalan" refers to a mandate of the public powers of Catalonia "to adopt the measures necessary to facilitate compliance with this duty".[409] In this context, the duty to know Catalan would create liability for Catalan public institutions to build up capacity to be able to communicate and teach in Catalan, whereas the duty to know Castilian applies to all citizens of the state.

---

408 Paragraph 12 of Decision 31/2010 of the CCS.
409 *Id.* at, paragraph 14. b.

Linguistic issues came also to the fore with regard to education. Article 35.1 NSAC stipulates that "each individual has the right to receive an education in Catalan", and that "Catalan shall be used as the teaching and learning language for university and non-university education". The CCS notes that even though this article does not refer to Spanish as a teaching language, this cannot be understood deliberately to order an exclusion. While "it is perfectly legitimate for Catalan to be the centre of gravity of this model of bilingualism … both languages must be not just taught, but also a means of communication in the educational process as a whole, both co-official languages constitutionally must be recognized by the public powers as teaching and learning languages and therefore each individual has the right to be taught in either of them".[410]

Another relevant part of CCS decision 31/2010 in relation to the Szekler case was the one pertaining to the internal administrative borders of Catalonia. Articles 83, 90, and 91 NSAC mention *Vegueria* as the new administrative unit of local government in Catalonia (responsible for the territorial organization of its services),[411] whose executive council should supersede that of the province.[412] The challenge of PP to the *Vegueria* system was dismissed by the CCS "because the territorial division of the State into provinces, generally speaking, is not affected by it, nor, more particularly, is the division of Catalonia into the four provinces currently existing… since the constitutional guarantee of the province as a local entity does not exclude the existence of other supra-municipal government entities".[413] The conclusion of the CCS was that the autonomous administration in practice is free to develop whatever internal administrative structure it deems appropriate for the organizations of services that fall in their competencies (even concurring, multi-level structures) as long as they maintain the administrative capacities for the fulfilment of state activities. In this sense, the NSAC's option of dividing the territory of Catalonia into veguerías, as unique administrative units that exist only here, does not harm the State's territorial division into provinces.[414]

As described earlier in section 2.2.2, one of the procedural objections against the reestablishment of the traditional Szekler Seats, as internal administrative

410 *Id.* at, paragraph 24.

411 The *vegueria* was the feudal administrative territorial division of the Principality of Catalonia between the 12th and 18th century.

412 Catalonia is currently divided into 948 municipalities, which are organized into 42 *comarques*, included in four provinces (Barcelona, Girona, Lleida, and Tarragona).

413 CCR (2014) *Supra note*, paragraph 40.

414 *Id.* at paragraph 40.

units of an autonomous Szeklerland, was that no such unit is mentioned in the constitution and that this would result in a three-level municipal structure, as opposed to the usual two-level system of any other county of Romania. In this perspective, it is worth mentioning that the CCS did not find anything unconstitutional in chapter VII NSAC, which concerns Aran's own institutions.[415] Aran is an autonomous entity within an autonomous entity. Addressing Aran's cultural specificities, they were granted an autonomous government called the *Conselh Generau*, which is vested with the power to decide the internal administrative division of Aran. Consequently, the Aranese executive established a territorial division that exists nowhere else in Spain, the so-called *terçons*. The *terçó* was the traditional territorial division of the Aran Valley from 1313 to 1834. The *Conselh Generau* decided to re-establish them in 1990, even though the traditional borders of the six *terçons* cross-cut that of the nine municipalities of Aran. Although Section 141.3 CS stipulates that groups of municipalities other than provinces may be formed, the lack of a similar provision in the Romanian constitution does not constitute a *de jure* ban on other forms of administrative units, e.g. the Szekler Seats.

While the interpretative descriptions of Decisions 31/2010 of the CCS generated a lot of discontent among Catalans, it also took away the edge of several claims of the PP in favour of the self-governance reform plans of Catalan lawmakers. This example shows that it is legally possible to conceptualize a multi-tier administrative system for a unitary state, which gives room for the expression of specific traditions in the shape of historical local administrative units (in this case the vegueria system, and the terçons of Aran). Furthermore, the example of Decisions 31/2010 of the CCS shows the relevance of how one perceives a provision and illustrates that the interpretative framework of legal provisions can be elaborated in a manner that, in many ways, fosters the accommodation of autonomy aspirations. From a comparative perspective, this approach of the CCS shows many substantial differences to that of the CCR, as exhibited in Decision 80/2014.

415 Aran is the northernmost *comarca* of Catalonia where the population speaks Aranese, a form of the Gascon dialect of Occitan, spoken in Val d'Aran.

# 4 Policy Implications

The preceding chapters already imply some conclusions *de lege ferenda.*[416] Consequently, I found it important to directly address the possible policy implications that can be deducted from this book. The rationale of this chapter would be to identify the corresponding action various actors (State, Minority Community, Kin-state, International community) could undertake in order to assist the establishment of the territorial autonomy of Szeklerland in Romania.

There have been many attempts within academia to gauge past events in order to assess possible "recipes of success" for the future. Shaykhutdinov, for example,[417] conducted a correlation and regression analysis on the self-determination movements of 168 ethnic groups in 87 states between 1945 and 2000 in order to assess the impact of violence on the success of those movements.[418] The statistical analysis showed that the employment of peaceful tactics when seeking greater self-rule is the sole strongest predictor of the formation of an autonomy arrangement. Non-violent movements were about three times more effective at achieving territorial autonomy than ethnic groups that employed violence.[419] Even though there were some cases where violent tactics played a significant role in an arrangement that introduced autonomy for that community, in most cases these tactics were found counterproductive as they generate mistrust and antipathy towards members of the movement and alienate representatives of the given state as well as actors of the international community. Furthermore, the study identifies some additional factors that are relevant to the Szekler case. A positive correlation with successful autonomy movements was found in cases where: the

416 Latin expression, meaning "with a view to the future law" as opposed to *de lege lata*, the "current law".

417 Shaykhutdinov (2010), pp. 179–191.

418 The analysis only included minority groups that constituted at least 1 % of their country's population or had 100,000 members or more, and had expressed a desire for territorial autonomy or independence at least once between 1945 and 2000. Additionally, groups included in the study resided in countries with a population of at least 500,000.

419 This viewpoint is shared also by Daftary in her comparative study between Corsica and the Åland-islands, where she notes that the low level of militarization of the Åland conflict along with the Finnish democratic political culture were major factors contributing to the success of the Ålandic autonomy movement relative to Corsica. See: Daftary, (2004).

autonomy demand came from larger and geographically concentrated communities (the latter being the more important factor); there were international mediators involved in the autonomy process (state actors were found to have more influence in this regard than international organizations); the political system of the host country could be characterized as democratic.

Cunningham examined the internal fragmentation of the primary actors of any autonomy process: the central governments of states and organizations representing a given minority community.[420] She argues that the internal structure of both movements for self-determination and national governments structures the negation process in these disputes and the incentives that both sides have for settlement. The author's findings fine-tuned the general *topos* that autonomy movements led by a sole and unified organization are more likely to succeed in winning autonomy than their organizationally fragmented counterparts. Unified movements have the competitive advantage that central governments are less able to deploy "divide and conquer" tactics against them. Thus, the negotiated agreement is more likely to echo the opinion of the whole group, which also makes this option more "costly" to central governments, insofar as it presupposes the fulfilment of all (or at least the majority) of the demands of that group. This scenario decreases the government`s manoeuvring space and pushes the dynamics of the autonomy process in the direction of a zero-sum game. The situation is not the same with internally fragmented movements where the government could use these internal divisions to their advantage by pursuing "*divide et impera*" strategy and offering autonomy deals that a subset of factions would agree to in an attempt to divide the moderates from the hardliners. This scenario would entail governments satisfying moderate factions with lesser concessions resulting in autonomy arrangements with a more limited scope of powers that are only accepted by a fraction of the group. This in turn could generate discontent among the minority group and make the arrangement more fragile and unstable.[421] From the government's point of view, this option is more favourable and easier to communicate as it does not jeopardize its own internal structure, which usually is not homogeneous but is composed of parties with discrepant preferences. Cunningham states that relatively

420 Cunningham (2007), pp. 6–12.

421 Salat and Constantine further point out that autonomy arrangements that are not accepted by the wider majority of the affected communities can produce severe legitimacy deficit. It was the case with Macedonia and the Ohrid Framework Agreement or the Jewish Autonomous Oblast in Russia. See: Salat et al. (2014), pp. 465–466.

higher levels of internal fragmentation of minority and majority actors constitute a hurdle for policy change, given that it increases the number of veto players on both sides, makes it more difficult for parties to assess each other's relative bargaining strength and decreases the chances of elaborating an autonomy arrangement that would satisfy the majority of both sides. In summary, Cunningham notes that the chances of reaching an autonomy arrangement are the highest in cases where you have a government with a moderate number of internal veto players[422] complemented by a minority group, which is either unified or fragmented in a way that allows governments to buy off moderates with lesser autonomy concessions.[423] In this latter case, the minority group can increase its chances for a deal with establishing a coordinating or deliberative body for the various stakeholders, which decreases the potential of hard-liners to block the acceptance of an autonomy proposal of the government.

Ghai and Woodman indicated on a five-point scale how strong the correlation was between specific factors and their contribution to the establishment of an autonomy arrangement in 13 different regions.[424] They found that the most salient factor that facilitated the granting of an autonomous status was general regime change in the host country. Ghai notes that times when the architecture of the state is under review present an opportunity for minorities to assert a variety of claims to the future order, including claims on autonomous status (this assertion was true to 11 of the 13 autonomies covered by the book, which shows the presence of a strong correlation).[425] The second strongest correlation was found in cases where the international community actively contributed to the establishment of that autonomy. Chances for autonomy were further increased in cases where the territory inhabited by the given national community was relatively small in size and economic significance. Lastly, the presence of a democratic political system and traditions of rule law were found to have helped facilitate autonomy (given that most of the autonomies can be found in liberal democracies). Other authors, however, contested the relevance of democratic political structures in autonomy arrangements and would allude to examples

---

422 As an example, she mentions the Corsican autonomy process whose outcome was very much shaped by the excessive number of veto players on the governmental level in 1982, 1991 and 2001.

423 As Cunningham mentions, this type of favourable fragmentation was present, for example, in the Northeast Indian movements of Naga, Mizo, and Bodo.

424 Ghai et al. (2013), pp. 449–486.

425 *Id.* at p. 452.

where the host country could not be characterized as a liberal democracy,[426] such as: Gagauzia in Moldova, Hong Kong in China, Aceh Darussalam in Indonesia, Bougainville in Papua New-Guinea, Muslim Mindanao in the Philippines, or Tatarstan in Russia.

Lapidoth highlighted 16 points which can contribute to a successful autonomy arrangement. Among these, one can find some factors I have already alluded to above (like the positive, mediating role of the international community) as well as new factors, such as the importance of the consent of the minority community that is supposed to be the subject of the newly established autonomy. Moreover, if there is a kin-state to which the given minority of a host country is attached to culturally, then that kin-state should be involved in the autonomy negotiation process (and be able to give its tacit or explicit consent to it), and the arrangement should be mutually beneficial for both the state and the population of the given region.[427]

## 4.1 Romanian State

Besides the already-mentioned historical resentment towards Hungarians, there are some traits of Romanian political culture that represent difficulties to be reckoned with, when seeking a lasting legal solution to Szekler autonomy demands. Such as: Byzantine power structures, meaning that informal mechanisms of decision-making often prevail over formal ones; weakness of rule-of-law traditions; high levels of corruption-proneness resulting in extensive patronage politics;[428] selective law enforcement; poorly phrased laws generating cacophony in interpretations of legislation; or the general lack of willingness to implement laws pertaining to minority rights.[429] Nonetheless, from a legal-doctrinal point of view, the following general categorization contains options that are theoretically available if state authorities wanted to accommodate minority autonomy aspirations:[430]

426 See, for example, Schulte (2015), pp. 75–84.

427 Lapidoth (1997), pp. 199–201.

428 Patronage politics refers to the process whereby political "patrons" use state resources to secure the loyalty of their "clients" in the general population.

429 On these traits of Romanian political culture see, for example, Varga (2002); Roper (2006); Dimulescu et al. (2013); Hein (2015).

430 A thought-provoking study on the theoretical challenges, and possible guiding principles of accommodating differences through law is provided by: Palermo (2007), pp. 63–83.

### 4.1.1 Options Requiring the Amendment of the Constitution or the Adoption of a New One

*Federalization*

The imaginary line that separates the Western civilization from the orthodox world runs right through the middle of Romania.[431] Szeklerland is actually the easternmost part of Western Christianity. The line of the Carpathians separates regions and communities with historically divergent views on shared motivations, social values, beliefs, identities and interpretation of common experiences.[432] In multi-ethnic polities shaped by such vast regional, historical, cultural, and linguistic differences, a federalized state can be considered as an appropriate constitutional structure. Such a shift would break with the "oppressive governance of cultural minorities" and offer a way to provide national minorities with equal rights, governance, and political participation – without dismembering the Romanian state, but transforming it from a nation state into a pluri-national state.[433] That is a state that accommodates several nations, as opposed to aiming to have one nation in one state. This option, however, would first require the Romanian political elite to admit that maintaining an ethnically unitary conception of Romania proves unable to solve the issue of the coexistence of the Hungarian and Romanian national communities. Furthermore, the stringent requirements laid down in Art. 152 of the Constitution means that such a federalization would only be possible if a new Constitution would be adopted. This option, however, would most likely come into the fore in case there is an overwhelming change that effects country as a whole. Such event would be, for example, if Romania was to unify with the Republic of Moldova, even though this is not a plausible scenario in the foreseeable future.[434] As the history of Romania shows, political elites have always been preoccupied with working

431 See Huntington (1996), 258.

432 For a detailed description about the cultural differences in Romania, see the findings of Bakacsi et al. (2006).

433 Payero-López - Nimni (2018), p. 102.

434 Such a unification would first require the settlement of the Transnistrian question between Moldova, Russia, and the population of Transnistria. Secondly, the Gagauzian autonomy statute foresees the region's secession from Moldova provided the country's independent status ceases to exist. Gagauzia even organized a consultative referendum on the issue in 2014, where the overwhelming majority opted against the unification with Romania as well against EU membership, and favoured independence and membership in the Russian customs union instead. A third obstacle would be the reluctance of Moldovans to become a part of Romania.

towards the establishment of a large but unitary and ethnically homogeneous nation state. Due to this fact, the Romanian political class would most likely accept any federalized power-sharing structure to a limited time-period only and would probably revert to a unitary structure as soon as the domestic and international environment allows for it, as it happened with the gradual phasing out of the Hungarian Autonomous Province in the late 1950s and early 1960s.

*Transformation into a regionalized state, characterized by asymmetric regionalism*

As Asbjørn Eide noted, a process of decentralization is often a "reaction to over-centralization, found unacceptable both because of bureaucratic overload, and for linguistic, cultural or other reasons".[435] In terms of Romania, both aspects are relevant. On the one hand, asymmetric regionalism could contribute to tackling governmental bureaucracy and the forms of corruption that can be linked to over-centralization. On the other hand, such regionalization would enable the state to avoid unnecessary inter-ethnic conflicts and create an administrative system that is often characterized as one of the best possible ways to ensure the effective participation of national minorities in public affairs.[436] As the Explanatory note of the Lund Recommendations reminds, "experience shows that powers can be divided even with respect to fields of public authority traditionally exercised by central government, including devolved powers of justice (both substantive and procedural) and powers over traditional economies".[437] One of the core features of the asymmetric regionalism that exists in Italy and the "quasi-federalism" that exists in Spain is that these systems have a firm general constitutional entrenchment. Consequently, a similar level of constitutional protection of devolved powers would only exist in the case of Szeklerland if the constitution would be amended. This, however, does not rule out the option to implement an asymmetric regionalism with a looser form of constitutional entrenchment (discussed in the following section).

### 4.1.2 Options Not Requiring Constitutional Amendments

Not requiring any legal reform, it would be possible to interpret the Constitution differently. A more open-minded central government, Parliament, and

435 See UN Commission on Human Rights - Sub-Commission on Prevention of Discrimination and Protection of Minorities (1993), at para. 257.

436 See, for example, Section III/B of the OSCE's Lund recommendations on the Effective Participation of National Minorities in Public Life.

437 See paragraph 20 of the Explanatory note, available at: http://www.osce.org/hcnm/32240?download=true, accessed: 2017.02.23.

Constitutional Court could arrive to an alternative interpretation on provisions of the Constitution that diverge from the ethnocentric understanding thereof. The main responsibility lies with the host country to protect its citizens belonging to a minority. The opportunity to engage in a dialogue with minorities is always open, and the administrative reform that has been on the agenda of Romanian politics for years is a suitable framework for such a dialogue. Under the auspices of an administrative reform, the central government could engage in a discussion with the representatives of the Hungarian community in order to elaborate an arrangement that would accommodate their aspirations but left the constitutional framework unchanged. Such a dialogue is even mandatory under the provision of Law 215/2001 and Law 3/2000. An administrative reform process could entail the rethinking of the distribution of power and further decentralization through organic or ordinary laws, but it should at least pertain to acknowledging cultural circumstances and aspects of minority protection when drawing the borders of future administrative units in accordance with the international and domestic legal obligations of the country (e.g. Law 2/1968). Pursuant to the provisions of Law 215/2001 and Art. 5 of the European Charter of Local Self Government, a local referendum should be conducted to establish the will of the local communities in this regard. It could be perceived as a major step forward both in Szekler–Romanian relations as well as in Szeklerland's path towards autonomy, if Szeklerland would be able to form one unified administrative unit, even if it was without special law-making competencies. Especially, if the historical seats, which are so deeply embedded in Szekler culture, would be administratively re-established. This option would be short of what is written in the draft statute of autonomy; still it would represent a meaningful step towards recognizing the existence and distinctiveness of Szeklerland,[438] contribute to building mutual trust between Hungarians and Romanians, and foster the de-securitization of autonomy aspirations, all of which are key components for establishing a sustainable autonomy arrangement.

From the above the most important prerequisite is the de-securitization of the autonomy discourse. What needs to be curbed is the majority's unfounded existential distress. "The majority needs to understand that the identity of a community with a different culture does not pose a threat to their identity, not even to the ethno-cultural character of the state; at most it may give it a special hue on

438 As Prina pointed out, the recognition of ethnicity-based territorial formations and its symbolic value have a potentially stabilising effect in inter-ethnic relations. See: Prina (2016), p. 268.

the local level. . . .The process, which could result in minority issues losing their security relevance, requires the cultural character of the majority political identity to fade away"[439]

## 4.2 Minority Community

While past events show that external (accession to international organizations) and internal (coalition forming with Hungarian parties) developments can trigger fluctuations in majority rhetoric on minority rights in Romania, this is not the case regarding attitudes towards autonomy.[440] As we saw in section 2.4, the majority political parties - regardless of their ideological affiliation - remain adamantly opposed to granting territorial autonomy to Szeklerland. Representative organizations of the Hungarian community are, thus, left without political allies among the majority parties in this regard. Hungarian parties can reach certain concessions if their presence is needed to produce a governing majority in the national parliament. Still, as long as the general opinion rejects dialogue on this topic, major public demonstrations need to be organized to raise both international and domestic public awareness and to generate a public discourse on autonomy arrangements. Given the reluctance of the Romanian political elite to engage in a dialogue about autonomy within domestic institutions, proactive presence of minority representatives in international fora is pivotal to provide external motivation for Romanian authorities to engage in a dialogue in order to accommodate minority claims. The best way the minority community can contribute to achieve this dialogue is to maintain a balance between international lobbying and domestic trust-building *vis-á-vis* the majority society and to remain coherent about the target and the instrument of the final goal. Consequently, Szekler self-determination needs to keep revolving around autonomy (and not secession) using, as in the past, peaceful and democratic means only.

An aspect which continuously comes to the fore when mentioning the minority actors of the autonomy struggle is the extent to which they are internally fragmented. Cunningham mentioned that while unified autonomy movements do not have to face "divide and conquer" tactics of the central government, certain degrees of organizational fragmentation can foster an autonomy deal. As far as Hungarian political parties are concerned, the Dominant party has always been DAHR, which has gained around 80 % of the valid Hungarian votes since the

439 Kardos (2015), pp. 41–42.
440 See finding of Andriescu (2007).

political transition even when they had smaller contenders (like the Hungarian Civic Party or the Hungarian People's Party of Transylvania, both of which are pro-autonomy parties).[441] Outside the party-political arena, the most relevant actor is the Szekler National Council, which, unlike DAHR, does not participate in elections and is rather involved in paradiplomacy and the organization of pro-autonomy events, as well as building the theoretical and strategic background for autonomy related action.[442] If we accept Cunningham's findings,[443] we can conclude that this type of fragmentation can potentially foster a moderate form of autonomy arrangement.

However, as scholars point out, DAHR has switched tactics step by step and shifted from the community building and mobilizing tactics of the 1990s to putting an emphasis on the absorption of state resources instead. This in turn allows for a phenomenon called "control-cooptation", whereby the central state is able to mitigate minority claims while not giving any concessions in return.[444] While DAHR was a member of various governments for over two decades from 1996 onwards, the privileges they managed to obtain (like state investments in Hungarian regions) were due to *ad hoc* political deals, the cost of which was to abandon claims on institutionalization of minority power-sharing or the use of international advocacy strategies. In 2013 – following the largest pro-autonomy rally to date, the so-called Great March of the Szeklers, which mobilized approximately 120,000 people (one-third of the Hungarian-speaking population of Szeklerland) – Prime Minister Victor Ponta made specific references to control-cooptation when he emphasized the importance of preventing the "radicalization" of Hungarian self-government claims by allowing DAHR into the central government.[445] This model thus reproduces the dominance of the titular nation and the marginalization of the Hungarian community, allowing the central state the opportunity to make continuous attempts at transforming a minority

441 Source: Kiss et al. (2013), pp. 7–8.

442 A partner organization of SzNC is the Hungarian National Council of Transylvania, which has a Transylvanian wide scope of activity, which is not narrowed down to Szeklerland, and advocates for various types of autonomy for the Hungarian community of Romania.

443 Cunningham (2007) *Supra note.*

444 Control-cooptation referrers to the process of neutralizing or overcoming the influence potential of a certain group (in this case a party representing a minority community) through assimilation into existing power-structures. For more detail see Kiss et al. (2013) *Supra note.*

445 See: Kiss (2015), p. 55.

representative organization into a channel that mediates and reproduces power asymmetry.

Due to the above, the relation of DAHR to Szekler autonomy is rhapsodical. On the one hand, the official party program of DAHR contains the pledge to „achieve the legal articulation, as well as the application through legislative means, various forms of autonomy, including territorial autonomy."[446] The program specifically refers to the autonomy of Szeklerland as a „public legal administrative framework and institutional structure that provides decision-making competencies for local authorities…" while at the same time grants "additional competencies to maintain the regions special cultural- and linguistic heritage and traditions.[447] On the other hand, however, DAHR never organized any autonomy protest on their own initiative, and their representatives usually refrain from speaking on pro-autonomy rallies organized by others (e.g. there were never any speakers from DAHR on the Day of Szekler Freedom events).[448] Additionally, the draft autonomy statutes were never submitted to the Romanian parliament as fraction proposals but as an initiative of individual or a group of individual MPs that sat in the DAHR fraction. Finally, while some candidates might make references to autonomy, DAHR as a party organization does not make any specific autonomy-related pledges in its electoral campaigns.

Based on the above quoted sources, one can argue that minority organizations that wish to achieve autonomy for Szeklerland might be better off resuming and amplifying strategies of community-building, international advocacy, and mobilization of members of the minority community to place the question of territorial autonomy on the domestic political agenda in order to achieve institutional solutions, as opposed to relying on haphazard political pacts.

---

446 A Romániai Magyar Demokrata Szövetség programja: https://rmdsz.ro/upload/dokumetumok/RMDSZProgram2017.pdf, p. 2, accessed: 2021.06.09.

447 *Id.* at p. 3.

448 An example where all political forces, including RMDSZ actively contributed to the organizations of an autonomy rally was the so called "Great March of the Szeklers" on 27 October 2013. The fact that all relevant representative organizations rallied behind this event resulted in an historical mobilization, as the approximately 120,000 participants formed a 55-km-long human chain in Southern Szeklerland between the communes of Bereck, and Kökös. On political comments see: https://szekelyhon.ro/aktualis/haromszek/megkezdodott-a-szekelyek-nagy-menetelese, accessed: 2021.03.02.

## 4.3 Kin-State

In his analysis on the impact of ethnic minorities on foreign policy, Moore argues that a systematic effect emerges in bordering countries in relation to an ethnic group that is split across that border. This effect, however, is asymmetric and has an impact mostly on the kin-state rather than the host country. He found that a country in which a given ethnic group is dominant or advantaged appears to be more hostile in its foreign policy toward the country where the group's kin are disadvantaged or persecuted.[449] His findings also imply that the foreign policy aspect of kin-state activism is a collateral consequence of the failure of a given territorial state to create equality among its citizens - irrespective of their cultural, linguistic, or ethnic background -, the magnitude of which is in correlation, among others, with the level of victimization the kin-minority is subject to in the host country (take the example of the South Tyrolean conflict, where the most critical and violent years generated the most intense kin-state activity from Austria in the 1960s, especially compared to Austria's conduct towards Italy after the so-called *Streitbeilegung* as of 1992 onwards).[450]

According to Kardos, "four types of action can be taken by a kin-state in favour of its kin minority: 1) actions in the context of international bodies and mechanisms; 2) actions in relation to the home state; 3) actions *vis-à-vis* other states; 4) and domestic legislation on the relationship with its kin minority".[451] Hungary as a kin-state has been active in all these spheres, the second one being the most salient from the perspective of an autonomy arrangement. The question of Hungarian minority autonomy in Romania, however, has not been on the agenda of bilateral talks between the two states. Relations between these two parties are burdened with many unresolved minority-related issues, which is further exacerbated by the fact that there is little to no intention in the Romanian party to discuss these issues in the framework of inter-state dialogue. To have a better understanding of the reasons for this reluctance, I conducted an interview

449 Moore (2002), p. 80.

450 The term *Streitbeilegung* refers to the cessation of the dispute between Austria and Italy opened in 1960 and 1961 before the UN concerning the application of the Gruber – de Gasperi Agreement relating to South Tyrol. See more in: Peterlini, Oskar (2017): Österreich-Italien 1992 - Streitbeilegung zu Südtirol vor der UNO, dem Europarat und dem IGH – Wiederveröffentlichung der Originaldokumente und der diplomatischen Noten anlässlich der 25 Jahrfeier. Auszüge aus: Peterlini, Oskar (2000): *Autonomie und Minderheitenschutz in: Südtirol und im Trentino*; und (2012): *Südtirols Autonomie und die Verfassungsreformen Italiens.*

451 Kardos (2006), p. 130.

with Mr. Ferenc Kalmár, Ministerial Commissioner for the Development of Hungary's Neighbourhood Policy, on 18 February 2021,[452] who said the following:

> Romanian diplomats negotiate with their Hungarian counterparts from a position of strength, as opposed to negotiating on an equal footing. There is a perception among Romanian diplomats that they can do so, given that Romania actually enjoys a more valuable geopolitical position for the Euro-Atlantic integration than Hungary. This mentality characterizes their approach also in issues pertaining to the Hungarian national community living in their country. There are questions where they simply deny even the possibility of engaging in a dialogue. One such issue is territorial autonomy. But even in less contentious topics related to the Hungarian minority we find it difficult to communicate with our Romanian counterparts. This is the main reason why the Hungarian-Romanian Joint Committee had its last plenary session way back in 2011, even though we should have one regular session each year according to the Bilateral Treaty on Understanding, Cooperation and Good Neighbourhood[453]

Having good neighbourly relations built on mutual trust between the kin-state and the host country is a crucial factor for the autonomy struggle. It is hard to imagine that Romania would grant autonomy to a minority whose kin-state they are suspicious of. Good relations and trust between Romania and Hungary can therefore be seen as a prerequisite for Szekler autonomy.

Furthermore, while some of the support that Hungary has so far granted for its kinspeople abroad stirred controversy in the host countries (like the Status Law in the late 1990s), financial and cultural support was much less contentious

452 Throughout the 1990s, Hungary concluded a series of bilateral treaties with its neighbours, all of which contain provisions on mutual minority protection. All of these treaties foresee the establishment of Joint Committees, which convene on a regular basis to discuss topical issues pertaining to the implementation of these bilateral treaties.

453 In the fifth Report submitted by Romania on the implementation of the FCNM on 8 November 2019, the central government assessed the quality of inter-state dialogue in a dissenting way: "In relation to Hungary, for the application of the provisions of Art. 15 of the Treaty of Understanding, Cooperation and Good Neighborhood between Romania and the Republic of Hungary (signed at Timisoara on 16 September 1996) a Romanian-Hungarian Specialized Cooperation Committee on National Minorities was established. The Protocol to the 8th Session of this Committee is currently under negotiation. On 13 July 2015, the text of the Protocol was initiated at the secretariat level. The last meeting at the level of co-chairs took place on 21 October 2016. Therefore, Romania's experience of dialogue under these agreements is long and very wide". Available at: https://rm.coe.int/5th-sr-romania-en/16809943af, pp. 54–56, accessed: 2021.02.24.

and has meant an important form of support that assisted minority communities in reproducing their societies. The maintenance of minority identity is a crucial question due to the rapid demographic decline Hungarian minorities have been suffering for many decades.[454] Such kin-state aid policies are not illegitimate or illegal given that Hungary concluded a series of bilateral treaties on good neighbourly relations and cooperation with surrounding states. Among others, these treaties contain reciprocal obligations for parties to protect and promote the rights and identity of minorities and obliges parties to settle all their disputes concerning the interpretation or implementation of that Treaty through direct consultations and negotiations or based on an international multilateral treaty on peaceful settlement of disputes both countries are parties to. Due to these, Hungary has a treaty-based, mutually agreed-upon opportunity to be involved in the management of minority affairs of neighbouring countries, including that of Romania. Given the general reluctance of the international community as a whole to address the yet unresolved issues of traditional minorities, the kin-state activity of Hungary will continue to be an important factor in assisting minority Hungarians to maintain and reproduce their communities, let their voices be heard by the international public opinion, initiate a dialogue with the host countries on their problems and aspirations, and to negotiate beneficial economic deals and promote cross-border development programs.

## 4.4 International Community

The limits of the main human rights/minority rights forum of Europe (the CoE) to create compulsory and judicially enforceable international norms on minority protection became obvious by 1993, the latest. Had the Committee of Ministers of the CoE adopted Recommendation 1201 (1993), Europe would have an additional protocol on the rights of minorities to the European Convention on Human Rights which would be enforceable before the European Court of Human Rights. Not even an armed conflict, as violent as the Yugoslav wars, proved to be enough of an incentive for European states to create a general legal framework through which an external actor would have been entitled to make legally binding decisions regarding minority protection.

Even so, Art. 1 of FCNM stipulates that the protection of national minorities and of the rights and freedoms of persons belonging to those minorities forms

454 Csángó Hungarian, for example, is already listed by UNESCO as one of the severely endangered languages of Europe.

an integral part of the international protection of human rights and as such falls within the scope of international co-operation. Consequently, while the responsibility to implement measures of minority protection lies primarily with the respective territorial states, the question itself is not merely an issue of any state's internal affairs. This is also relevant for autonomy arrangements, as these represent a form of implementing the effective participation of minorities in public life. As Gilbert puts it, there is nothing to suggest that international organizations "could not require a State to enter into negotiations in good faith regarding autonomy".[455] With this in mind, the importance of international organizations is mainly to provide platforms to develop the global or regional legal regimes of minority protection; to motivate states to develop their legal framework or even to engage in negotiations to resolve minority-related disputes; and - within the given possibilities - to hold them accountable for the implementation of those international documents that were ratified by them. The importance of the active involvement of other states and international institutions in autonomy arrangements was already mentioned.[456] What can be added is that the international community can also foster the durability of autonomy arrangements, as seen in the case of both South-Tyrol and the Åland Islands. Drawing on the experiences of this latter region, Hannikainen even asked the question why not authorize an international organ to work for the creation of regional autonomies in States?[457] In the case of the Åland Island, the League of Nations actively participated in the formation of the regional autonomy in close cooperation with both the minority community and its host country, who were both able to communicate their viewpoints to the League Council, and if these pertained to legal questions, the Permanent Court of International Justice could have been consulted. More importantly, the Ålanders had the opportunity to turn to the League of Nations, as the external guarantor agency, in the event of Finland breeching its commitments.

As we saw earlier, Romanian constitutional culture was heavily influenced by foreign models. Constitutional transplants following mostly the French and the Belgian constitutions were present in many cases. After the political transition of 1989, the Euro-Atlantic integration provided for a set of different external requirements from both the CoE and the EU, some of which even entailed the amendment of the constitution. While the incentive from the side of the

455 Gilbert (2002), p. 312.
456 Ghai et al. (2013), p. 452.
457 Hannikainen (1998), p. 95.

Romanian state to accommodate its legal system to external standards is not as strong as it has been during the processes of accession to the CoE and the EU, international influence has proven to be a strong factor in shaping minority-related norms of the Romanian legal system. In fact, the historical overview presented in section 1.6 showed that the active involvement of external forces, especially state powers, was always a major factor in some form to develop the domestic circumstances of minority protection in Romania. Even though there appears to be a diminishing readiness from the side of the international community to actively engage in resolving issues of traditional national communities of Europe, the mechanisms of the CoE, the UN, and the EU, along with the involvement of foreign states, could still play a salient role in promoting dialogue between the parties and in fostering the improvement of autonomy-related practices and legislation in Romania.

# 5 Conclusions

History shows that there has always been a certain readiness from the side of Romania to adopt Western constitutional patterns and legal solutions, the full implementation of which mostly failed due to discrepancies in political culture. The adoption of such "western" standards, however, was mostly neglected when they pertained to best practices of minority protection, decentralization, or power-sharing. It appears in many cases that Romanian political elites and public officials have rather been preoccupied with generating the appearance that the country abides by its international commitments regarding minority protection as opposed to actually abiding by them. This is the reason why public institutions fail to fully implement minority rights–related international documents signed and ratified by Romania and the reason why state policies towards the Hungarian/Szekler community are characterized by general mistrust, linguistic inequality, restrictions on the use of symbols, and the securitization of autonomy aspirations. The long-term aim that has spanned various governments and different regimes has continued to be the establishment of an ethnically homogeneous nation state, an endeavour which is tangible in the practices of local and national public institutions, parliamentary debates and decisions, court judgements, fines and protocols of law enforcement agencies, or activities of the secret services and other actors of the Romanian state. All these different public institutions exhibited in their own peculiar way some typical traits of "nation-state thinking" in their conduct towards the Szekler/Hungarian minority: the majority is dominant and superior to the extent that it can impose on the minority separate forms of behaviour to follow and dissenting rules to abide by; autonomy aspirations are being construed as an imminent threat to the constitutional order and to public safety; exercising certain rights might be contingent on the approval of authorities in the case of the ethnic Hungarian minority but not for the ethnic majority (as we saw in the case of the DSF or with the use of the Hungarian language in public administration). Ultimately, it is the ethnic majority that is entitled to tell the minority how to live, what language to speak, which identity to pledge allegiance to, and what legal status to enjoy.

As described in section 1.7.2, territorial autonomy, on the one hand, is the demand of a minority community that wishes to obtain a more effective way of protecting its identity and participating in public life as a response to the widespread and multifaceted rights violations they have been subject to for many decades. On the other hand, and from a legal point of view, one would hardly find a legal construction that could be potentially more efficient in providing adequate and comprehensive solutions at once to all of the outlined rights violations and problems in minority–majority group-relations, then an autonomy arrangement. The appeal of territorial autonomy thus lies in the fact that it indeed possesses the capacity to solve or at least redress and remedy long-standing, complex problems in a single, sustainable framework, which, if implemented in good faith, would be mutually beneficial for both the minority as well as the majority community.

Irrespective of the unwillingness of the ethnic majority to accept the legitimacy of Szekler autonomy claims, the arguments of the preceding chapters prove that territorial autonomy as an institutional solution does not contradict the constitutional order of Romania. There are no provisions in the Romanian legal system whatsoever, which would constitute a legal obstacle to the creation of an autonomous administrative unit. The indivisibility clause (Art. 1 CR) and the eternity clause (Art. 152) of the Constitution of Romania, so frequently referred to in the autonomy discourse, are thus of no legal relevance and cannot be understood as an effective constitutional legal barrier. On the contrary, the notion of autonomy is not alien to the Romanian constitutional system at all, as it recognizes personal, functional, as well as a certain degree of territorial administrative autonomy.

The only existing obstacle to a Szekler autonomy arrangement is a political one. The assumption that autonomy contradicts the constitutional order and violates the unitary, indivisible, and national character of the state arises from the misinterpretation of the connection between state and autonomy. These misconceptions can be traced back to the historic resentment that is present in Romanian political culture towards Hungarians and the parallel nation-building processes of Hungarians and Romanians that have been unfolding for more than a century now. Fears of autonomy are also fuelled by weak rule of law traditions and insufficient experiences in democratic governance. The omnipresence of preferences for an ethnically homogenous nation state among Romanians, and the tacit agreement on full rejection of autonomy that comes with it, produces conceptual restraints, which disables relevant office holders to be receptive to alternative and possibly more effective ways the state could function, that is, less centralized. This is how referring to Art. 1 of the constitution becomes a mental shortcut to avoid a meaningful discussion on power-sharing, decentralization, and territorial autonomy. This is also where the inspiration came from to invite readers of this book to engage in a "mind-game" in order to deconstruct the "constitutional myth". What this writing intended to achieve was to shed a new light on prevailing Romanian doctrinal claims concerning the constitutionality of an autonomy aspiration and illustrate that a "simple" change in one's mindset can remove an unnecessary and unjustified, albeit seemingly robust, obstacle to a legitimate minority aspiration.

With this in mind, the most relevant conclusion that can be deducted from the different forms of legal entrenchment presented in this book is that in the presence of political will, minority claims can be accommodated even if the resolution requires the central state to resort to special legal measures. In the case of the Åland Islands, the autonomy statute was provided with a firm constitutional entrenchment and protection against unilateral amendment by the central governments. As an act of exception, this statute was unique in its kind and stood alone in the Finnish legal system for over seven decades. International entrenchment further strengthened this autonomy arrangement, given that the guarantor of the autonomy of the islands was the League of Nations. South Tyrol was equally special within the Italian constitutional system, on the one hand, because among the five regions with special statutes, it is the only one to have an international legal entrenchment through the Gruber-de Gasperi agreement, and, on the other hand, because in their case the autonomous competencies were granted on a provincial level, while in the other four cases autonomous powers were granted on the regional level. Both Åland and South Tyrol show the importance of active participation of the international community in facilitating a dialogue between a state and its constituent parts striving for greater self-rule. These examples, especially the case of South Tyrol, also show that kin-states can have a pivotal role in assisting the aspirations of their compatriots abroad.

The devolution of Scotland required the common law system of the UK to change and develop, including its pivotal doctrine on parliamentary sovereignty, which has been fine-tuned by the Sewel Convention. With the devolution process, the UK Parliament has chosen to exercise its legislative sovereignty in devolved matters through an elected body other than the UK Parliament and reinforced this decision in its political conventions.[458] Similarly, the Faroese case also shows the importance of political culture and political thinking in the establishment and functioning of an autonomy arrangement. The relations between Faroe and Denmark are developed under the auspices of equality, consensus building, and the respect of Faroese peculiarities, even though in the absence of a general constitutional entrenchment, there are no constitutional provisions that

458 Some scholars even argue that autonomy in Scotland and Northern Ireland defies a feature of the Parliamentary Sovereignty doctrine, namely that all statutes are of the same constitutional value. See: Tierney (2014), pp. 159–180.

would compel successive Danish governments to follow suit with this approach. The example of Gagauzia and the Hungarian Autonomous Province in Romania shows that territorial autonomy can be achieved within Central-Eastern Europe as well, even though most of the territorial autonomies of the continent can be found in western Europe. Parallel with the numerous flexible legal solutions that were mentioned, the case of the New Catalan Statute of Autonomy before the Constitutional Court of Spain showed the importance of how state institutions conceptualize and think of the constitutional framework, decentralization, and the aspirations of a national community. Judgement 31/2010 of the CCS showed that a different mindset might be enough to remove a perceived threat (greater autonomy to sub-state entities) by simply presenting an alternative interpretation of a given legal provision. This observation is particularly relevant in the case of Romania, where the political culture and the constitutional traditions are both ethnocentric.

That being said, the text of the Constitution of Romania is not, "all in all, ethnocentric in itself: it allows an opposite, pluralistic interpretation. What must be changed, therefore, is not the constitutional text but the ethnocentric mentality".[459] Indeed if one reads the Romanian constitution without an ethnocentric mindset and in line with international documents ratified by Romania, it is very much possible to adopt an interpretation of the constitution that is open to accommodate minority claims on regional power-sharing.

One can draw inspiration from the examples and solutions mentioned in this book and apply them to the Szekler case. The DL could blend into the Romanian legal system as an organic law based on Art. 117 (3) of the Constitution. Besides this semi-general constitutional entrenchment, a regional entrenchment would also be present as the DL stipulates that any amendment to the statute should be approved in a local referendum before it can enter into force. While such an arrangement could be flexible enough to follow the changes that inevitably occur in group relations over time, it might also make it doubtful whether such an arrangement would be sufficient enough to protect the local Szekler community in the long run and to ensure the effective participation of the citizens of the autonomous polity in public decision-making. Due to the weakly embedded nature of democratic political culture, a political entrenchment that functions effectively in Denmark or the UK cannot be achieved within a reasonable time-frame in Romania. For this reason, an international entrenchment of some kind would be desirable to counterbalance the possible shortcomings of the lack of a general

459 Selejan-Gutan (2016) *Supra note*, p. 43.

constitutional entrenchment. Theoretically, such a treaty-based entrenchment would be possible under the auspices of an international organization (as it happened in the case of the Åland-islands) or can take a bilateral form, as concluded between Hungary and Romania.[460] However, as noted by an author, it is more likely for such internationalized solutions to come into being, and work effectively, if they stay "outside the realm of strict sovereignty over land",[461] which is how the Romanian party tends to perceive the question of territorial autonomy. Furthermore, as I explained in the fourth chapter, an additional difficulty for any international entrenchment is the reluctance of the international community to engage in such issues, which is paired with a non-existent bilateral dialogue on the topic between Romania and Hungary.

Even so, the bottom line is that "the constitution is not a straitjacket".[462] It is a human construction. A product of collective choices and political struggles that can be reshaped by members of the community that give legitimacy to it as a social contract that inevitably changes over time. Given the simple fact that popular sovereignty rests with all citizens of any democratic country, citizens can at any given time invoke their constituent power and aspire to achieve changes in the exercise of public authority. As Pitkin put it: "constitutions are made, not found. They do not fall miraculously from the sky or grow naturally on the vine", which is why there is "nothing particularly sacred or inviolable about a constitution". Drafters of constitutions were "men, not gods", and the same power they exercised in framing the constitution is latent in present generations as well,

460 It should be pointed out here that Romania was keen to include in the Annexes of the Bilateral Treaty between Hungary and Romania on Understanding, Cooperation and Good Neighbourhood a declaration stipulating that Recommendation 1201 of the CoE – one of the international documents referred to in this treaty – does not refer to collective rights, nor does it impose upon the parties any obligations to grant any right to a special status of territorial autonomy based on ethnic criteria. This declaration, however, does not dispose of a right under this bilateral treaty to autonomy based on paragraph 35 of the Copenhagen Document, another international document referred to in the treaty. Additionally, as mentioned earlier, Romania pledged to base its policy regarding the protection of minorities on the principles laid down in Recommendation 1201 (1993) as part of their application for membership in the CoE. Art. 17.2 of PACE Resolution 1115 (1997) clearly stipulates that member states should continue honouring commitments entered into by the authorities of member states on their accession to the CoE.

461 Nicolini et al. (2016), p. 141.

462 Supreme Court of Canada, Reference re Secession of Quebec, [1998] 2 S.C.R. 217, at para. 150.

"in our ordinary human capacity for creative action, particularly for collective, shared creativity".[463]

As a closing remark, one could refer to the thoughts of Count Esterházy János[464] regarding good minority policy, which is also applicable to regional autonomy: "Righteous national minority policy is a considerably bigger security coefficient than a number of written laws, it is more secure than any Maginot line, for nothing makes a state stronger than the fact that not only the majority citizens but also the minority citizens feel completely at home".[465]

---

463 Pitkin (1987), p. 168.

464 Count János Esterházy was an ethnic Hungarian politician in Czechoslovakia during the inter-war era as well as in the First Slovak Republic (a puppet state of Nazi Germany). He was the only parliamentarian of the First Slovak Republic who voted against the law on the deportation of Jews in 1942. Based on fabricated allegations, he was sentenced to 10 years of forced labour in Siberia. Additionally, the Slovak National Court sentenced him to death in his absence for contribution to the dissolution of the Czechoslovak state. He was not executed due to a presidential pardon but was transferred around instead from prison to prison over the next 10 years. He died in prison in 1957.

465 Quoted by Kardos (2015), p. 40.

# Appendix

**Tab. 1:** Demographic trends of Hungarian minority communities living in countries adjacent to Hungary (1989–2011)

| Country | 1989–1992 | 2001–2002 | % | 2011 | % |
|---|---|---|---|---|---|
| Austria | 33,459 | 40,583 | 21.3 | ~ 60,000 | 47.8 |
| Croatia | 22,355 | 16,595 | -25.8 | 14,048 | -15.3 |
| Romania | 1,624,959 | 1,434,377 | -11.7 | 1,268,444 | -11.6 |
| Serbia | 344,147 | 293,299 | -14.8 | 251,136 | -14.4 |
| Slovakia | 567,296 | 520,528 | -8.2 | 458,467 | -11.9 |
| Slovenia | 8,503 | 6,243 | -26.6 | ~ 5,000 | -19.9 |
| Ukraine | 155,711 | 151,516 | -2.7 | ~ 141,000 | -6.9 |
| Total | 2,756,430 | 2,463,141 | -10.61 | 2,198,095 | -10.76 |

Source: Répás (ed.) (2013), p. 24.

**Tab. 2:** Proportion of GDP/capita in the CDR counties, relative to the CDR's GDP/capita average (in %)

| County | 2007 | 2008 | 2009 | 2010 | 2011 |
|---|---|---|---|---|---|
| CDR | 100 | 100 | 100 | 100 | 100 |
| Alba/Fehér | 108 | 103 | 102 | 99 | 107 |
| Brasov/Brassó | 122 | 124 | 118 | 122 | 126 |
| Covasna/ Kovászna | 81 | 78 | 80 | 80 | 74 |
| Harghita/Hargita | 82 | 81 | 81 | 81 | 77 |
| Mures/Maros | 83 | 82 | 85 | 83 | 80 |
| Sibiu/Szeben | 109 | 115 | 117 | 119 | 116 |

Source: Annex FB 3 of the Intervention of Kovászna County in Case T-529/13. http://nemzetiregiok.eu/dokumentumok/t-529-13.sz.per-kovaszna-megye-beavatkozasi-kerelme.doc, accessed: 2021.03.21.

**Tab. 3:** Annual increment of GDP/capita in the counties of the Central Development Region

| County | 2008 (Euro) | 2013 (Euro) | Increment |
|---|---|---|---|
| Alba/Fehér | 6,318 | 7,111 | 12.5 % |
| Brasov/Brassó | 7,285 | 8,681 | 19.2 % |
| Covasna/Kovászna | 4,923 | 5,009 | 1.7 % |
| Harghita/Hargita | 5,013 | 5,243 | 4.6 % |
| Mures/Maros | 5,269 | 5,953 | 12.9 % |
| Sibiu/Szeben | 7,25 | 8,011 | 10.9 % |

Source: Annex FB 4 of the Intervention of Kovászna County in Case T-529/13. http://nemzetiregiok.eu/dokumentumok/t-529-13.sz.per-kovaszna-megye-beavatkozasi-kerelme.doc, accessed: 2021.03.21.

**Fig. 1:** Administrative borders of the Austro-Hungarian Empire

Source: Hungarian version available at Bereznay (2011), p. 173 (English version of the illustration was received directly from historian-cartographer András Bereznay)

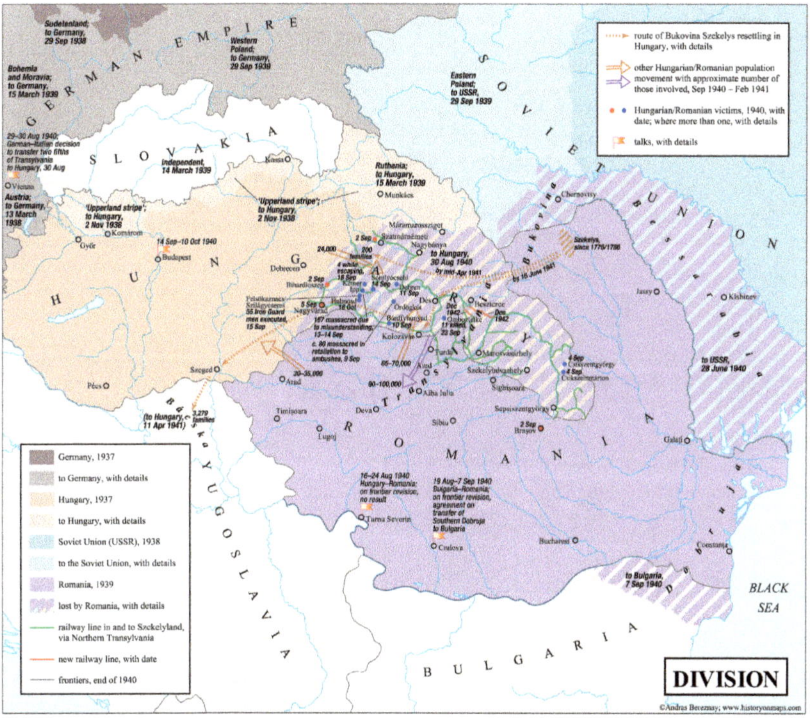


**Fig. 2:** Territorial changes due to the 1st and 2nd Vienna Arbitrations in 1938 and 1940

Source: Hungarian version available at Bereznay (2011), p. 195 (English version of the illustration was received directly from historian-cartographer András Bereznay)

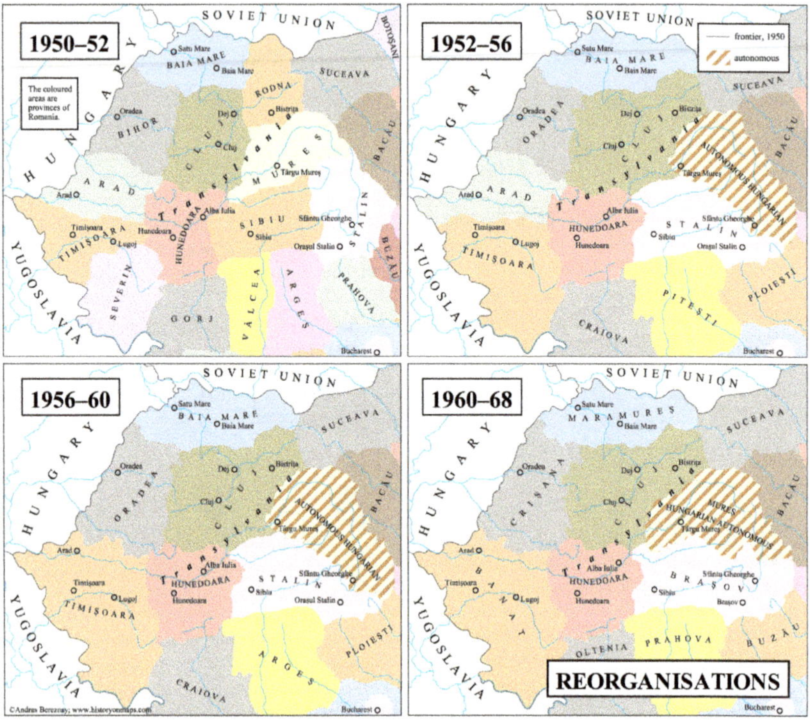


**Fig. 3:** Changing borders of the Hungarian Autonomous Province in communist Romania

Source: Hungarian version available at Bereznay (2011), p. 205 (English version of the illustration was received directly from historian-cartographer András Bereznay)

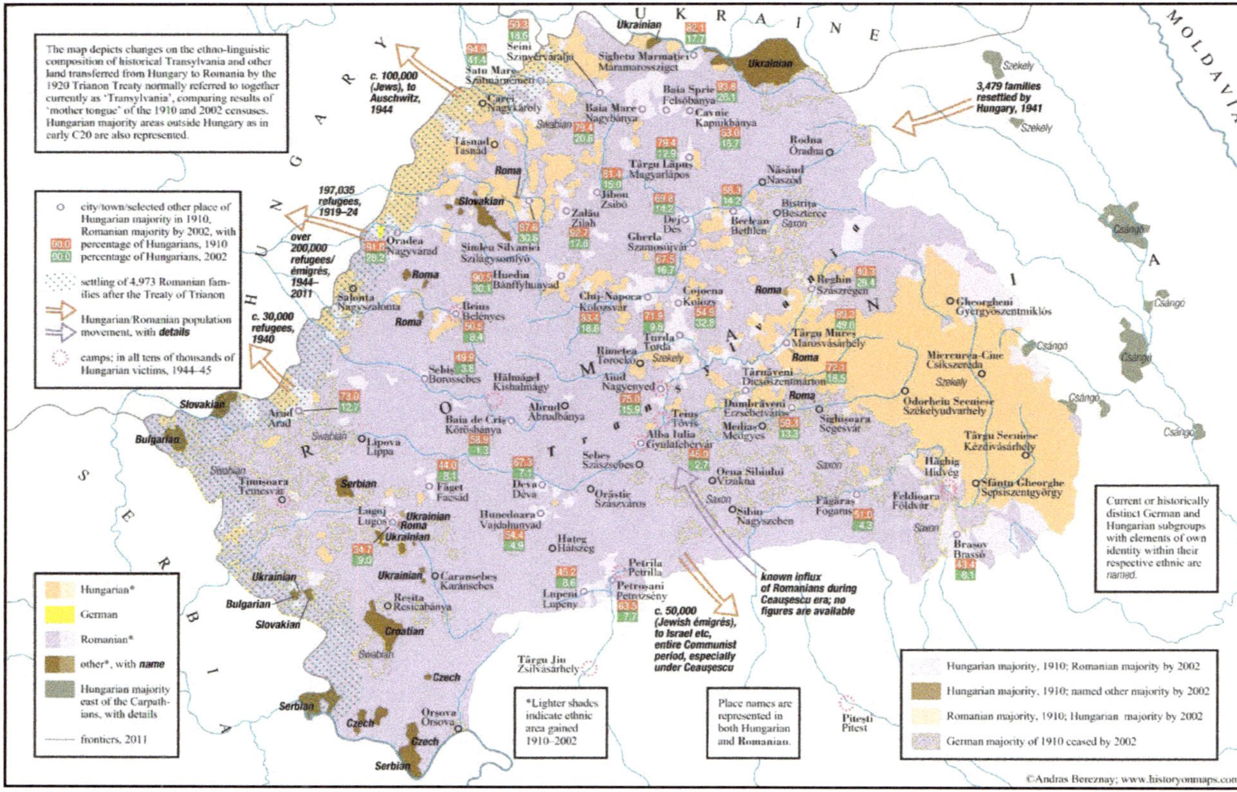


**Fig. 4:** Changes in the ethno-linguistic composition of Transylvania comparing results of the 1910 and 2002 censuses

Source: Illustration received from historian-cartographer András Bereznay

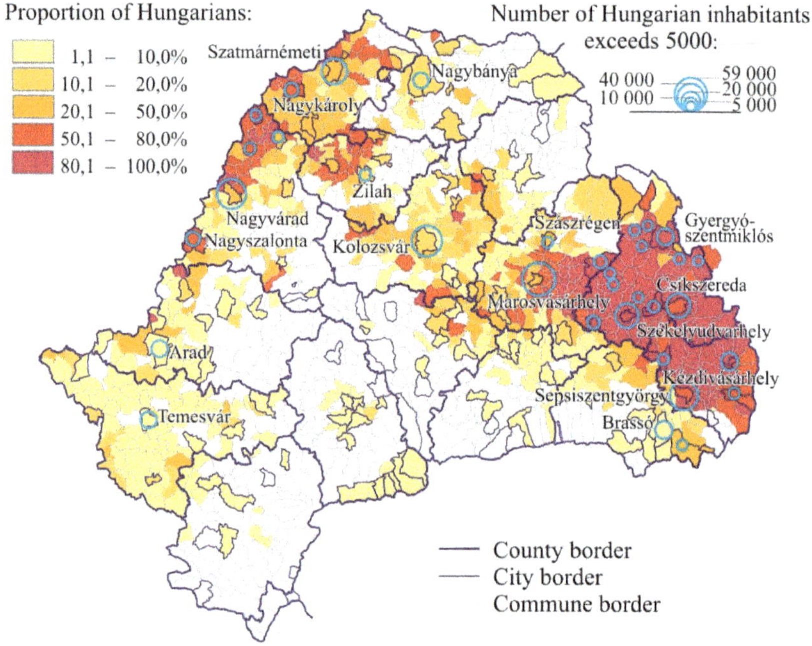


**Fig. 5:** Ethnic map of Transylvania (based on the census of 2011)

Source: Illustration received directly from cartographer László Sebők

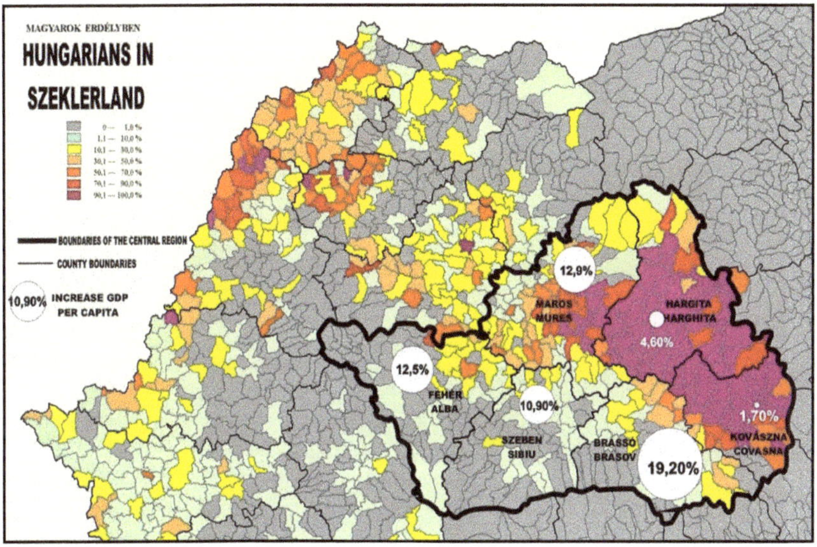


**Fig. 6:** Ethnic map of Transylvania, juxtaposed with borders of the administrative and the Central-Romanian NUTS II Development Region (with bold outlines), as well as the increment of their GDP per capita income 2007–2013

Source: https://www.erdely.ma/a-eu-kohezios-politikajanak-kudarca-a-kozep-romaniai-fejlesztesi-regioban/, accessed: 2021.03.21

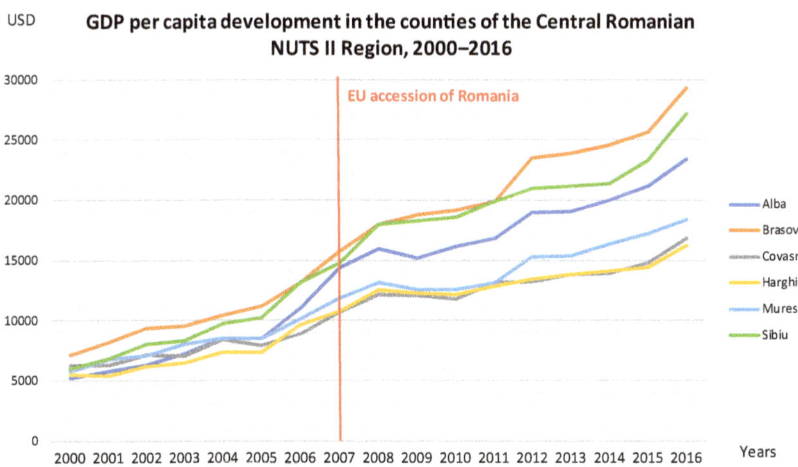


**Fig. 7:** GDP per capita development in the counties of the Central-Romanian NUTS II Region, calculated in current price USD based on purchasing power parity (2000–2016)

Source: Own chart based on OECD statistics, available at: stats.oecd.org, accessed: 2021.03.21

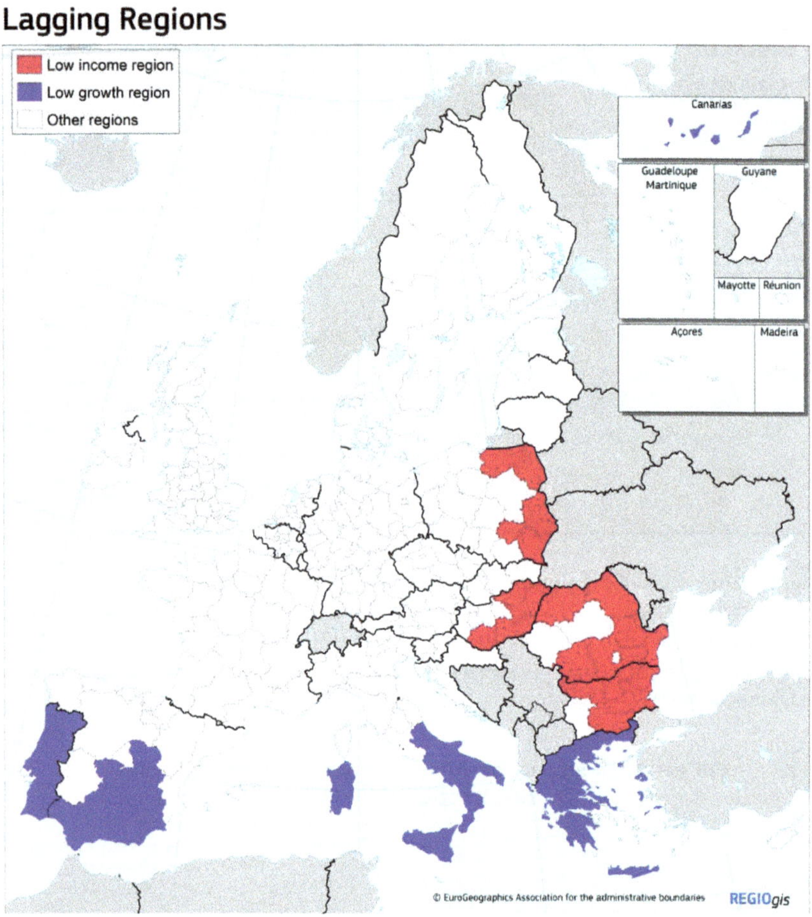


**Fig. 8:** Low income (red), low growth (blue), and other NUTS II regions (white)

Source: European Commission (2017), p. 1, available at: https://ec.europa.eu/regional_policy/sources/docgener/studies/pdf/lagging_regions%20report_en.pdf, accessed: 2021.03.21

# Bibliography

## Scientific Literature


Alfredsson, Gudmundur (1996): Different Forms of and Claims to the Right of Self-Determination. In: Clark, D. & Williamson, R. (eds.): *Self-Determination – International Perspectives.* London: Palgrave Macmillan, pp. 58–86.

Åkermark, Sia Spiliopoulou (2013): Internal Self-Determination and the Role of Territorial Autonomy as a Tool for the Resolution of Ethno-Political Disputes. In: *International Journal on Minority and Group Rights, 20(1)*, pp. 5–25.

Andreescu, Liviu (2007 May): The Construction of Orthodox Churches in Post-Communist Romania. In: *Europe-Asia Studies, 59(3)*. Glasgow: University of Glasgow, pp. 451–480.

Andriescu, Monica (2007): Rhetorical Patterns on Minority Language and Education Rights in Post-Communist Romania: Finding the Middle Ground (1996–2004). In: *CEU Political Science Journal, 2(4)*. Budapest: CEU.

Arday Lajos (2010): *Kisebbségek, kisebbség politikák Kelet-Közép Európában.* Available at: http://www.grotius.hu/doc/pub/KHXPKJ/dke_02_ma_kk_arday.pdf, accessed: 2015.04.25.

Arzoz, Xabier (2012): New Developments in Spanish Federalism. In: *Dans L' Europe en Formation, 2012/1(n° 363)*, pp. 179–188.

Bakacsi Gyula et al. (2006): *Final Report on the Results of GLOBE-Romania Project.* Manuscript.

Bakk Miklós (2004): Az autonómia-tervek két szakasza Erdélyben 1989 után. In: *Magyar Kisebbség, IX évf. 2004. 1–2 (31–32.) sz.* Kolozsvár: Jakabffy Elemér Alapítvány.

Bakk Miklós (2010): Politikai közösség és identitás az alkotmányban. In: *Magyar Kisebbség XV. évf. 2010. 1–2. (55–56.) sz.* Kolozsvár: Jakabffy Elemér Alapítvány, pp.15–44.

Barelli, Mauro, Guliyeva, Gulara, Errico, Stefania & Pentassuglia, Gaetano (2011). *Minority Groups and Litigation: A Review of Developments in International and Regional Jurisprudence.* Minority Rights Group Guide Series (ed.), London: Minority Rights Group International. Available at: https://www.refworld.org/docid/4ed6105b7e.html, accessed: 2021.03.21.

Bárdi Nándor (2004): Javaslatok, modellek az erdélyi kérdés kezelésére – A Magyar elképzelések 1918–1940. In: *Konfliktusok és kezelésük Közép-Európában, TLA, pp. 137–180* and *Magyar Kisebbség 2004. 1–2. sz., pp. 329–376.* Kolozsvár: Jakabffy Elemér Alapítvány.

Bárdi Nándor, Fedinec Csilla & Szarka László (eds.) (2008): *Kisebbségi Magyar közösségek a 20. században*. Budapest: Gondolat - MTA Etnikai- Nemzeti Kisebbségkutató Intézet.

Beauséjour, Anthony (2018): *Secession and Secessionist Movements: A Comparative Impact Analysis of Indivisibility and Secession Constitutional Clauses*. LLM dissertation, Cambridge: University of Cambridge.

Benedikter, Thomas (2007): *The World's Working Regional Autonomies – An Introduction and Comparative Analysis*. London, New York, Delhi: Anthem Critical Studies.

Beran, Harry (1984): A Liberal Theory of Secession. In: *Political Studies, 32(1)*, pp. 21–31.

Bereznay András (2011): *Erdély történelmi atlasza*. Somorja: Méry Ratio.

Bernhardt, Rudolf (1981): Federalism and Autonomy. In: Dinšṭein, Yôrām (ed.): *Models of Autonomy*. New Brunswick, New Jersey: Transaction Books, Rutgers.

Bianchi, Andrea (2008): Human Rights and the Magic of Jus Cogens. In: *The European Journal of International Law, 19(3)*, pp. 491–508.

Blokker, Paul (2013): Constitutional Amendment in Romania: Analyses and Perspectives. In: *Romanian Journal of Comparative Law, 3(2)*, pp. 187–204.

Bolleyer, Nicole, Swenden, Wilfried & McEwen, Nicola (2014): A Theoretical Perspective on Multi-Level Systems in Europe: Constitutional Power and Partisan Conflict. In: *Comparative European Politics (2014) 12*. University of Copenhagen, Denmark; New York University, USA: Palgrave Macmillan, pp. 367–383.

Bonell, Lukas & Winkler, Ivo (2006): *Südtirols Autonomie*. Bozen: Herausgegeben von der Südtiroler Landesregierung.

Bottoni, Stefano (2008): *Sztálin a Székelyeknél. A Magyar Autonóm Tartomány története. (1952–1960)*. Csíkszereda: Pro-Print Könyvkiadó.

Boyron, Sophie (2013): *The Constitution of France: A Contextual Analysis (Constitutional Systems of the World)*. Oxford: Hart Publishing.

Bölöny József (1940): A román alkotmányok és a kisebbségi kérdés. In: *Kisebbségi körlevél, 1940. évi szeptember havi szám*. Kecskemét: Első Kecskeméti Hírlapkiadó és Nyomda Rt, pp. 1–12.

Brubaker, Rogers (1996): National Minorities, Nationalizing States, and External National Homelands in the New Europe. In: *Nationalism Reframed: Nationhood and the National Question in the New Europe*. Cambridge: Cambridge University Press, pp. 55–76.

Brunner, Georg & Küpper, Herbert (2004): Európai autonómia-megoldások: A kisebbségi önkormányzatok autonómia-modelljeinek tipológiája, In: *Magyar Kisebbség. 2004. 1–2. sz.* Kolozsvár: JakabffyElemérAlapítvány, pp. 466–498.

Cassese, Antonio (1995): *Self-Determination of Peoples: A Legal Reappraisal.* Cambridge, New York: Cambridge University Press.

Cornell, Svante E. (2002): Autonomy as a Source of Conflict: Caucasian Conflicts in Theoretical Perspective. In: *World Politics, 54*, pp. 245–276.

Cunningham, Kathleen Gallagher (2007): *Divided and Conquered: Why States and Selfdetermination Groups Fail in Bargaining Over Autonomy*. San Diego: University of California Electronic Theses and Dissertations.

Dabis Attila (2013): Dél-Tirol Autonómia-statútuma. In: *Magyar Kisebbség 3–4. szám*, pp. 43–95.

Dabis Attila (2021): Sustainability of Cultural Diversity and the Failure of Cohesion Policy in the EU: The Case of Szeklerland. In: Bisello, A., Vettorato, D., Haarstad, H., Borsboom-van Beurden, J. (eds.): *Smart and Sustainable Planning for Cities and Regions. Results of SSPCR 2019. Green Energy and Technology.* Cham: Springer, pp. 355–369.

Daftary, Farimah (2004): Insular Autonomy; a Framework for Conflict Resolution? Corsica and the Åland-Islands. In: Schenker, Ulrich Wolff, Stefan (Eds.): *Managing and Settling Ethnic Conflicts: Perspectives on Successes and Failures in Europe, Africa, and Asia*. New York: Palgrave Macmillan.

Dawn, Oliver & Fusaro, Carlo (2011): *How Constitutions Change: A Comparative Study*. Oxford: Hart Publishing.

Dimulescu, Valentina, Pop, Raluca & Doroftei, Irina Mădălina (2013): Risks of Corruption and the Management of EU Funds in Romania. In: *Romanian Journal of Political Science, Summer 2013, 13(1)*, pp. 101–123.

Emich Gusztáv, Edvi, Illés Aladár & Halász, Albert (Eds.) (1920): *Magyarország Gazdasági Térképekben – 1920/The Economies of Hungary in Maps – 1920.* Első reprint kiadás. Budapest: Szabadkéz Kft.

Ferrari, Paolo (2009a): *Das neu Autonomiestatut. 14., ergänzte Auflage.* Bozen: Südtiroler Landesregierung. Available at: https://www.provinz.bz.it/lpa/download/statut_dt.pdf, accessed: 2021.07.27.

Ferrari, Paolo (ed.) (2009b): *Südtirol Handbuch 27.* Überarbeitete Auflage. Bozen: Südtiroler Landesregierung. Available at: https://www.provinz.bz.it/politik-recht-aussenbeziehungen/autonomie/downloads/Suedtirol_Handbuch.pdf, accessed: 2021.07.27.

Friend, Julius W. (2012): *Stateless Nations: Western European Regional Nationalisms and the Old Nations*. Houndsmills: Palgrave McMillan.

Ghai, Yash (2011): Ålands Autonomy in Comparative Perspective. In: Åkermark, Sia Spiliopoulou (ed.): *The Åland Example and Its Components – Relevance for International Conflict Resolution*. Mariehamn: The Åland Islands Peace Institute.

Ghai, Yash (2013): Introduction: Nature and Origins of Autonomy. In: Ghai, Yash & Woodman, Sophia (eds.): *Practising Self-Government. A Comparative Study of Autonomous Regions*. Cambridge: Cambridge University Press, pp. 1–31.

Ghai, Yash & Woodman, Sophia (2013): Comparative Perspectives on Institutional Frameworks for Autonomy. In Ghai, Yash & Woodman, Sophia (eds.): *Practising Self-Government. A Comparative Study of Autonomous Regions*. Cambridge: Cambridge University Press, pp. 449–486.

Gilbert, Geoff (2002): Autonomy and Minority Groups: A Right in International Law. In: *Cornell International Law Journal, 35(2), Article 2*, pp. 307–353.

Guibernau, Montserrat (2006): National Identity, Devolution and Secession in Canada, Britain and Spain. In: *Nations and Nationalism 12(1)*. New Jersey: Blackwell Publishing Ltd., pp. 51–76.

Guțan, Manuel (2013a): The Challenges of the Romanian Constitutional Tradition I. Between Ideological Transplant and Institutional Metamorphoses. In: *Journal of Constitutional History, Issue 25*, pp. 223–252.

Guțan, Manuel (2013b): The Challenges of the Romanian Constitutional Tradition II. Between Constitutional Transplant and (Failed) Cultural Engineering. In: *Journal of Constitutional History, Issue 26*, pp. 217–241.

Hannikainen, Lauri (1988): *Peremptory Norms in International Law. Historical Development, Criterea, Present Status*. Helsinki: Finnish Lawyers` Publishing Company.

Hannikainen, Lauri (1997): The International Legal Basis of the Autonomy and Swedish Character of the Åland Islands. In: Hannikainen, Lauri & Horn, Frank (eds.): *Autonomy and Demilitarisation in International Law: The Aland Islands in a Changing Europe*. The Hague: Kluwer Law International.

Hannikainen, Lauri (1998): Self-Determination and Autonomy in International Law. In: Suksi, Markku (ed.): *Autonomy: Applications and Implications*. The Hague; Boston: Kluwer Law International, pp. 79–95.

Hannum, Hurst (1996): *Autonomy, Sovereignty, and Self-Determination. The Accommodation of Conflicting Rights, Revised Edition*. Philadelphia: University of Pennsylvania Press.

Hannum, Hurst & Lillich, Richard B. (1981): The Concept of Autonomy in International Law. In: *American Journal of International Law, 74(4), Oct 80*. Washington DC: American Society of International Law, pp. 858–889.

Hein, Michael (2015): The Fight against Government Corruption in Romania: Irreversible Results or Sisyphean Challenge? In: *Europe-Asia Studies, 67(5)*, pp. 747–776.

Heintze, Hans-Joachim (1998): On the Legal Understanding of Autonomy. In: Suksi, Markku (ed.): *Autonomy: Applications and Implications*. The Hague; Boston: Kluwer Law International, pp. 6–32.

Henders, Susan J. (2010): *Territoriality, Asymmetry, and Autonomy – Catalonia, Corsica, Hong Kong, and Tibet*. New York: Palgrave Macmillan.

Hepburn, Eve (2014): Forging Autonomy in a Unitary State: The Åland Islands in Finland, In: *Comparative European Politics (2014) 12*. University of Copenhagen, Denmark; New York University, USA: Palgrave Macmillan, pp. 468–487.

Himsworth, Chris (2013): The Autonomy of Devolved Scotland. In: Ghai, Yash & Woodman, Sophia (eds.): *Practising Self-Government. A Comparative Study of Autonomous Regions*. Cambridge: Cambridge University Press, pp. 349–382.

Huntington, Samuel P. (1996): *The Clash of Civilizations and the Remaking of World Order*. [First Edition]. London: Simon & Schuster.

Ibarra, Pedro & Irujo, Xabier (eds.) (2011): *Basque Political Systems*. University of Nevada, Reno: Center for Basque Studies.

Kapitány, Balázs (2015): Ethnic Hungarians in the Neighbouring Countries. In: Monostori, Judit, Őri, Péter & Spéder, Zsolt (eds.): *Demographic Portrait of Hungary 2015*. Budapest: Hungarian Demographic Research Institute.

Kardos Gábor (2006): Role for the Kin-states? In: Osamu Ieda (ed.): *Beyond Sovereignty: From Status Law to Transnational Citizenship?* Hokkaido: Slavic Research Center, pp. 127–137.

Kardos Gábor (2015): Fear of Autonomy for Minorities. In: Láncos Petra Lea, Varga Réka, Molnár Tamás & Szabó Marcel (eds.): *Hungarian Yearbook of International Law and European Law 2014*. The Hague: Eleven International Publishing, pp. 35–43.

Kincses Előd (1990): *Marosvásárhely fekete márciusa*. Budapest: Püski.

Kiss Tamás (2015): Marginalizáció, etnikai párhuzamosság és aszimmetrikus akkomodáció. Az erdélyi magyar közösséget érintő társadalmi és politikai folyamatok. In: *Magyar Kisebbség. XX. évf. 12. (75–76.) sz.*, pp. 30–64. Kolozsvár: Jakabffy Elemér Alapítvány.

Kiss Tamás, Barna Gergő & Székely István Gergő (2013): A társadalomépítéstől a klientúra-építésig. Az RMDSZ és a magyar választók közötti kapcsolódás átalakulása. In: *Magyar Kisebbség 68. sz. = 18. évf. (2013.) 2. sz.*, pp. 7–40. Kolozsvár: Jakabffy Elemér Alapítvány.

Kiss Tamás, Csata István & Toró Tibor (2020): *Regionális Barométer 2019. Fejlődési idealizmus, regionális identitások, korrupciópercepció, demokráciafelfogás és magyarellenesség Romániában.* Kolozsvár/Sepsiszentgyörgy: Székelyföldi Közpolitikai Intézet/Bálványos Instézet.

Kocsis Károly (2013): Historical Predecessors and Current Geographical Possibilities of Ethnic Based Territorial Autonomies in the Carpathian Basin. In: *Autonomies in Europe: Solutions and Challenges*. Budapest: Nemzetpolitikai Kutatóintezet, L`Harmattan.

Krasner, Stephen D. (1999): *Sovereignty: Organized Hypocrisy.* Princeton: Princeton University.

Lapidoth, Ruth (1997): *Autonomy – Flexible Solutions to Ethnic Conflicts.* Washington D.C.: US Institute of Peace Press.

Larsen, Bárður & á Rógvi, Kári (2012): A New Faroese Constitution? – Faroe Islands between Parliamentary Sovereignty and Sub-Sovereign Constitutionalism, between Statutory Positivism and Pragmatic Reasoning. In: *The Yearbook of Polar Law, IV(1)*, pp. 341–363.

Lauterpacht, Hersch (1958): Some Observations on the Prohibition of 'Non Liquet' and the Completeness of the Legal Order. In: F. M. van Asbeck (ed.): *Symbolae Verzijl: Présentées au Prof J.H.W. Verzijl, à l'occasion de son LXX-ième anniversaire*. The Hague: Nijhoff, pp. 196–221.

Légaré, André & Suksi, Markku (2008): Rethinking the Forms of Autonomy at the Dawn of the 21st Century. In: *International Journal on Minority and Group Rights, 15(2)*, pp. 143–155. Leiden: Brill Publishing.

Leyland, Peter (2012): *The Constitution of the United Kingdom: A Contextual Analysis.* (Constitutional Systems of the World). Oxford: U.K. Hart.

Mackinder, Halford John (1904 April): The Geographical Pivot of History. In: *The Geographical Journal, 23(4)*. London: Royal Geographical Society.

Mentzelopoulo, Maria Margarita & Dumbrava, Costica (2018): *Acquisition and Loss of Citizenship in EU Member States – Key Trends and Issues.* Brussels: European Parliamentary Research Service. Available at: https://www.europarl.europa.eu/RegData/etudes/BRIE/2018/625116/EPRS_BRI(2018)625116_EN.pdf, accessed: 2021.03.18.

Miklósné Zakar Andrea (2010): *Interetnikus értelmiségi diskurzusok az erdélyi autonómiáról.* Doktori Értekezés. Győr: Széchenyi István Tudományegyetem.

Moore, Will H. (2002): Ethnic Minorities and Foreign Policy. In: *SAIS Review, XXII(2) (Summer–Fall 2002)*, pp. 77–91.

Packer, John (1999): Problems in Defining Minorities. In: Bowring, Bill & Fottrell, Deirdre (eds.): *Minority and Group Rights in the New Millennium.* The Hague: Martinus Nijhoff Publishers, pp. 223–273.

Palermo, Francesco (2007): Legal Solutions to Complex Societies: The Law of Diversity. In: Ruiz Vieytez, Eduardo Javier & Dunbar, Robert (eds.): *Human Rights and Diversity: New Challenges for Plural Societies*. Bilbao: Humanitarian Net, University of Deusto, pp. 63–83.

Payero-López, Lucía & Nimni, Ephraim (2018): The Liberal Democratic Deficit in Minority Representation: The Case of Spain. In: Pentassuglia, Gaetano (ed.): *Ethno-Cultural Diversity and Human Rights: Challenges and Critiques*. Leiden, Boston: Brill Nijhoff, pp. 90–121.

Peterlini, Oskar (2013): Foundations and Institutions of South Tyrol's autonomy. In: Ghai, Yash & Woodman, Sophia (eds.): *Practising Self-Government. A Comparative Study of Autonomous Regions*. Cambridge: Cambridge University Press, pp. 118–162.

Peterlini, Oskar (2017): Österreich-Italien 1992 – Streitbeilegung zu Südtirol vor der UNO, dem Europarat und dem IGH – Wiederveröffentlichung der Originaldokumente und der diplomatischen Noten anlässlich der 25 Jahrfeier. Auszüge aus: Peterlini, Oskar (2000): *Autonomie und Minderheitenschutz in: Südtirol und im Trentino*; und (2012): *Südtirols Autonomie und die Verfassungsreformen Italiens*.

Pitkin, Hanna Fenichel (1987): The Idea of a Constitution. In: *Journal of Legal Education, 37(2)*, pp. 167–169.

Prina, Federica (2016): Shrinking Autonomy for Tatarstan and Gagauzia: The Perils of Flexible Institutional Design. In: Nicolini, Matteo, Palermo, Francesco & Milano, Enrico (eds.): *Law, Territory, and Conflict Resolution: Law as a Problem and Law as a Solution. Series: Studies in Territorial and Cultural Diversity Governance (6)*. Leiden: Brill, pp. 244–269.

Radbruch, Gustave (1956): *Rechtsphilosophie* [5. Auflage]. Stuttgart: Koehler.

Répás Zsuzsanna (ed.) (2013): *Magyar Nemzetpolitika – A Nemzetpolitika Stratégiai Kerete*. Budapest: Magyar Közlöny Lap- és Könyvkiadó Kft.

Roe Paul (2004): Securitization and Minority Rights: Conditions of Desecuritization. In: *Security Dialogue. 2004; 35(3)*, pp. 279-294.Roper, Steven D. (2006): The Influence of Party Patronage and State Finance on Electoral Outcomes: Evidence from Romania. In: *Journal of Communist Studies and Transition Politics, 22(3)*, pp. 362–382.

Rosas, Allan (1993): Internal Self-Determination. In: Tomuschat, Christian (ed.): *Modern Law of Self-Determination*. Boston: Martinus Nijhoff Publishers, pp. 225–252.

Salat Levente, Constantin, Sergiu, Osipov, Alexander & Székely István Gergő (eds.) (2014): *Autonomy Arrangements around the World: A Collection of Well and Lesser-Known Cases*. Kolozsvár/Cluj-Napoca: Romanian Institute for Research on National Minorities.

Schulte, Felix (2015): Conflict Regulation through Self-Rule – Success Factors of Territorial Autonomy Systems. In: *Report from the Åland Islands Peace Institute, Nr. 1, April 2015*. Available at: http://www.peace.ax/images/FINAL_Report_1_2015_FS_online.pdf, accessed: 2016.04.25.

Selejan-Gutan, Bianca (2016): *The Constitution of Romania: A Contextual Analysis* (Constitutional Systems of the World series). Oxford: Hart Publishing.

Shaykhutdinov, Renat (2010): Give Peace a Chance: Nonviolent Protest and the Creation of Territorial Autonomy Arrangements. In: *Journal of Peace Research, 47(2)*, pp. 179–191.

Smith, David J. & Hiden, John (2012): *Ethnic Diversity and the Nation State. National Cultural Autonomy Revisited*. London and New York: Routledge.

Smooha, Sammy (2001): The Model of Ethnic Democracy. In: *ECMI Working Paper # 13*. Flensburg: European Centre for Minority Issues.

Stanomir, Ioan et al. (2010): A romániai politikai és alkotmányos rendszert elemző államfői bizottság jelentése – a jogállam megerősítése érdekében. In: *Magyar Kisebbség, XV. évf. 2010. 1–2. (55–56.) sz.* Kolozsvár: Jakabffy Elemér Alapítvány, pp. 9–89.

Stepan, Alfred, Linz, Juan & Yadav, Yogendra (2011): *Crafting State-Nations: India and Other Multinational Democracies*. Baltimore: Johns Hopkins University Press.

Stone, Julius (1964): *Legal System and Lawyers' Reasonings*. Stanford: Stanford University Press.

Suksi, Markku (1993): *Bringing in the People: A Comparison of Constitutional Forms and Practices of the Referendum*. Dordrecht: Martinus Nijhoff.

Suksi, Markku (ed.) (1998): On the Entrenchment of Autonomy, In: Suksi, Markku (ed.): *Autonomy: Applications and Implications*. The Hague; Boston: Kluwer Law International, pp. 151–171.

Suksi, Markku (1999): *On the Constitutional Features of Estonia*. Turku/Åbo: Åbo Akademis Tryckeri.

Suksi, Markku (2011): *Sub-State Governance through Territorial Autonomy: A Comparative Study in Constitutional Law of Powers*. Berlin Heidelberg: Springer Verlag.

Summers, James (2013): The Internal and External Aspects of Self-Determination Reconsidered. In: *Statehood and Self-Determination*. Cambridge: Cambridge University Press, pp. 229–249.

Szalayné Sándor Erzsébet (2003): *A kisebbségvédelem nemzetközi jogi intézményrendszere a 20. században*. Budapest: MTA – KKI.

Thompson, Wayne C. (1998): Citizenship and Borders: Legacies of Soviet Empire in Estonia. In: *Journal of Baltic Studies, 29(2), Summer 1998*, pp. 109–134.

Thornberry, Patrick (1993): The Democratic or Internal Aspect of Self-determination with Some Remarks on Federalism. In: Tomuschat, Christian (ed.): *Modern Law of Self-determination*. Boston: Martinus Nijhoff Publishers, pp. 101–138.

Tierney, Stephen (2014): Flexible Accommodation: Another Case of British Exceptionalism? In: Lluch, Jaime (ed.): *Constitutionalism and the Politics of Accommodation in Multinational Democracies*. New York, Basingstoke: Palgrave Macmillan, pp. 159–179.

Tkacik, Michael (2008 June): Characteristics of Forms of Autonomy. In: *International Journal on Minority & Group Rights, 15(2/3)*. Nacogdoches: Stephen F. Austin State University SFA Scholar Works, pp. 369–401.

Tomuschat, Christian (1992): Democratic Pluralism: The Right to Political Opposition. In: Rosas, Allan & Helgesen, Jan (eds.): *The Strength of Diversity and Pluralist Democracy*. Dordrecht: Nijhoff, pp. 27–48.

Tóth Norbert (2014): *A kisebbségi területi autonómia elmélete és gyakorlata: Nemzetközi jogi és összehasonlító jogi analízis*. Budapest: L'Harmattan.

Turp, Daniel & Sanjaume-Calvet, Marc (2016): *The Emergence of a Democratic Right to Self-Determination in Europe*. Brussels: Centre Maurits Coppieters.

Turp, Daniel (2020): Self-Determination, the Right of Peoples to Decide and the Obligation of States to Negotiate. In: Dabis Attila (ed.) (2020): *Minority Protection - Special Issue*. Budapest: Institute for the Protection of Minority Rights

Turpin, Colin & Tomkins, Adam (2011): *British government (7th ed.)*. Cambridge: Cambridge University Press.

Varga Attila (2002): Nacionalizmusok a politikai és kulturális nemzet határán. In: *Regio –Kisebbség, politika, társadalom, 13/4*, pp. 194–211.

Vitucci, Maria Chiara (2016). Internationalised Territorial Regimes as Solution to Conflicts? In: Nicolini, Matteo, Palermo, Francesco & Milano, Enrico (eds.): *Law, Territory and Conflict Resolution. Law as a Problem and Law as a Solution. Studies in Territorial and Cultural Diversity Governance series, Volume: 6*. Leiden: Brill | Nijhoff.

Watts, Ronald L. (2008): *Comparing Federal Systems*. London: McGill-Queen's University Press.

Weber, Max (1922): *Wirtschaft und Gesellschaft*. Tübingen: Mohr.

Weller, Marc (2005): The Self-Determination trap. In: *Ethnopolitics, 4*, pp. 3–28.

Weller, Marc & Nobbs, Katherine (eds.) (2010): *Asymmetric Autonomy and the Settlement of Ethnic Conflicts*. Philadelphia: University of Pennsylvania Press.

Woelk, Jens, Palermo, Francesco & Marko, Joseph (eds.) (2008): *Tolerance through Law – Self-Governance and Group Rights in South Tyrol*. Leiden, Boston: Martinus Nijhoff Publishers.

Wolff, Stefan (2013): Conflict Management in Divided Societies: The Many Uses of Territorial Self-governance. In: *International Journal on Minority and Group Rights, 20(1)*, pp. 27–50.

## International Instruments, National Laws, Autonomy Statutes, Court Cases, Monitoring Reports, and Policy Documents

AC (2001): *First Opinion on Romania*, adopted on 6 April 2001 – ACFC/INF/OP/I(2002)001. Available at: https://rm.coe.int/CoERMPublicCommonSearchServices/DisplayDCTMContent?documentId=090000168008bd1c, accessed: 2021.07.23.

AC (2005): *Second Opinion on Romania*, adopted on 24 November 2005 – ACFC/OP/II(2005)007. Available at: https://rm.coe.int/168008c2ba, accessed: 2021.07.23.

AC (2012): *Third Opinion on Romania*, adopted on 21 March 2012 – ACFC/OP/III(2012)001. Available at: https://rm.coe.int/CoERMPublicCommonSearchServices/DisplayDCTMContent?documentId=090000168008c6a3, accessed: 2021.07.22.

AC (2017): *Fourth Opinion on Romania*, adopted on 22 June 2017 – ACFC/OP/IV(2017)005. Available at: https://rm.coe.int/fourth-opinion-on-romania-adopted-on-22-june-2017/168078af76, accessed: 2021.07.22

Civic Engagement Movement (2016): *Shadow Report to the Second Periodical Report on the Implementation of the European Charter for Regional or Minority Languages in Romania*. Marosvásárhely: CEMO.

CLRAE (2013): *Resolution 361 (2013) on Regions and Territories with Special Status in Europe & Explanatory Memorandum*, adopted on 31 October 2013. Available at: https://rm.coe.int/regions-and-territories-with-special-status-in-europe-resolution-recom/1680719502, accessed: 2021.07.26.

CLRAE - Institutional Committee (2002): *Information Report No. CG/INST (8) 55 rev/2002 on Local and Regional Democracy in Romania*, adopted on 25 April 2002. Available at: https://rm.coe.int/168071919c, accessed: 2021.07.27.

CLRAE (2011): *Recommendation 300 (2011) on Local and Regional Democracy in Romani*a, adopted on 22 March 2011. Available at: https://rm.coe.int/local-and-regional-democracy-in-romania-20th-session-of-the-congress-o/168071b146, accessed: 2021.07.30.

CoE (1950): *Convention for the Protection of Human Rights and Fundamental Freedoms*, opened for signature on 4 November 1950. Strasbourg: Directorate of Information. Available at: https://www.echr.coe.int/Documents/Convention_ENG.pdf, accessed: 2021.07.29.

CoE (1994): *Framework Convention for the Protection of National Minorities & Explanatory Report*, adopted by the by the Committee of Ministers on 10 November 1994. Available at: https://rm.coe.int/16800c10cf, accessed: 2021.07.26.

CoE (1992): *European Charter for Regional or Minority Languages*, adopted by the by the Committee of Ministers on 25 June 1992. Available at: https://rm.coe.int/1680695175, accessed: 2021.07.26.

CoE - Committee on Legal Affairs and Human Rights (2005): *Doc. 10762 – The Concept of "Nation"*. Strasbourg: PACE.

COMEX (2011): *First Report on the application of the Charter in Romania*, adopted on 30. November 2011 - ECRML(2012)3. Available at: https://www.coe.int/t/dg4/education/minlang/Report/EvaluationReports/RomaniaECRML1_en.pdf, accessed: 2021.07.22.

COMEX (2017): *Second Report on the application of the Charter in Romania*, adopted on 23 June 2017 - CM(2018)4. Available at: https://rm.coe.int/CoERMPublicCommonSearchServices/DisplayDCTMContent?documentId=09000016807766d3, accessed: 2021.03.16.

*Consolidated versions of the Treaty on European Union and the Treaty on the Functioning of the European Union* (TEU & TFEU) [2016] OJ C202/1. Available at: https://eur-lex.europa.eu/legal-content/EN/TXT/HTML/?uri=OJ:C:2016:202:FULL&from=FR, accessed: 2021.07.29.

Constitutional Court of Romania (2014): *Decision Nr. 80 of 16.02.2014, on the Legislative Proposal on the Revision of the Constitution of Romania*. Published in the Official Journal of Romania (No. 246) on 07.04.2014. Available at: http://www.ccr.ro/files/products/Decizie_80_2014.pdf, accessed: 2015.03.27.

Constitutional Court of Spain (2010): *Decision No. 31/2010 on the Constitutionality of Provisions of the Statute of Autonomy for Catalonia, as amended by Organic Law No. 6/2006*, dated 19 July 2006. Available at: https://www.tribunalconstitucional.es/ResolucionesTraducidas/31-2010,%20of%20June%2028.pdf, accessed: 2021.07.26.

Constituent Assembly of Italy (1947): *Constitution of the Italian Republic*, adopted on 22 December 1947. Available at: https://www.senato.it/documenti/repository/istituzione/costituzione_inglese.pdf, accessed: 2021.07.28.

CSCE (1990): *Document of the Copenhagen Meeting of the Conference on the Human Dimension of the CSCE*, adopted on 29 June 1990. Available at: https://www.osce.org/files/f/documents/9/c/14304.pdf, accessed: 2021.07.23.

CSCE (1991): *Report of the CSCE Meeting of Experts on National Minorities in Geneva*, adopted on 19 July 1991. Available at: https://www.osce.org/files/f/documents/4/3/14588.pdf, accessed: 2021.07.23.

Directia Centrala de Statistica – Directia Regionala de Statistica (1960): *Anuarul Statistic al Regiunii Autonome Maghiare, 1960/A Magyar Autonómtartomány Statisztikai Évkönyve*. Bucharest: Central Directorate of Statistics – Regional Directorate of Statistics.

ECRI (2005): *Third Report on Romania*, adopted on 24 June 2005 - CRI(2006)3. Available: https://rm.coe.int/third-report-on-romania/16808b5b90, accessed: 2021.07.23.

ECRI (2014): *Fourth Report on Romania*, adopted on 19 March 2014 - CRI(2014)19. Available at: https://rm.coe.int/fourth-report-on-romania/168094d771, accessed: 2021.07.25.

ECRI (2019): *Fifth Report on Romania*, adopted on 3 April 2019 - CRI(2019)20. Available at: https://rm.coe.int/fifth-report-on-romania/168094c9e5, accessed: 2021.07.22.

ECtHR (1979): *Rassemblement Jurassien and Unité Jurassienne v. Switzerland*, Application No. 8191/78, Decision of 10 October 1979 on Admissibility.

ECtHR (1998): *Socialist Party and Others v. Turkey*, Application No. 21237/93, Judgment of 25 May 1998.

ECtHR (2000): *Sener v. Turkey*, Application No. 26680/95, Judgment (Merits and Just Satisfaction) of 18 July 2000.

ECtHR (2001): *Stankov and United Macedonian Organisation (UMO) Ilinden v. Bulgaria*, Applications nos. 29221/95 and 29225/95, Judgment (Merits and Just Satisfaction) of 2 October 2001.

ECtHR (2006): *Oya Ataman v. Turkey*, Application No. 74552/01, Judgment of 5 December 2006.

ECtHR (2007): *Bukta v Hungary*, Application No. 25691/04, Judgment of 17 July 2007.

ECtHR (2012): *Catholic Archdiocese of Alba Iulia v. Romania*, Application no. 33003/03, Judgement of 25 September 2012.

ECtHR (2021): *Guide on Article 10 of the European Convention on Human Rights – Freedom of Expression*. Available at: https://www.echr.coe.int/Documents/Guide_Art_10_ENG.pdf, accessed: 2021.07.29.

Eide, Asbjørn (2001): *Final Text of the Commentary to the Declaration on the Rights of Persons Belonging to National or Ethnic, Religious and Linguistic Minorities*. Geneva: UN. Sub-commission on the Promotion and Protection of Human Rights – Working Group on Minorities. Available at: https://digitallibrary.un.org/record/439563?ln=en, accessed: 2021.07.29.

European Commission (2017). *Competitiveness in Low-Income and Low-Growth Regions. The Lagging Regions Report. Commission Staff Working Document*. Brussels: European Commission.

European Convention (2000): *Charter of Fundamental Rights of the European Union (2000/C 364/01)*, proclaimed on 7 December 2000. Available at: https://www.europarl.europa.eu/charter/pdf/text_en.pdf

European Parliament (2015): The Principle of Subsidiarity. In*: Fact Sheets on the European Union. Luxembourg: Office for Official Publications of the European Communities*. Available at: http://www.europarl.europa.eu/ftu/pdf/en/FTU_1.2.2.pdf, accessed: 2021.03.21.

Finlands Riksdag (1920): *Riksdagen Protokoll i Sammandrag*. Helsingfors: Statsrådets Tryckeri.

Government of Finland (2009): *Report of the Government on the Application of Language Legislation*. Oikeusministerio: Helsinki. Available at: http://www.oikeusministerio.fi/material/attachments/om/julkaisut/6FiopvJGh/KielikertomusENG_060432009_netti.pdf, accessed: 2017. 02. 21.

Government of Romania (2012): *National Strategic Reference Framework 2007–2013*. Bucharest: Ministry of Economy and Finance.

Government of Romania (2014): *Romanian Partnership Agreement for the 2014–2020 Programming Period*. Bucharest: Ministry of European Funds.

Legislative Council of the Parliament of Romania (2004): *Opinion Nr. 405/2004 on the Rejection of the Draft Law on the Statute of Autonomy of Szeklerland*. Hungarian version. Available at: http://adatbank.transindex.ro/html/cim_pdf540.pdf, accessed: 2021.03.23.

Minority Rights Group (2012): *Introduction to Minority Rights, Regional Human Rights Mechanisms, and Minority Rights Advocacy* [online material for the Global Advocacy Programme]. Available at: https://www.minorityrightscourse.org/mod/page/view.php?id =1613&lang=ur, accessed: 2021.03.03.

OSCE High Commissioner on National Minorities (1999): *The Lund Recommendations on the Effective Participation of National Minorities in Public*

*Life & Explanatory Note*, adopted on 1 September 1999. Available at: https://www.osce.org/files/f/documents/0/9/32240.pdf, accessed: 2021.07.23.

PACE (1993): *Recommendation 1201 (1993) on the Additional Protocol on the Rights of Minorities to the European Convention on Human Rights*, adopted on 1 February 1993. Available at: https://pace.coe.int/en/files/15235/html, accessed: 2021.07.26.

PACE (1993): *Opinion No. 176 (1993) on Application by Romania for Membership of the Council of Europe*, adopted on 28 September 1993, available at: http://assembly.coe.int/nw/xml/XRef/Xref-XML2HTML-en.asp?fileid=13915&lang=en, accessed: 2021.07.26.

PACE (2003): *Resolution 1334 (2003) on the Positive Experiences of Autonomous Regions as a Source of Inspiration for Conflict Resolution in Europe*, adopted by the Assembly on 24 June 2003. Available at: http://www.assembly.coe.int/nw/xml/XRef/Xref-XML2HTML-en.asp?fileid=17120&lang=en, accessed: 2021.07.27.

PACE (2003): *Resolution 1335 (2003) on Preferential Treatment of National Minorities by the Kin-state: the Case of the Hungarian Law of 19 June 2001 on Hungarians Living in Neighbouring Countries ("Magyars")*, adopted by the Assembly on 25 June 2003. Available at: http://www.assembly.coe.int/nw/xml/XRef/Xref-XML2HTML-en.asp?fileid=17121&lang=en, accessed: 2021.07.27.

PACE (2014): *Resolution 1985 (2014) on the Situation and Rights of National Minorities in Europe*, adopted by the Assembly on 8 April 2014. Available at: https://assembly.coe.int/nw/xml/XRef/Xref-XML2HTML-en.asp?fileid=20772&lang=en, accessed: 2021.07.27.

Parliament of Denmark (1948): *Act No. 137 on Home Rule of the Faroe Islands*, adopted on 23 March 1948. Available at: https://www.government.fo/en/the-government/the-home-rule-act/, accessed: 2021.07.28.

Parliament of Denmark (1953): *Constitutional Act of Denmark*, adopted on 5 June 1953. Available at: https://www.thedanishparliament.dk/-/media/pdf/publikationer/english/my_constitutional_act_with_explanations.ashx, accessed: 2021.07.28.

Parliament of Denmark (2005): *Act no. 578 relating to the Takeover of Affairs and Fields of Affairs by the Faeroe Islands Public Authorities*, adopted on 24 June 2005. Available at: https://www.faroeislands.fo/government-politics/constitutional-status/the-takeover-act/, accessed: 2021.07.28.

Parliament of Finland (2003): *Language Act No. 423/2003*. Available at: https://www.finlex.fi/en/laki/kaannokset/2003/en20030423.pdf, accessed: 2021.07.27.

Parliament of Finland (1919): *Constitution Act of Finland*, promulgated on 17 July 1919. Available at: https://www.refworld.org/docid/3ae6b53418.html, accessed: 2021.07.28.

Parliament of Finland (1920): *Act No. 124/1920 on the Self-government for Åland*, adopted on 6 May 1920. Available at: https://www.lagtinget.ax/sites/www.lagtinget.ax/files/alands_sjalvstyrelselag_124-1920.pdf, accessed: 2021.07.28.

Parliament of Finland (1999): *Constitution Act of Finland (731/1999, including amendments up to 817/2018)*, adopted on 11 June 1999. Available at: https://www.finlex.fi/en/laki/kaannokset/1999/en19990731.pdf, accessed: 2021.07.28.

Parliament of France (1958): *Constitution of France*, adopted on 4 October 1958. English translation available at: https://www2.assemblee-nationale.fr/langues/welcome-to-the-english-website-of-the-french-national-assembly/legal-texts/constitution, accessed: 2021.07.26.

Parliament of France (1991): *Law No. 91-428, Statute of the territorial community of Corsica*, adopted on 13 May 1991. Available at: https://www.legifrance.gouv.fr/loda/id/JORFTEXT000000536085/, accessed: 2021.07.28.

Parliament of Hungary (1993): *Law No. LV. of 1993 on Hungarian citizenship*, adopted on 1 June 1993. Available at: https://net.jogtar.hu/jogszabaly?docid=99300055.tv, accessed: 2021.07.26.

Parliament of Hungary (2001): *Law No. LXII of 2001 on Hungarians Living in Neighbouring States*, adopted on 19 June 2001. Available at: https://net.jogtar.hu/jogszabaly?docid=a0100062.tv, accessed: 2021.07.26.

Parliament of Hungary (2011): *Fundamental Law of Hungary*, adopted on 25 April 2011. Available at: https://net.jogtar.hu/jogszabaly?docid=a1100425.atv, accessed: 2021.07.26

Parliament of Hungary (2011): *Law No. CLXXIX of 2011 on the Rights of Nationalities*, adopted on 19 December 2011. English translation available at: https://www.legislationline.org/download/id/6547/file/Hungary_act_rights_of_nationalities_2011_en.pdf, accessed: 2021.07.26.

Parliament of the Republic of Moldova (1994): *Constitution of the Republic of Moldova*, adopted on 29 July 1994. Available at: https://www.presedinte.md/eng/constitution, accessed: 2021.07.28.

Parliament of the Republic of Moldova (1994): *Law No. No 344-XIII on the Special Legal Status of Gagauzia (Gaguz Yeri)*, adopted on 23 December 1994. English version available at: http://www.regione.taa.it/biblioteca/minoranze/gagauziaen.pdf, accessed: 2021.07.28.

Parliament of Romania (1968): *Law No. 2 of 1968 on the Administrative Organization of the Territory of Romania*, adopted on 16 February

1968. Available at: http://legislatie.just.ro/Public/DetaliiDocument/189, accessed: 2021.07.26.

Parliament of Romania (1991): *The Constitution of Romania*. Available at: http://www.cdep.ro/pls/dic/site.page?id=371, accessed: 22021.03.21.

Parliament of Romania (1991): *Law No. 21/1991 on Romanian citizenship*, adopted on 1 March 1991. Available at: http://legislatie.just.ro/Public/DetaliiDocument/121439, accessed: 2021.07.27.

Parliament of Romania (1991): *Law No. 51/1991 on the National Security of Romania*, adopted on 29 July 1991. Available at: http://legislatie.just.ro/Public/DetaliiDocument/1517, accessed: 2021.07.26.

Parliament of Romania (1991): *Law No. 60/1991 on the Organization and Conduct of Public Gatherings*, adopted on 23 September 1991. Available at: http://legislatie.just.ro/Public/DetaliiDocumentAfis/156395, accessed: 2021.07.30.

Parliament of Romania (1991): *Law No. 61/1991 on Sanctioning the Acts of Violation of Certain Rules of Social Coexistence, Public Order and Peace*, adopted on 27 September 1991. Available at: http://legislatie.just.ro/Public/DetaliiDocument/125693, accessed: 2021.07.30.

Parliament of Romania (2000): *Law No. 3/2000 on the Organization of the Referendums*, adopted on 22 February 2000. Available at: http://legislatie.just.ro/Public/DetaliiDocument/21139, accessed: 2021.07.27.

Parliament of Romania (2001): *Law No. 215/2001 on Local Public Administration*, adopted on 23 April 2001. Available at: http://legislatie.just.ro/Public/DetaliiDocumentAfis/79638, accessed: 2021.07.26.

Parliament of Romania (2004): *Law No. 535/2004 on Preventing and Combating Terrorism*, adopted on 25 November 2004. Available at: http://legislatie.just.ro/Public/DetaliiDocument/57494, accessed: 2021.07.26.

Parliament of Romania (2006): *Law No. 489/2006 on Religious Freedom and the General Regime of Denominations*, adopted on 28 December 2006. Available at: http://legislatie.just.ro/Public/DetaliiDocument/78355, accessed: 2021.07.26.

Parliament of Romania (2010): *Law No. 135/2010 on the Criminal Procedure Code*, adopted on 1 July 2010. Available at: http://legislatie.just.ro/Public/DetaliiDocumentAfis/120609, accessed: 2021.07.26.

Parliament of Romania (2011): *Law No. 1/2011 on National Education*, adopted on 5 January 2011. Available at: http://legislatie.just.ro/Public/DetaliiDocument/125150, accessed: 2021.07.26.

Parliament of Romania (2015): *Law No. 141/2015 on the Display and Use of the Flags of Administrative-territorial Units*, adopted on 10 June 2015.

Available at: http://legislatie.just.ro/Public/DetaliiDocumentAfis/168736, accessed: 2021.07.26.

Parliament of Spain (1978): *The Spanish Constitution*, approved by the Cortes Generales on 31 October 1978. Available at: https://www.boe.es/legislacion/documentos/ConstitucionINGLES.pdf, accessed: 2021.07.26.

Parliament of Spain (1979): *Organic Law 4/1979 on the Statute of Autonomy for Catalonia*, adopted on 18 December 1979. Available at: https://www.boe.es/buscar/doc.php?id=BOE-A-1979-30178, accessed: 2021.07.28.

Parliament of Spain (1979): *Organic Law 3/1979 on the Statute of Autonomy for the Basque Country*, adopted on 18 December 1979. Available at: https://www.boe.es/buscar/act.php?id=BOE-A-1979-30177, accessed: 2021.07.28.

Parliament of the United Kingdom (1998): *The Scotland Act 1998 (c. 46)*, Royal Assent received on 19 November 1998. Available at: https://www.legislation.gov.uk/ukpga/1998/46/contents, accessed: 2021.07.28.

President of the Republic of Italy (1972): *Decree No. 670 on the Approval of the Unified Text of the Constitutional Laws Relating to the Special Statute for Trentino-Alto Adige*, adopted on 31 August 1972. Available at: http://lexbrowser.provinz.bz.it/doc/de/dpr-1972-670/dekret_des_pr_sidenten_der_republik_vom_31_august_1972_nr_670.aspx, accessed: 2021.07.27.

Romániai Magyar Demokrata Szövetség (1993): Törvény a nemzeti kisebbségekről és autonóm közösségekről. In: *Magyar Kisebbség III. Évf. - 1997. 1–2. (7–8.) szám*. Kolozsvár: Jakabffy Elemér Alapítvány, pp. 314–329.

Secretary-General of the United Nations (2014): *Guidance Note on Racial Discrimination and Protection of Minorities*. Geneva: UN.

Secretary-General of the United Nations (2019): *Report of the Secretary-General on SDG Progress 2019 – Special Edition*. New York: UN- Department of Economic and Social Affairs.

SRI (2014): *Raportul de activitate al Serviciului Român de Informațiiînanul 2014*. Available at: https://www.sri.ro/fisiere/rapoarte/Raport_SRI_2014.pdf, accessed: 2021.07.30.

Supreme Court of Canada (1998): *Reference re Secession of Quebec, [1998] 2 S.C.R. 217*. Available at: https://scc-csc.lexum.com/scc-csc/scc-csc/en/item/1643/index.do, accessed: 2021.07.26.

Szekler National Council (2009): *The Autonomy Statute of Szeklerland*. Sepsiszentgyörgy: T3 Kiadó.

*Treaty of Understanding, Cooperation and Good Neighbourhood between Romania and the Republic of Hungary*, signed at Temesvár/Timisoara on 16 September 1996. English version available at: https://treaties.un.org/doc/Publication/UNTS/Volume%201966/volume-1966-I-33604-English.pdf, accessed: 2021.07.27.

UN Human Rights Council (2018): *Universal Periodic Review of Romania – Thematic list of Recommendations*. Geneva: Official Documents System of the United Nations. Available at: https://lib.ohchr.org/HRBodies/UPR/Documents/Session29/RO/UPR29_Romania_Thematiclist_of_recommendations_E.docx, accessed: 2021. 02. 16.

UN Commission on Human Rights - Sub-Commission on Prevention of Discrimination and Protection of Minorities (1993): *Possible ways and means of facilitating the peaceful and constructive solution of problems involving minorities*. Report submitted by Asbjørn Eide, 10 August 1993, E/CN.4/Sub.2/1993/34. Available at: http://www.refworld.org/pdfid/3b00f4344.pdf, accessed:2021.07.29.

UN Working Group on Minorities (2005): *Commentary of the Working Group on Minorities to the UN Declaration on the Rights of Persons Belonging to National or Ethnic, Religious and Linguistic Minorities*. Geneva: UN – Commission on Human Rights. Available at: http://www.ohchr.org/Documents/Events/Minority2012/G0513385_en.pdf, accessed: 2021.07.30.

Venice Commission (1999): *Report nr. CDL-INF (2000) 2 on Self-determination and Secession in Constitutional Law*, adopted by the Commission at its 41st meeting in Venice on 10–11 December 1999.

www.ingramcontent.com/pod-product-compliance
Ingram Content Group UK Ltd.
Pitfield, Milton Keynes, MK11 3LW, UK
UKHW021009120926
8556IPUK00029B/247

9 783631 855805